LEGAL INFORMATION ONLINE ANYTIME

24 hours a day

www.nolo.com

AT THE NOLO.COM SELF-HELP LAW CENTER, YOU'LL FIND

- **Nolo's comprehensive Legal Encyclopedia filled with plain-English information on a variety of legal topics**
- **Nolo's Law Dictionary—legal terms without the legalese**
- **Auntie Nolo—if you've got questions, Auntie's got answers**
- **The Law Store—over 200 self-help legal products including Downloadable Software, Books, Form Kits and eGuides**
- **Legal and product updates**
- **Frequently Asked Questions**
- **NoloBriefs, our free monthly email newsletter**
- **Legal Research Center, for access to state and federal statutes**
- **Our ever-popular lawyer jokes**

Quality LAW BOOKS & SOFTWARE FOR EVERYONE

Nolo's user-friendly products are consistently first-rate. Here's why:

- A dozen in-house legal editors, working with highly skilled authors, ensure that our products are accurate, up-to-date and easy to use

- We continually update every book and software program to keep up with changes in the law

- Our commitment to a more democratic legal system informs all of our work

- We appreciate & listen to your feedback. Please fill out and return the card at the back of this book.

OUR "NO-HASSLE" GUARANTEE

Return anything you buy directly from Nolo for any reason and we'll cheerfully refund your purchase price. No ifs, ands or buts.

Read This First

The information in this book is as up to date and accurate as we can make it. But it's important to realize that the law changes frequently, as do fees, forms and other important legal details. If you handle your own legal matters, it's up to you to be sure that all information you use—including the information in this book—is accurate. Here are some suggestions to help you do this:

First, check the edition number on the book's spine to make sure you've got the most recent edition of this book. To learn whether a later edition is available, go to Nolo's online Law Store at www.nolo.com or call Nolo's Customer Service Department at 800-728-3555.

Next, because the law can change overnight, users of even a current edition need to be sure it's fully up to date. At www.nolo.com, we post notices of major legal and practical changes that affect a book's current edition only. To check for updates, go to the Law Store portion of Nolo's website and find the page devoted to the book (use the "A to Z Product List" and click on the book's title). If you see an "Updates" link on the left side of the page, click on it. If you don't see a link, there are no posted changes—but check back regularly.

Finally, while Nolo believes that accurate and current legal information in its books can help you solve many of your legal problems on a cost-effective basis, this book is not intended to be a substitute for personalized advice from a knowledgeable lawyer. If you want the help of a trained professional, consult an attorney licensed to practice in your state.

Dedication

We dedicate this book to . . .

Those grappling with the enormity of divorce and, thus, most in need of guidance. Our clients who remind us of the pain, personal struggle and growth that divorce causes.

Our families and friends, who kept us sane through the writing process.

Larry Woodhouse, for his continued friendship, and our children, Brooke and Tyler, all of whom have taught me the value of communication, negotiation and compromise.

Table of Contents

Introduction

CHAPTER 4

The Hardest Part: Is My Marriage Really Over?

CHAPTER 5

The Separation: What Happens When One Spouse Moves Out?

CHAPTER 6

Closing the Books: What Do We Do With Joint Accounts?

CHAPTER 7

Getting Help: To Whom Can I Turn?

CHAPTER 8

Financial Fact-Finding: What Must I Know and When Must I Know It?

CHAPTER 9

Facing the Future: What Must I Plan For?

Introduction

You've just been through the worst week of your life when the person you're divorcing suddenly calls and demands copies of your tax returns for the past five years.

You brown-bag your lunch and take the bus to work so you can make ends meet while the divorce settlement is pending. One day, you receive an unexpected bill in the mail. Your soon-to-be-ex-spouse charged an expensive vacation on your joint credit card, and now you have to pay for it.

No ... divorce is not the best time in the world to deal with money. But it may be the most crucial. In fact, making financial decisions is possibly the most important job you have when a marriage ends.

How can you make the right decisions? How can you deal with tedious financial details when you're going through such a stressful event? Unfortunately, it's hard to find answers to those questions.

Legal advice is plentiful, and therapists or support groups can help you through emotional upheavals. But who can show you how to make sense of your financial life?

That's where this book comes in. It explains what you must know to avoid the financial disasters of divorce. Specifically, this book draws on our years of experience as financial planners to help you understand:

- what you own and owe
- how divorce affects you tax-wise
- how best to divide your property, investments and other assets
- what can happen to your retirement nest egg or your business
- what to do about alimony and/or child support

- how to prepare for negotiating a final settlement, and
- how to gain financial stability in your new life as a single person or single parent.

Each divorce is different, of course, so we cannot promise to provide complex financial advice for every possible situation you may encounter. At the very least, however, we *can* let you know where—and to whom—to turn in finding answers for yourself.

As we see it, divorce is a crash course in managing personal finances—a course you must take whether you signed up for it or not. And the first lesson in that course is to understand that there is a big difference between legal reality and financial reality.

The financial truth about divorce is this—just because you "get it in writing" doesn't mean you will get it for real. In other words, even though your settlement may be perfectly legal and fair, it can still be costly in financial terms. For example:

*How will you pay for debts that mounted during the marriage if your spouse refuses to come up with his or her share—even if you were **not** supposed to pay those bills under your settlement agreement?*

If you leave the division of your property up to the courts, the future tax consequences of your transactions will most likely be ignored. But the IRS will still collect those taxes.

What will you do if your spouse agreed to pay child support but is consistently late?

As you divorce, you must be on the alert for the limitations of the law. Throughout this book, we will show you how to craft a strong financial settlement without ignoring the blind spots of the legal system.

Keep in mind that divorce does not have to be messy and expensive. Even if you have a great deal of property, you need not spend a fortune. One couple we worked with had $5 million in assets, yet they spent only $5,000 in legal fees. This couple evaluated their property, analyzed tax consequences and negotiated fairly.

By contrast, another couple, whose property totaled only $100,000, ended up spending $20,000 on attorneys' fees alone—all because they could not be realistic about their personal finances, and instead let their emotions interfere with reason.

Whether you and your spouse have a little money or a lot, it is important that you look at your divorce from the perspective of financial reality. It means protecting your financial well-being, whether or not your spouse cooperates. Without this perspective, you may one day find yourself painted into a financial corner, saddled with debts or burdened with assets you cannot afford or hope to sell.

The choice is yours. Divorce is painful enough. Don't let money problems make it worse.

If You Are Feeling Overwhelmed . . .

Congratulations. You're normal. Feeling overwhelmed is a very common experience during divorce. Even people who are extremely capable under other circumstances may suddenly find it difficult to balance a checkbook or perform a simple task.

If that happens to you, try to slow down.

Although every divorce is different, the process seems to have one universal effect: temporary paralysis. Whether you're a hard-driving executive or a stay-at-home spouse, in the midst of a traumatic separation, competent people become immobilized by the gravity of the financial questions they face. Should the house be sold? How

much alimony will be awarded? What will happen at tax time? Who will support the children?

Feeling overwhelmed, confused, angry or depressed—these are normal responses to the stress of divorce. Our advice, as with any major undertaking, is to break it down into small, manageable pieces. And because the hectic pace of life today puts so many demands on your time, we present this plan in step-by-step segments. When you complete several small goals each day, you are less likely to become overwhelmed and immobilized. That feeling of accomplishment helps you stay out of the crisis mode and works to your benefit both emotionally and financially.

How to Use This Book

Before you jump ahead and try to figure out what your house is worth or what you will need to do about alimony or child support, we recommend that you read Chapters 1 and 2, which give the framework on legal and financial reality that you *must* understand as your divorce progresses.

For tips on dealing with emotional upheavals, read Chapter 3.

Chapters 4 through 7 cover "The First 30 Days" and are especially important if you are in the initial stages of divorce. Chapters 8 and 9 help you start gathering financial data and thinking about the future.

In Chapters 10 through 12, you begin to seriously evaluate your assets and debts, and income and expenses. Whether you are a "do-it-yourselfer" or you consult an attorney, you must figure out what you own and owe, and what it costs you and your family to live. We've provided several worksheets in Chapter 12 to help you.

Chapters 13 through 16 cover specific assets—family home, retirement benefits, investments and other employee benefits. Chapter 17 deals with your debts. And in Chapter 18, you will evaluate the likelihood of paying or receiving alimony and/or child support—and in what amounts.

Your analysis and calculations from Chapters 12 through 18 are brought together in Chapter 19 to help you structure your final settlement. Finally, Chapter 20 gives you guidelines for establishing a healthy financial life once the marriage has officially ended.

Icons

Throughout the book, we use icons to alert you to certain information. These icons are:

Fast Track
We use this icon to let you know when you can skip information that may not be relevant to your case.

Warning
Our warning icon alerts you to financial pitfalls during divorce or other information that needs emphasizing because of the potential consequences.

Attorney or Other Professional
This icon lets you know when you probably need the advice of an attorney or other professional.

Steps
This icon alerts you to a series of tasks designed to help you reach certain decisions.

Additional Resources
When you see this icon, a list of additional resources that can assist you in researching a particularly technical point follows.

Time
This icon lets you know it's time to make a decision about how to divide your assets.

Web
This icon alerts you to websites that may be helpful. ■

CHAPTER

1

Legal vs. Financial Realities of Divorce

Sooner or later during a divorce, you will discover the one insight that is central to this book *and* to the successful outcome of your settlement:

Legal reality and financial reality are fundamentally different.

A seemingly simple idea—but you'd be surprised at how long it takes to sink in. To help you understand why this concept is so important, take a few moments to consider the following real-life divorce stories. In each, read the Legal Reality first. Then, see the true outcome in the Financial Reality side.

Legal Reality	*Financial Reality*
Jonathan and Penny were married for five years before they divorced. During that time, Penny frequently ran their credit cards to the limit buying clothing, and had trouble balancing their checkbook.	After the divorce, however, Penny didn't pay off the credit cards, and creditors began hounding Jonathan for the money. Jonathan ended up footing the bills, because a divorce settlement assigning debts—even one included in a divorce judgment—cannot change a couple's original joint obligation to their creditors.
When they reached the final settlement hearing, Jonathan was greatly relieved when the court ordered Penny solely responsible for paying the $10,000 in credit card debts she had accumulated during their marriage. The settlement was included in the final divorce judgment, which made Jonathan feel safe.	Had Jonathan raised the issue before their settlement was finalized, he could have demanded more property in exchange for paying Penny's debts or insisted that they sell some jointly held property to pay off their creditors.

Moral of the story:
Getting something "in writing" from the court
doesn't always mean you'll get it for real.

Legal Reality	**Financial Reality**
During their 15-year marriage, Sharon and Bill were committed to building up a good portfolio of stocks and mutual funds for their retirement.	Sharon paid attention to basic financial facts which Bill ignored: costs and taxes that decrease the value of an asset.
Because Sharon avidly followed the market, she wanted to keep a batch of stocks she had recently purchased and asked Bill to take stocks of equal value, which they had purchased early in their marriage. After negotiating over a few other assets, Bill and Sharon reached an agreement in which each of them would receive the exact same dollar amount in cash or assets at the end of the divorce. The court accepted the terms of their settlement, and the books on their marriage were quickly closed.	Sharon wisely picked the stocks most recently purchased. Because these stocks had not increased substantially in value, the taxable capital gains were low. Bill, however, blithely accepted the older stocks, which had gone up a lot in value since the time of purchase. Even at the capital gains rate of 20%, he owed substantial taxes when he sold the stocks. Had he taken the time to calculate his potential tax burden before agreeing to the settlement, he could have suggested splitting the stocks so that each spouse took half of the older stocks and half of the newer stocks.

Moral of the story: A 50-50 settlement isn't always equal.

A. Lessons in Legal Reality

Ending a marriage with no assets or huge debts is the hard way to learn about divorce. Your lessons do not have to be so costly. You would never try to play basketball with football rules or to cook Chinese food using classic French recipes, would you? Similarly, you must learn to follow the correct "rules" for playing in the legal league versus the financial field.

The following five guidelines explain the legal basics of divorce:

- Most divorces are settled out of court.

- Generally, divorce law is local.

- Don't expect the legal system (or a lawyer) to take care of you.

- Your future is in your hands—not the court's.

- It's easier to write laws than to enforce them.

1.   Most Divorces Are Settled Out of Court

You may imagine that you'll have a divorce trial like those on an old *Perry Mason* or *L.A. Law* episode— everything settled in an hour with the "good guys" winning. Perhaps you're waiting for your day in court when you can explain to a wise and kindly judge the exact wrongs your spouse has visited upon you.

Don't count on it.

An estimated 90% of divorce cases are settled without a court trial. Most of your settling will be done through meetings between you and your spouse or between your lawyers, often on the courthouse steps. As the final settlement date nears, you will quite likely be rushed into conferences in the courtroom hall or coffee shop. In these frantic meetings, your spouse and/or the attorneys may confront you, demanding instant decisions on issues that will affect the rest of your life.

Realize, too, that most divorce courts today are primarily concerned with money, not morals. The main job of the legal system is to resolve property disputes and to ensure the welfare of any children. Spousal misconduct, of course, could affect custody,

and economic mischief (such as hiding assets) can change the outcome of the final settlement. But, by and large, you will not get a chance to vent feelings about your mate in the courtroom.

The impersonal atmosphere of the legal world may baffle you. But in fact, it is often to your advantage to stay out of the courtroom. As long as you and your spouse work toward a settlement without involving the court, you can trade property, negotiate terms and still maintain some measure of control over your destiny. *If you cannot reach a settlement and must have a trial, however, you put your fate into the hands of a judge—a stranger who knows nothing about your children or property.* You'll have to live with whatever that judge decides.

2.   Divorce Law Is Local

Divorce laws not only differ from state to state, but interpretations of divorce law can vary from judge to judge. Whether or not you ultimately hire an attorney or have a court trial, you should ask local lawyers to assess the most likely outcome of a divorce like yours. Ask about the types of settlements local judges tend to approve. Find out how the local courts and individual judges view mediation. Also ask about judges' attitudes toward women or men, and the prevailing mood regarding, for example, joint custody, moving away with the children or alimony.

Understand, too, that divorce courts are unlike other courts. They are called "courts of equity," which means that the judge has wide discretion in making decisions. While a lawyer can educate you on the law, a lawyer cannot ethically or realistically promise what the judge will do in your case.

You may not like what you hear. A lawyer may tell you that the things you want in your divorce are impossible to get. Another attorney may promise you everything, but ultimately deliver nothing. Interviewing several people for a cross section of opinion can give you a more accurate picture of your situation. (See Chapter 7 for information on hiring an attorney.)

If you know how individual judges normally rule in your locale, your expectations will be more realistic. Even if you don't have a trial to settle matters (remember, 90% of cases are resolved before a trial), divorce lawyers tend to give advice that is consistent with local court rulings. Granted, it's hard to ignore sensational newspaper stories about big-dollar divorces in other parts of the country. But those cases are irrelevant. You must concentrate on what happens in your backyard, because that is where your divorce and your financial future will be decided.

Affording Attorneys

Throughout this book, we may tell you to "check with an attorney" on various questions. We say this because the individual circumstances of your divorce may require legal information beyond the scope of this book.

But who is going to pay for this costly legal advice?

Attending a brief consultation with a lawyer should not bankrupt you. Organize your thoughts and questions before you seek legal advice so you can save time when the attorney's meter is running. At an initial visit, spend an hour—not a day. Then go home and think about how much more you may have to spend on an attorney.

In some cases, your spouse may have to pay all or some of *your* lawyer's fee. The lawyer should be able to advise you about this at the initial consultation.

If you have very little money and feel you truly need advice from an attorney, consider borrowing money, holding a garage sale or taking a short-term second job to get some money to pay legal fees. As an inexpensive alternative, see if a local law school has a divorce clinic where law students can assist you.

For more information on finding—and working with—lawyers, see Chapter 7, Section B1.

NOTE: Do not let your spouse's attorney or anyone else chosen by your spouse be the one to represent you. If your spouse is represented by an attorney, you should be also. Except in very limited circumstances, one attorney cannot represent both parties in a divorce action.

---

3. Don't Expect the Legal System to Take Care of You

One of the most costly illusions in divorce is the idea that the judicial system will protect all of your rights and meet all of your needs. You cannot afford to make that assumption. *You* are the one who must make the decisions in your divorce, because *you* are the one who will have to live with them.

Attorneys and other professionals can help you understand your rights during divorce, but they should not determine what your financial needs will be once the marriage ends. Just because you are "entitled" to a certain property (say, the house), that does not mean you can afford to keep it. Even though you may want to remain a freelancer, you may have to get a steady job so you can support your family after a divorce. Only you can make these decisions.

Instead of passively going through the motions of divorce, you might do better by adopting the active attitude of an entrepreneur. Business people starting a new company go to lawyers to have them formalize agreements and assess legal risks—not to ask whether or not they are making a smart financial move. The entrepreneur sits down with accountants and financial professionals to crunch the numbers and determine whether a business will turn a profit. Only then, after examining the financial aspects of a venture, do they consult with attorneys about potential legal problems.

Likewise, you must be the one to call the shots in your divorce. Don't expect the legal system to make the decisions that are best for you.

Don't Be Afraid to Ask Questions

Don't be intimidated or afraid to ask questions if something is unclear. One divorcing woman admitted that some of her troubles resulted from her own unwillingness to appear ignorant. In an interview with sociologist Terry Arendell in the book *Mothers and Divorce*, the woman recalled her divorce and commented, "Part of the problem was my own fault. I gave the appearance of being knowledgeable. I knew more about buying property and bank accounts than my lawyer did, but I didn't understand all the tax things. And so I was reluctant to ask some of the things I should have asked."

4. Your Future Is in Your Hands— Not the Court's

Once the divorce is final, you will have to make all the decisions about your financial future. The legal system is not designed to help you with your finances once the divorce is granted.

You may legally and fairly split the benefits of a pension plan in a divorce settlement, but when the time comes to retire, you may have less income than you need to live on. The court cannot resolve that problem for you. You cannot leave complex, multifaceted money questions about your future to the one-dimensional perspective of divorce law.

Further, the implications of future taxes on property are not taken into account in settlement agreements in most states. Generally, only existing—or impending—taxes can be factored into a division of assets. Anything beyond these taxes is considered speculation—and speculation is not normally welcome in the courtroom. For example, if, as part of the divorce settlement, you and your spouse will sell $40,000 of stock at a profit, the taxes owed on the profit will be factored into the settlement and could be split between you. If you keep the stocks and your spouse gets another asset of the same value, the court will not grant you more at the time of the settlement to cover whatever amount of taxes you may owe in the future.

Again, you are the one who must secure your future financial life, because the legal system cannot do that job.

> ### Definition: Settlement Agreement
>
> Throughout this book, we refer to marital settlement agreements, property settlement agreements, settlement agreements or simply agreements. They all mean the same thing. A settlement agreement is a written contract between you and your spouse outlining how you will divide your property and debts, the amount of alimony and child support, who will pay it and who will receive it, who will have custody of or visitation with the children and other major issues. If you and your spouse are unable to reach an agreement on these issues (on your own or with the help of a mediator), you will have to go to court to have a judge resolve them. Once these issues are finalized, they are incorporated into the final divorce decree.

5. It's Easier to Write Laws Than to Enforce Them

Laws concerning child support payments are among the most stringent on the books. Yet every year, millions of parents don't receive the money to which they are legally entitled. Nonenforcement of court orders is one aspect of legal reality for which you must prepare yourself. As you go through each step of your negotiations, ask, "How will I handle this if my ex refuses to abide by the judge's orders? What options do I have to enforce this agreement?"

And most important, "How much will enforcement cost me?"

When you recognize these risks ahead of time, you can take steps to minimize them.

If you have to enforce your divorce agreement, you will probably have to go to court. The process is expensive, time-consuming and emotionally draining. If at all possible, keep animosity to a minimum after the divorce so that both parents' custodial or visitation time with the children goes smoothly. That will make it more likely that your ex will make alimony and child support payments on time.

B. Your Best Strategy: Think Financially—Act Legally

Make your financial concerns the centerpiece of your divorce, and work within the framework of the law. That is the most powerful position you can take. If you think financially and act legally, you will be able to anticipate risks and assess your needs, before a financial disaster hits.

No one wants to negotiate for an asset in a divorce and then be unable to sell it because they'd owe too much in taxes. Why should you go through the nightmare of settlement negotiations only to end up losing everything you fought for six months after the divorce is over?

Remember: The legal process of divorce is something you will live *through*—but the financial reality is what you will have to live *with* for the rest of your life.

In a divorce, it's not what you get that counts—it's what you keep.

Covenant Marriages

Three states (Arizona, Arkansas and Louisiana) provide marrying couples with the option of entering into a "covenant" marriage. A covenant marriage makes it more difficult to get a divorce and is an alternative to a traditional marriage permitting divorce without restrictions. In addition to undergoing premarital counseling prior to their wedding, a couple wanting to end a covenant marriage must wait a full two years before proceeding, and may divorce only for reasons such as adultery or alcoholism. Parties are free to enter into a traditional marriage if they prefer. Opponents claim covenant marriages will force some women to stay in an abusive relationship.

Although most states that have considered covenant marriage laws have rejected them, Arkansas adopted covenant marriage as recently as 2001, and such laws are still pending in several other states.

C. Legal vs. Financial Stages of Divorce

Use the following table to help understand the relationship between the legal and financial stages of divorce. These stages will be explored in more detail throughout the book. Keep in mind that few divorces will follow these steps in this exact order.

 Nolo's website, www.nolo.com, contains legal information and resources that will help you through your divorce. In addition, several sites specialize in divorce information. Typically, these sites include forums, message centers and chat rooms on topics such as custody, mediation, infidelity, parenting, child support, debt, grandparent issues and divorce in the military. Many contain articles and books on divorce-related subjects and state-by-state explanations of the law. Some can help you find professionals—lawyers, therapists or financial advisors—to assist you in your divorce.

Some require small membership fees for full participation.

- www.aaml.org
- www.divorcecare.com
- www.divorcecentral.com
- www.divorceinfo.com
- www.divorcenet.com
- www.divorcesource.com
- www.divorcesupport.com
- www.flyingsolo.com

Legal Stages	Financial Stages
Consult an attorney or do some research at a law library to learn about your legal rights and responsibilities. In particular, investigate how your state's laws regarding separation impact custody, alimony, child support, debts incurred after separation and increases and decreases in the value of marital assets after separation.	Gather together your financial papers and make copies of all documents. Investigate the financial impact of separation. Close or freeze access to joint accounts. (See Chapter 6, Section A.) Open accounts in your own name before filing for divorce.
Physically separate. For some couples, this means moving apart. For others, it's no longer sleeping together and living in different parts of the house. Additionally, your state law may use its own criteria to define the date of marital separation. Consult with an attorney to determine the rules in your state.	Keep track of debts incurred before and after separation, joint bills paid and improvements made to property during separation. Keep receipts for moving and other expenses. Update insurance as necessary. Will you file taxes jointly or separately?
One spouse files a complaint or petition requesting a divorce. This begins the formal divorce proceedings. The other spouse must file an answer or response.	
One spouse files a request for temporary orders regarding custody, visitation, alimony and/or child support. The request may also ask that the other spouse pay his or her attorney fees.	Document all temporary alimony payments made. These payments may be tax deductible as long as there is an agreement in writing or a court order concerning the payments.
Conduct legal discovery (the procedures used to obtain information during a lawsuit) or win spouse's cooperation to share documents. Determine the amount of alimony, child support and attorney fees you will pay or receive, if applicable.	Conduct financial fact-finding. Complete the net worth and cash flow statements in Chapter 12. Hire a forensic accountant if necessary to search for hidden assets. Analyze your assets and debts—use appraisers, accountants, tax advisors, actuaries and others to help you assess values, tax consequences and other risks of keeping or giving up property.
Begin settlement negotiations, using one of these possible scenarios: • Negotiate through your attorneys. • Use mediation to negotiate the settlement. • Negotiate between yourselves. • If you are unable to settle certain issues, bring those issues to a judge.	Before settlement negotiations, make a list of all items you want the agreement to cover. Be sure to carefully analyze the tax ramifications and other financial pitfalls of each offer and counteroffer. Reduce attorneys' fees by doing much of the legwork on your own, settling without an attorney, keeping anger out of your negotiations and avoiding a trial. Remember that a trial can be very expensive. You'll have to pay lawyers' fees as well as the fees of the experts (accountants, actuaries and the like) whom you bring in to testify.
Your marital settlement agreement is drafted to incorporate terms of the settlement or the court order. The agreement is incorporated into the final judgment of divorce.	If you settle by agreement, carefully check it against your wish list.
Your divorce is over. Double-check all legal papers, including deeds, registration forms and other ownership documents.	Your divorce is over. Double-check all financial papers, such as beneficiary designations of insurance, wills, retirement plans and the like. Change where needed.

Financial Realities
No One Talks About

The true cost of divorce is rarely discussed openly.

You probably know more about negotiating to buy a car than you do about negotiating a divorce settlement. At least when you're buying an automobile, you have an idea of what to expect. Entering a showroom, you see the sticker price on a shiny new car. But that price is not the final one. There's often a "dealer markup." You will have to pay taxes or other fees before you actually drive the car off the lot. And once you get the car home, you will have to spend money on insurance, registration fees, repairs and maintenance.

In divorce, however, many transactions are conducted as though the "sticker" price were the total cost.

When it comes to property settlements, courts do not consider the taxes, maintenance fees, insurance, commissions and other expenses that are a normal part of any money exchange today.

Look at the family home, for instance. If you were going to sell your house under any conditions other than divorce, you would plan to fix up the place and pay a commission to a real estate agent (unless you sold it yourself). You might have to repair the roof or get a termite inspection. And once you sell the house, you may have to pay a capital gains tax. Under current tax law, you must pay taxes on any profit beyond the first $250,000

($500,000 if you are married and file jointly with your spouse).

In divorce, however, no one seems to talk about these very real costs that they would routinely discuss under any other circumstances. Spouses commonly pay their ex-partners for a full share of the equity—totally ignoring the other normal costs and benefits, and possible tax consequences, of a house sale. Only after selling the house does one spouse recognize the benefits or risks of carrying these costs alone. In our experience, most people *do* sell the family home, often within five years after the divorce.

At divorce, you and your spouse are essentially selling everything you own—either to each other or to an outsider.

If you were making a deal at any other time in your life, you would no doubt consider the hidden or additional costs that might crop up. That is how to handle the financial reality of divorce—looking at your situation from a realistic perspective that takes many factors into account, especially any tax-related consequences.

Financial reality begins where legal reality ends. To help you close the gap between the two, we provide you with worksheets and instructions on specific issues. We also suggest that you keep in mind five general observations on financial reality. We call them the basic "truths" about money and divorce, and you should refer to them any time you have to make tough decisions:

- In divorce, everything takes longer and costs more.

- When you're connected to another person financially, you're at risk.

- The IRS is watching your divorce—even when you're not.

- Cash is king.

- You're playing for keeps; don't sell off tomorrow for today.

A. In Divorce, Everything Takes Longer and Costs More

One of the universal misconceptions about divorce is the idea that it will be over quickly. Then all the parties can get on with their lives as though nothing happened.

In fact, your divorce can cost more money and take a longer time to settle than you ever imagined. For many couples, the whole process usually takes one to two years—even simple divorces that both parties thought would take only six months. The cost can range from several hundred dollars to several thousand. (One couple we knew took three years, spent $1 million and still hadn't settled when last seen ….)

To understand the costly nature of divorce, you must recognize the high price of splitting one economic unit in half. On the surface, an equitable property division would seem to mean each person walks away with half of what was shared by two, and is therefore left with enough to support one.

But in the mathematics of divorce, the equation does not work out that way. Spouses have unequal salaries and earning potential. And many people today live beyond their means. When it comes time to divide one household into two, there is rarely enough money to go around. That holds true as much for young married couples with little property as it does for wealthy couples with assets accumulated over many years. When a catastrophic event such as divorce hits, the fragile economic base for these couples is torn apart much as an earthquake loosens a house from its foundation, leaving everything in disarray.

Recognizing that everything takes longer and costs more can help you through those moments when you are suddenly faced with an unexpected debt or an unwanted delay in your divorce.

Accept the Fact That Money Is Tight

Maybe you have gotten used to the idea that your divorce will cost you dearly. What do you do with that knowledge?

Be willing to accept a change in your lifestyle. Face it, you may have to borrow money, move, get a second job or buy a used car instead of a new one. Be prepared for an economic pinch—at least for a while.

You will have to resist the very understandable temptation to splurge when your marriage is ending. The fact that you have to prepare for lean times also means that you must pay special attention to each financial decision you will make in divorce. In the end, the expense of the divorce itself means you must begin conserving your financial resources now.

B. When You're Connected to Another Person Financially, You're at Risk

This truth seems obvious, yet it's often ignored. Divorcing partners tend to resist or "forget" the fact that they must cut or minimize the financial ties that bind them. And they pay for those ties long after the marriage ends.

You are at risk any time you hold a joint interest with, have responsibility with or are financially dependent upon your spouse or ex-spouse. You have no control over what may happen in the future should your former husband or wife default on payments, commit fraud, go bankrupt, die or become disabled. Any one of these events could jeopardize your financial future.

There are many reasons for overlooking these risks; simple resistance to change is one of them. If you've been accustomed to a joint checking account for 20 years, it may feel strange to suddenly close it. It's possible that the act of reorganizing your financial position will force you to recognize that the marriage is really over. This can be a difficult period of adjustment if you're having trouble accepting the reality of the divorce.

Also, if you're denying the divorce, you'll likely avoid other things you need to do—like closing joint accounts or having your spouse's name taken off charge cards.

In other cases, a spouse feels overly responsible for the other partner's welfare—and so continues paying for something like a car long after it's appropriate. Resentments over an affair or some other perceived wrongdoing, such as lying, losing money, gambling or abusing alcohol, can also cause one partner to remain financially entangled with the other.

People often leave themselves at risk with their former partners because they simply do not think about it. As you work through this book and your divorce, we will point out the most common financial risks divorcing couples face and give you tools for protecting yourself. Because your divorce is unique, however, you must stay alert to the risks in your particular case. Identify the areas where you and your spouse could remain connected financially, then work to break those connections whenever possible.

C. The IRS Is Watching Your Divorce

Throughout the process of a divorce, you must consider the tax implications of each major financial move you make. To you, selling your property may seem like a simple business transaction—but to the Internal Revenue Service, those actions may create something called a "taxable event." Be sure you're managing those "events" to your best advantage. Factor in tax costs anytime you make a financial decision in your divorce, because, someday, the IRS will want to be paid.

As a general rule, a transfer of property between spouses incident to divorce is a nontaxable event. There may be major tax consequences to face in the future, however, when that asset is sold. With anything you keep as part of your settlement, you become totally and solely responsible for the taxes due on all gain (profit) on that asset from the time the two of you originally purchased it.

It is in your interest to consult with tax accountants or other financial professionals who can help you calculate the impact of taxes on your property division.

You will also need to decide how you will file tax returns once a divorce is underway. If you expect refunds on joint returns, decide how you will split the money. Be sure you know how the tax bill will be paid if money is due. And get all agreements in writing.

You'll also need to understand the tax consequences of alimony or support payments. The point is not to become paralyzed with worry about the IRS, but to recognize that your changing marital status definitely affects your tax status. Throughout the rest of the book, we give you guidance and formulas regarding tax matters.

 The IRS has made some significant improvements in the area of user-friendliness. The IRS website offers plain-English answers to many different tax questions, at www.irs.gov.

D. Cash Is King

Quick—which would you rather have:

- a retirement plan that promises to pay $125,000 in ten years, or $100,000 today?

- a Mercedes currently valued at $35,000, or a mutual fund with a current market value of $35,000?

- a secured note from your spouse promising to pay you $500 a month for the next five years, or a lump sum payment of $30,000 today?

The simple answer is: Take the money and run.

Women and Men—Divorce and Money

Throughout this book, we aim to provide an objective, professional view of money issues in divorce without regard to gender. We cannot honestly address personal financial realities, however, without giving recognition to the economic conditions of the larger society.

For instance, although the wage gap has been decreasing in recent years, men still tend to earn more than women in the U.S. And divorce can increase the disparity. A 1985 book by sociologist Lenore J. Weitzman, *The Divorce Revolution* (Free Press), reported that in the first year after divorce, women's standards of living decrease by an average of 73%, while men's increase by an average of 42%.

Those figures were disputed in 1996 by Richard R. Peterson, a sociologist at the Social Science Research Council in New York. He found that the drop in women's living standards was much smaller than Dr. Weitzman had calculated. According to the *New York Times* (May 9, 1996), Dr. Peterson reported that

after divorcing, women's standards of living decrease by an average of 27%, and men's increase by an average of 10%. He also stated that 9% of the men in the study had their standards of living decline after divorce by an average of 73%.

This debate is significant because Dr. Weitzman's data have long influenced legislators, policy makers and media reports on divorce issues. We mention these statistics to encourage both women and men to mentally prepare for the possibility of a reduced standard of living after divorce. Take time to accurately calculate your post-divorce potential income, child care needs, housing costs and other financial commitments.

Certainly, some individuals have used their divorce settlements as a launching pad to begin a business or pursue an education in order to increase their earning potential. But such an outcome takes careful planning and tough negotiating. Only by pursuing a divorce strategy that focuses on long-term financial interests can most people hope to avoid an economic struggle.

Like the proverbial "bird in the hand worth two in the bush," a dollar you get today is worth more than a promise of one tomorrow. In the examples above, the retirement plan may be riskier than you think, the Mercedes will depreciate and could be expensive to repair and your spouse might never make good on the promised payments. (While the $35,000 mutual fund is not exactly in cash, a mutual fund is a liquid asset—it can be converted to cash much more quickly than a car that is depreciating in value.) "Cash is king" holds true whether you are speaking of actual cash or cash-equivalent liquid assets.

Three basic financial concepts explain why cash is king: inflation, the time value of money and the risk-free nature of cash.

Inflation. This is the rise in the prices of goods and services. In other words, your dollar may not be capable of buying as much tomorrow as it will today. Suppose you currently have $1,000. With an inflation rate as small as 3.5% per year, your $1,000 would only have the power to buy $503 in goods in 20 years.

What if you and your spouse agree that you will be paid $10,000 as part of your settlement? If you're paid at the time of the divorce, you'd get $10,000 in today's dollars. If you have to wait three years for your money, that $10,000 will be worth less. Consequently, if you are offered a divorce settlement payment to be collected in the future, you must account for inflation.

Time value of money. Quite simply, if your money is working for you today—by growing in a quality mutual fund, producing profits in your business or even earning interest in a bank account—you are getting more value than if you have to wait until tomorrow to put that money to work. Why should you have to wait, and give your spouse the use of your money for months or years to come? Better to get your payments in cash at the time of the divorce than to miss the opportunity of using your money to best advantage.

Risk-free nature of cash. The value of a lump-sum payment doesn't fluctuate and is not taxed upon receipt. That may make it attractive enough for you to accept cash in exchange for getting less than the full amount owed.

E. You're Playing for Keeps

In the rush to reach a settlement, some divorcing couples seek the quickest way out—regardless of the future cost. When the dust settles, mistakes may surface that could cost you far more in money and time.

To manage money effectively, you need alternatives to help solve unexpected problems and to meet your goals. When you trade away long-term options for short-term needs, you're forcing yourself into a corner. You literally take future choices away from yourself. Accepting property—without considering maintenance costs and your future lifestyle—can strap you with debt for years to come. Agreeing to pay your spouse's bills just to hasten the divorce process may take care of some emotional needs, but it probably does not make sense financially. Nor should you calculate your finances based on a situation or arrangement that may prove only temporary.

Example: *Marla was divorcing and calculating her cost of living. During the divorce, Marla's mother provided free child care, and Marla assumed that care would continue indefinitely. She did not stop to think of what would happen should her mother become unable to babysit. After Marla's divorce was final, her mother found a new part-time job and could no longer care for her grandson. Marla spent a great deal of time and money renegotiating her support payments to reflect her true cost of living.*

When you are in the middle of a divorce, obvious problems may be overlooked unless you apply long-term thinking to your divorce decisions. Anytime you feel rushed or pressured, either by your spouse or the legal calendar of your divorce proceedings, take a moment to step back and look at your divorce from a future-oriented perspective. That view should help you withstand the pressures and make more informed decisions.

Money Is Not Math

Anxieties and phobias about math might hamper your ability to make financial decisions when a marriage ends. Do not feel embarrassed if you are intimidated by columns of numbers and fine-print paperwork. We have purposely simplified the formulas in this book so that everyone can understand the financial information needed at divorce.

Don't worry about mastering math. You need only gather current and accurate information about your financial situation. Getting the right numbers to plug into the formulas is much more important than learning how to make complicated tax or other calculations.

Years ago, computer scientists used the jargon term "GIGO," which stood for "Garbage In/Garbage Out." If they fed the computer the wrong data (garbage in), they would get the wrong answers (garbage out). Likewise, if you try to calculate your cost of living or the value of your property using outdated information or guesswork, you will end up with "garbage" in your final settlement. So gather the correct data; if you don't want to plug the numbers into the formulas yourself, you can hire a bookkeeper, accountant or financial planner to work with you.

■

CHAPTER

3

Emotional Divorce: Managing the "Money Crazies"

To make the best financial decisions during divorce, you must be aware of the emotional sabotage that can wreck your settlement negotiations.

Be on guard if you find yourself attempting to:

- get even

- get it over with, or

- get back together.

These three "gets"—plotting revenge, rushing through the divorce or pushing for a reconciliation—will hamper your ability to think clearly and act in your own best interest.

Check your attitude. Do any of the following sound like you?

"I'm going to get even no matter what it takes. You're going to pay for what you did to me. Just you wait. I'll see you in court."

It's normal to be angry during divorce, but if you're using the "get even" approach, you'll probably never be satisfied. A settlement may be totally equal according to the numbers on paper, but people with this attitude continue to complain years later. Not only will you harbor bitter feelings, but it's likely you will use poor judgment on important financial questions if you are motivated by revenge. And your attorney's fees will soar.

Realize, too, that if you insist on getting even, a court trial will likely cost you *three times* as much as an out-of-court settlement. Besides that, there is no guarantee that an ex-spouse will comply with court orders, or that the court will give you what you want. While you should certainly pursue your legal rights, the judicial system is no place to get satisfaction for your emotional demands.

"I don't care what happens. I just want to get it over with."

Stop right here. This is a major blind spot. The decisions you make during your divorce will affect you (and your children) for the rest of your life. It's no time to rush. While you may feel uncomfortable, your financial survival depends on participating in each step of your divorce settlement—regardless of how long it takes. And if you take too many shortcuts, you could find yourself paying for them because of unresolved resentments or unexpected money problems. In a year or two, your emotional life will be different. The financial agreements you make during divorce, however, affect you permanently.

"Maybe if I don't cause problems financially, we can work it out. I won't make waves. I'll just give in so we can get back together."

This is one of the most damaging misconceptions during divorce. Certainly you want to work things out if it's appropriate and if *both* of you are committed to a fair and equitable settlement. But it's futile to think that you can save the relationship by surrendering your financial leverage. Why should someone come back into a faltering relationship if you are giving the person everything he or she wants anyway? In any event, if you and your partner do get back together, your relationship will be much healthier if you are on an equal level financially and emotionally.

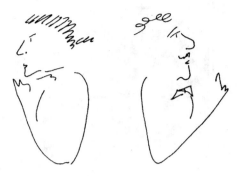

You may agree with all of the advice you have just read. But in reality, how do you deal with money when you are so involved emotionally with your spouse?

That is the central question you must answer for yourself, and that is what we will help you do throughout this book.

Basically, the better you manage your emotions, the better you will be able to manage your money during divorce. It's a difficult task. The emotional toll of divorce is so high that therapists and counselors use the label "crazy time" to describe it.

Ironically, you are being asked to make calm and rational financial decisions that will affect the rest of your life at a point when you are under some of the heaviest emotional pressures you are ever likely to experience. Those two tasks—the logical and linear management of money and the release of emotional tension—pull you in opposite directions. Attempting to balance these poles is an insane proposition. No wonder you feel as if you have the "money crazies."

Your best approach to managing these "money crazies" is to understand the divorce process in emotional terms and then take action to avoid some of the common pitfalls. Forewarned is forearmed.

A. Reduce Stress Whenever You Can

You can begin to resolve the financial-emotional struggle of divorce by recognizing just how stressful it is. Research has shown that divorce is second only to the death of a spouse in terms of the amount of stress produced. Some counselors contend that when other factors such as separation anxiety, moving from a long-term residence and loss of status are added to the equation, divorce becomes the most stressful event in life.

On top of all this, money is a difficult—sometimes taboo—subject, and even happily married couples can have a hard time talking about it. You may also feel pressure because you now have to take on tasks and responsibilities that were shared, or handled exclusively by your spouse. And most likely, you can no longer "talk things over" with your mate.

Here are some of the ways stress affects you during divorce:

- sleeplessness
- fatigue
- loss of appetite
- inability to cope with routine tasks
- disruption in work patterns
- emotional explosions, and
- frustrations over any challenge, large or small.

You can help combat these conditions by nurturing yourself. Do whatever is necessary for you to take care of yourself. If you have children, good self-care becomes even more important. Your frustrations are less likely to spill over onto the children if you are attending to your own needs.

Have a massage, go out to dinner or a movie, stroll through a museum—those are a few quick fixes that can see you through a rough period. Do not fall back on the excuse that you have little money or time to take care of yourself. Sitting under a tree or watching a sunset costs nothing, and can work wonders on your bruised emotions.

Even if you don't feel like it, try to keep your eating patterns close to normal. Good nutrition can be good medicine for your nerves. Also, exercising is one of the smartest things to do while divorcing. Besides relieving physical tension and helping to fight fatigue, vigorous workouts often improve your mental state.

These stress reduction techniques sound simple on paper—but simple or not, they are crucial to practice. The stress of your divorce will last for a while—you have to learn to live with it and manage it.

B. Safeguard Your Sanity

During a divorce, it is important to safeguard your emotional well-being. Spend more time with people who can give you positive reinforcement and less with those who may be critical of you or your divorce. Join a support group or see a therapist if necessary. In the long run, any money you spend on your mental health will be less than you'd lose if you got fired from your job or went on a shopping spree to deal with the "money crazies."

Rely more on your phone answering machine or e-mail. Not only can you screen nuisance calls or messages if your spouse is hostile, but also you can let others know that you are unreachable when you need to be alone.

There will be days when you feel like talking, and other days when it is the last thing you want to do. You may have just calmed down, and then, when you run into a friend and retell your story, emotions rise again—the catch in the throat, the anger, the frustration. That may be a healthy experience, but if you're feeling that it's "too much," limit your personal conversations just as you would your phone calls.

Take control of your home environment. Clean a closet, paint a room or move the furniture. There's an almost universal tendency during divorce to think about the past—obsessively and excessively. Most people find it is simply easier to put away the family pictures, the mementos and the visual cues that can trigger feelings of loss and depression.

You are not only affected by what you see, but also by what you hear. Instead of sitting back and passively allowing a favorite old song to make you sad, reach over and snap off the radio. The same goes for those heart-tugging commercials on television featuring happy couples—change the channel or turn off the TV. You'll be amazed at how good it can feel to exert control over something when so much of your life seems to be out of control.

C. Watch Out for Sore Spots

Probably, you already know which financial issues are likely to get you upset. All couples have sore spots—resentments about an unpaid bill, spending sprees, bounced checks, interfering in-laws, loans to relatives or gifts to a lover.

If you know that you will be dealing with an issue that's been a particular long-term irritation, prepare yourself for it instead of merely reacting to the inevitable pressure. Get a good night's sleep before tackling such a problem, or postpone a confrontation until you feel strong enough to be at your best. Taking these basic steps can go a long way toward reducing the tension in your life. Remember, reducing stress means increasing your ability to make sound financial decisions.

"No, We Can't Afford It Now"

Few parents enjoy denying their children toys, gifts or other pleasures. During divorce, you may find yourself repeating the phrase, "No! We can't afford it now!" more times than you care to count. Disappointing your children can only add to your level of frustration. But while you may want to protect them from harsh realities, you must also be honest and help your family adjust to the new circumstances.

Your children may be too young to understand the concept of money, much less the lack of it, so you may need an extra supply of parental patience. You can take heart in the fact that millions of couples have divorced, and millions of children have survived it. Teaching children to live on a tight budget may be more valuable in the future than giving in to their every whim today.

D. Be Prepared for Bad Scenes

Some emotional problems of divorce offer no easy solutions—when people are under stress, they tend to revert to their base, survival behaviors. That can lead to excessive drinking, shouting matches and other bad scenes. If someone tends to be absent-minded, selfish or nagging, those tendencies will be even more exaggerated when a marriage is ending.

During divorce, couples are facing the psychological task of separating, and consciously or unconsciously look for ways to break their connection to each other. During courtship, partners do everything possible to build the relationship, while in divorce, energy goes into destroying it. The stress, coupled with these "relationship destroying" behaviors, creates many of the horror stories of divorce. The sweet irrational gestures of romance are reversed by the equally ridiculous acts of "vengeance" during separation.

Maybe that will help you understand why your spouse is behaving so badly toward you—even if you thought you'd have a "civilized divorce."

Being prepared for the actions of someone who is determined to cut off any connection to you—by wiping out the checking account, running off to another state or ruining the family's credit—can help you short-circuit potential damage. Seeing bizarre behavior within the framework of the separation process may help you take it less personally. You may even find you are more detached from the short-term drama of divorce and therefore better able to concentrate on the long-term money questions that are important to you.

Don't Let Threats Throw You

In the process of divorce, your soon-to-be-ex-spouse may try to threaten you in some of these ways:

"Unless you play this my way, you'll never get a dime."

Keep calm. Of course the person making such a threat wants to scare and intimidate you and to continue the power plays that have worked in the past. When you hear such statements, tell yourself that coercion won't work. The property will be divided fairly, and support will be awarded in accordance with schedules.

"I'll go to jail before I'll pay you a dime of support."

Don't panic. Know that support can be enforced through a wage assignment, which means that your check will come directly from your ex-spouse's employer. If your ex-spouse doesn't work for someone else and falls behind in support payments, there are a number of enforcement methods. Ultimately, failing to pay support can mean a jail term, but most people pay voluntarily before going to jail.

"I'll quit my job before I'll pay you that kind of money."

Try to get witnesses to this kind of comment. If you can show a court that your ex-spouse quit a job to avoid support obligations, the court will probably continue support at the same level, and your ex will have to find a way to comply.

"I will reconcile with you only if you put everything in my name."

Nice try. If you are going to reconcile, why do you need an agreement that is lopsidedly in favor of the person making such a demand? Be extremely suspicious of such statements, and don't sign anything without consulting your attorney.

If you are on the receiving end of a threat, you may be intimidated to the point of giving in. Do not. Ignore threats as best you can and continue to work for a reasonable resolution.

E. Develop a Financially Focused Mental Attitude

To combat a devious spouse during divorce, you must develop a strong mental attitude and a solid legal strategy. Certainly you are entitled to feelings of outrage and betrayal. You can utter the cry, "How can you do this to me?!?" as much as you want to. In fact, that phrase is a common chorus in divorce cases. Yes, many things that happen in divorce *are* unfair.

But the fact remains that you will have to keep going and keep fighting for your financial life regardless of the injustices, which may be perpetrated by your spouse and/or your spouse's attorney. You can stand up for yourself. If you stay focused on the future and the financial realities of your life, you will be in a much stronger position as your divorce progresses.

F. Avoid the "All at Once" Syndrome

Most likely, you will experience a wide range of feelings and moods: anger, hatred, elation, excitement, sadness, loss, depression, bitterness, rejection, loneliness, guilt and hostility. Sometimes it will feel as though you're experiencing those feelings all at once. In fact, the "all at once" phenomenon seems to be part of the "money crazies" of divorce.

You may also feel that everything is coming apart all at once. Just as soon as you get the car fixed, the washer or the stove breaks down. One explanation is that you simply notice problems more because of your stressful state. Moreover, by the time most people separate, a great deal of their energy has been focused on the relationship—not on the normal chores that can keep a household running. You may not be in the mood to defrost the refrigerator or check the oil in the car as usual. That lack of maintenance can catch up with you as the machinery in your life begins breaking down.

The "all at once" syndrome in divorce can manifest itself in other ways as well. Some people decide that since they are changing a mate, they should change everything else in their lives as well. They try to lose weight, quit smoking, get a new job and redecorate the house, all at the same time. Give yourself time. Go slowly. You will have your hands full just getting through the divorce.

G. Manage the Ebb and Flow of Emotions

Keep in mind that emotions tend to be experienced in waves. One day you may feel fine; the next day, life is awful. Such fluctuations are common in divorce, and eventually the wave action subsides. Do not attempt to handle important money tasks on the bad days—wait until the storm subsides.

Because the level of tension in a divorce is often compared to the stress that accompanies the death of a loved one, some psychologists claim the grief processes are also similar. Elisabeth Kubler-Ross's groundbreaking work on death and dying pinpointed five stages of grief: denial, anger, bargaining, letting go and acceptance. These stages do not necessarily occur in this order. How you go through these stages is unique to you, but it is important that you experience them.

Marriage counselors note that people who avoid grieving by jumping into a new relationship too quickly are only prolonging the process. Those who do allow themselves to grieve for the marriages

they had (or the marriages they wished they had) actually get through their divorces more quickly— and carry less psychological baggage when the marriage is over. As a consequence, they are often able to manage their financial lives better, too.

While the grief processes are similar in death and divorce, some important differences do exist. Social attitudes have changed greatly, but widows and widowers still get more sympathy than those who have divorced. With divorce, too, the door to your relationship does not close with the same finality. You may still have contact with your former spouse for years and go through the grieving process many times as you make contact and separate.

Ambivalence—the love-hate relationship with your former spouse—is common when marriages end. Actually, the push and pull in and out of the relationship characterizes the separation process that began before the actual divorce. Commonly, one person in the relationship becomes discontented before the other, and this "initiator" is usually the one to ask for the divorce.

If your partner was the initiator, don't be surprised if he or she seems to have already moved on. In fact, that person had a head start on the psychological work needed to separate. Just don't let yourself lag behind financially, or get pushed into doing something you're not ready for.

The initiator may already be out the door and pressuring you to "get on with it"—to sign over the condo, to sell the house, to separate the silverware. Meanwhile, you may still be at the "starting gate," emotionally shocked and dazed, unable to finalize a process you have only begun.

If you initiated the divorce, realize that it is probably in your best financial and family interests to be sensitive to your partner's rate of accepting the separation. Your negotiations are likely to be more successful if you present your financial proposals to someone who has had a chance to assimilate what is happening in the relationship on a personal level.

Psychologists have found that the hardest part of the divorce process tends to be the time just before the actual physical separation. Tensions often mount dramatically until the real break occurs. Some couples separate and reconnect several times in an attempt to save the marriage. Whatever is happening to you emotionally, continue taking steps to put your financial life in order. Should you and your partner ultimately reunite, your relationship will be stronger if you have not used money as a weapon against each other.

Mixed Emotions—Working With Attorneys

Controlling your emotions is important—particularly when it comes to working with an attorney on your divorce settlement. Remember, your attorney is not your therapist or longtime confidante. As you proceed through this book and through your divorce settlement, be honest with yourself about whether you are being a model client (and one who will save attorney's fees) or a client whom your attorney would like to avoid. The following questions will help you make that determination:

- Have I given my attorney accurate and complete information on time?

- Have I thought through the objectives of my divorce agreement?

- Do I waffle in making decisions or compromises?

- If I'm not clear on a legal issue, do I ask for clarification?

- If I have a disagreement with my attorney, am I willing to talk it through to resolution?

- Do I neglect to cover issues and later blame my attorney for forgetting certain items?

- On a continuum between being a pest and being unavailable, where might I be?

- Am I paying my bills on time?

H. Don't Let Financial Tasks Overwhelm You

As you move through your divorce, it will be easy to become overwhelmed with the financial details. You may suffer from math anxiety or money phobias. Or perhaps you and your partner shared a complicated financial life, one that will take effort to untangle.

Whatever form your feelings take, you can get some relief by breaking down your tasks into small steps. Reward yourself for completing an item. Hire a math whiz to help you when necessary. If you are upset, do not hesitate to see a counselor or join a therapy group. That strategy makes much more sense, and is less costly, than using your attorney as a therapist or asking your friends to help you understand a situation that calls for expert analysis.

Anything you can do to build your self-esteem is important now. Divorce tends to make you feel worse about yourself, and it is easy to confuse money issues with your sense of self-worth. Besides the stress-management techniques already described, you may also find it helpful to keep a journal. Having a notebook handy to jot down feelings throughout the day helps dissipate tense moments. This record can serve as an "invisible calculator" to tally the emotional costs of financial decisions. Tracking feelings and reactions in this way can make it easier to reach those bottom-line decisions.

While it may seem as though the inner turmoil from your divorce will never end, it is a finite process which only takes time. For some people, the process lasts one or two years, while for others, recovery from a divorce may take longer. You are very likely to become a different person in that time, with different needs and attitudes. Keep that in mind as you manage the "money crazies" of your divorce—and make sure the financial choices you make today will work for you tomorrow.

Divorce—On a Spiritual Level

For some people, divorce stress is more than emotional. It becomes a religious or spiritual crisis. We cannot attempt to address such a crisis in this book. You can, however, contact local churches, synagogues or clergy members for referrals to divorce ministries.

One note of caution: No matter how you feel about your divorce from the spiritual point of view, you cannot ignore its legal and financial consequences.

For example, one client insisted on working exclusively with attorneys and other professionals who shared her faith. While there is nothing inherently wrong with this, it didn't work in her case. She didn't judge the professionals she hired on their competence or abilities. In the end, she had to go through the costly process of finding a new attorney and accountant to help her complete the divorce.

For more information on selecting professionals, see Chapter 7.

■

The Hardest Part:
Is My Marriage Really Over?

Legally, a final decree from the court marks the termination of your married life.

Emotionally, it may be years before you feel complete peace of mind about the end of your marriage. But from a strictly financial standpoint, the marriage ends when you or your spouse begin to take unilateral actions, regardless of the effect on the other person.

It's that moment when one spouse stops acting like a trusted friend or partner and starts putting the other spouse in economic jeopardy. One spouse might empty a bank account, leaving the other with nothing to pay the bills or hire an attorney. Or a soon-to-be-ex might run up debts unbeknownst to the other.

A great deal of financial damage can take place in the early stages of divorce. You must protect your interests whether or not you feel the marriage is over.

Couples often go through several phases of splitting up and getting back together before the final break. While you are going through this push and pull of separation, you may find yourself walking a tightrope between conflicting demands and emotions—watching out for your personal property without antagonizing your spouse, or taking care of your individual needs while not letting your spouse off the hook for joint responsibilities.

Eventually, you will recognize when the marriage has reached a point of no return. Even then, you may hold out hope for a reconciliation. There's nothing wrong with hope—as long as you continue taking care of business. That means knowing precisely where your financial risks lie, and what to do about them. The following stories illuminate the dilemma you are in at this stage of divorce—and the danger of ignoring its consequences.

A Happy Ending	An Unhappy Ending
When you're in the midst of a crumbling relationship, it may be hard to believe that resolving money problems can sometimes help clear up other troubling issues in a marriage. Alice came in for a financial consultation and said she was considering a divorce. Although she had always worked outside the home, her husband managed the finances and kept her in the dark. Unwilling to tolerate the situation any longer, Alice began educating herself and learning about the couple's cash flow, taxes and investments. She also consulted an attorney to assess her legal rights. Secure with her knowledge, she confronted her husband and demanded a greater financial role in the marriage. They argued bitterly and almost divorced at several points along the way. Through patience and counseling, however, they resolved their differences and kept the marriage intact.	The infamous Palm Beach divorce of Roxanne and Peter Pulitzer in the 1980s demonstrates what can happen if both parties are not equally committed to a reconciliation. Roxanne claimed that in trying to save her marriage, she lost her financial power and leverage as a mother. Upon receiving divorce papers concerning hearings and proceedings, she said she followed her husband's instructions to throw them in the garbage because he did not intend to end the marriage. Doing just that placed Roxanne at a great disadvantage when her husband did, in fact, continue the divorce proceedings. "I lost the case before it even started," she said once it was over. Instead of focusing on the reality of her situation, she put her energy into reconciliation—and lost.

No one can really predict which marriages will come apart or stay together, because every couple, and the dynamic between them, is unique. If you are still questioning whether you have a viable marriage or not, some options available to you are:

Counseling. Now is the time to find out if your marriage is worth saving. Some people cannot—and perhaps should not—let go until they have explored every avenue of reconciliation. But if your spouse refuses to cooperate, you may have little choice but to accept the inevitable and move on with the divorce.

Temporary separation. For some couples, time apart becomes a time for healing. Make a list of your joint obligations and expenses. Through mediation or counseling, you and your spouse may be able to reach agreements about dealing with the practical demands of life while you work on your emotional relationship.

After you give yourself some time to consider this information and your options, you must confront the main decision presented in this chapter: Is your marriage really over? This question is not meant to rush you toward divorce, but rather to help you clarify your position. You can afford to leave some questions open in life—but this isn't one of them. Once you've made this decision it will be significantly easier for you to tackle the hard tasks ahead. But if you're unclear on this, all decisions that follow become much harder to make.

Okay—take a deep breath. Write out your answer below, or speak it out loud to someone you trust. Either way, the time has come to make the decision which only you can.

Is my marriage really over?

Whatever Stage You're in, Don't Ignore Legal or Financial Realities

⚠ Whether you attempt counseling, a trial separation or some other method of resolving conflicts in your marriage, do not ignore your financial responsibilities and potential liabilities. Just as you would regard legal notices or documents as important matters at any other time in your life, so too must you recognize the serious implications of any legal actions in the early stages of divorce—even if your spouse tries to convince you otherwise. Do not ignore court orders or papers. And, if you have any reason to suspect your spouse is moving assets or taking funds from your joint accounts, you should quickly read Chapter 6 for information on how to protect your interests.

■

The Separation: What Happens When One Spouse Moves Out?

"I told him I wanted him out by the end of the month."

"I can't stand it another minute—I'm getting out of here."

"It's over and it would be easier on all of us if you would just go."

Don't be surprised if you find yourself saying—or hearing—any of these statements before you separate. Feelings run high, and emotions seem to dictate the schedule of events in your life. Old arguments and long-held resentments commonly surface in this most difficult period, just before or during the actual physical separation. Power plays may become more troublesome as one of you may try to "force" the other out.

No matter how you feel about your spouse, neither of you necessarily "has to" move—unless you or your children would be in physical danger if your spouse stayed. In such a case, you could get a restraining order from the court, prohibiting your spouse from remaining in the family home. In many states, you may be able to find a kit you can use to do this yourself, without a lawyer's assistance. In other states, however, court clerks must assist you in completing papers to apply for a restraining order. Many women's clinics also provide help—including

assistance in applying for restraining orders—for victims of domestic violence. (See the Appendix.)

Even when violence is not an issue in your marriage, practical reasons might dictate that one spouse move out. For example, many divorcing couples who live under the same roof find making agreements difficult. If one of the spouses moves out, the divorce often proceeds more smoothly and with less pain.

In the midst of ending a marriage, you may not want to look at your situation in the cold, harsh light of financial reality. But that denial could ultimately cost you thousands of dollars. Before you insist on leaving or having your spouse move out, take a little time to consider the financial consequences of the separation date.

Whether you view this time period as a trial separation (while you continue to work on your marriage) or a separation for real (as in the beginning of divorce), the following information is important to you.

Protect Your Rights to Custody of Your Children If You Plan to Move Out

⚠️ If you have children, the primary caretaker might want to stay in the family home while the other spouse rents a place, house-sits for someone else or moves in with a friend. Realize, however, that by moving out of the family home without your children, you could jeopardize your chances of getting physical custody of them. This is because few judges like to change the status quo when it comes to kids. So before you move out, be sure to make arrangements with your spouse as to the conditions under which you will each see the children. Define each parent's schedule with the children, including who will drive them to and from school, softball practice, ballet lessons and worship services.

If you have any question or doubt about your rights as a parent or feel that you are being pushed away from your children by moving out of the house, be sure to consult an attorney who can help you establish custody arrangements prior to moving out.

A. The Separation Date

After you think about who will move, the second question becomes even more crucial: by when? Depending on your state's laws, the date on which you formally separate can affect your credit, pension benefits or other assets. Think of that date as a legal benchmark.

Before that date, you and your spouse are still married and are subject to the same laws you've been living under since you first wed. After that date, however, you enter a gray area of financial and legal reality which is not fully clarified until the divorce becomes final. You have no control over the actions of your spouse in this time period, yet you are still tenuously connected—which means you could potentially be responsible for your spouse's bills. In addition, the value of a retirement plan or other assets can be thousands of dollars more or less at settlement time, depending on whether your state values and defines marital property from the date of separation or the date of divorce.

The definition of the separation date differs among states. This is a question you will need to ask your attorney (see Section B, below). In a few states, the separation date is the date you or your spouse physically move out of your joint residence or conduct your life differently, indicating a final breakup of the marital relationship. Other states consider that the separation begins the day you or your spouse files divorce papers. And in other states, the day on which you formally tell your spouse that you intend to get a divorce is the date on which you are considered separated. In either of the latter two situations, couples may continue living together after the separation date, perhaps because neither can afford to move. This arrangement may be very uncomfortable.

Determining a particular date to be the date of separation may have certain financial advantages for one spouse or the other. If you are going to be responsible for the credit card charges your spouse incurred during the marriage, for instance, you'd want the date of separation to be prior to your spouse's shopping spree. Or, if your company adds a tidy sum to your pension plan each May, you might want to move out in April.

Granted, it's difficult to take such factors into account before you separate. In six months to a year, however, you will have the advantage of hindsight and a different perspective. Instead of having regrets later, take a little time right now to think about how the separation will affect you.

What follows is an overview of how the separation date affects these financial issues:

- debts and credit
- retirement plans and pension benefits
- income and income taxes
- investments and business assets, and
- alimony.

D-Days

During your divorce, you may see or hear these abbreviations used to refer to certain milestones:

DOM   Date of Marriage

DOS   Date of Separation

DOD   Date of Divorce

If You Must Move

Although you may not like the idea, it's possible that you will have to move from your home. You can make life easier by preparing for the pressures you will face. Moving is stressful at any time; divorce only compounds the stress. Not only are you losing a mate, but you're letting go of a home and all that it has been to you.

Feelings of separation and abandonment can be exacerbated by anxiety about where you will live next. To cope with your emotional reactions, look at your situation in practical terms, which helps separate real concerns from unfounded fears. Here are a few things to remember:

- Movers often charge a premium for their hectic summer season, while offering lower prices between October and April. The first and last days of the month are also busy times for movers, so you may be able to save money by moving mid-month. The American Movers Conference suggests that you question a mover carefully about rates, liability, pickup and delivery and claims protection. To move locally, you'll probably be charged an hourly rate or a flat fee. Long-distance movers usually charge by the weight and mileage.

- In addition to the cost of the move itself, you'll need money to hook up utilities, phones and other services. You'll have other "new house" costs like buying kitchen staples, cleaning products and other basics. Count on eating out a lot, too, before you restock your kitchen or unpack your dishes and pots and pans.

- If you move your children out of state without your spouse's consent, a judge may order you to return the children to the state immediately and could ultimately deny you custody. Judges do not look favorably on parents who move their children away from the other parent, school, friends and other community ties. Before making such a move, consult an attorney to make sure you do not jeopardize your rights as a parent.

- Under changes created by the Taxpayer Relief Act of 1997, if you move out of the house during the divorce, it can still be considered your principal residence for tax purposes. This happens when ownership of the house is transferred to one spouse in a divorce and that spouse moves out. In other words, if you have to move out of the house during the divorce, you can still claim it as your principal residence for tax purposes, as long as you and your spouse have a written agreement about your intention that the house will remain your primary residence.

1. Debts and Credit

Bill collectors do not suddenly stop sending their statements just because you are going through a divorce. When you enter the limbo of separation, pay particular attention to its impact on your debts and credit standing.

a. Debts

In general, both spouses are responsible for paying debts generated during the marriage. Once the divorce is final, neither is responsible for the debts created by the other. Debts incurred during separation, however, can be tricky. The general rule is that debts incurred after the separation date but before the divorce is final are the responsibility of the spouse who incurred them and must be paid by that person.

One exception is for "family necessities." For example, if, during the period of separation, one spouse incurs a debt for food, clothing, shelter or medical care, the other spouse may be obligated to pay a portion of that bill. Children's expenses, too, usually fall into this category. The law views a spousal support or child support obligation as more important than one to a creditor.

The general rule—that debts generated during separation must be paid by the person who incurred them—does not always protect you, however. If your partner defaults or simply refuses to pay, the creditors no doubt will come after you for payment. And because you were still married when the debts were created, the creditor will assert a right to collect from you. Your only remedy may be to try to get reimbursed by your ex-spouse.

Example: *Janet's husband, Jim, had dental work done after he moved out of their apartment, but he never paid the bill. Janet did not know anything about his dental work, and Jim left town as soon as the divorce was final. The dentist turned the bill over to a collection agency, which then went after Janet for the money. Eventually she settled the bill, but not without spending her time, energy and money to resolve the problem.*

b. Credit

Remember the warning given in Chapter 2: When you're financially connected to someone else, you're at risk. You are responsible for any use of a credit or charge card by either cardholder on a joint account.

Most of the time it is best to close joint credit accounts, because you cannot control your spouse's use of them. But before angrily closing all joint credit accounts, check first to see how your individual credit will be affected by such an action. If you do not have credit in your own name, be sure to establish it before you separate.

There may be certain circumstances in which you'll need joint credit. For instance, if you'll both be buying maintenance items for your house, rental property or children, it may be convenient to have a joint checking account to which both you and your spouse contribute. You can make a formal,

written agreement as to how the account will be used and even require that all checks written on the account must have both spouses' signatures. Keep in mind, however, that even though you may need to retain joint accounts, you should not consider starting any new joint financial ventures.

Extensive information on debts, creditors, establishing credit in your own name and other similar issues can be found in *Money Troubles: Legal Strategies to Cope With Your Debts* and *Credit Repair*, both by Robin Leonard & Deanne Loonin (Nolo). You can also find a variety of informative articles on this subject on Nolo's website at www.nolo.com.

2. Retirement Plans and Pension Benefits

In most situations, the marital portion of your retirement plan is determined as of the date of your divorce. This means you'll probably be entitled to any growth in the account, even if you separate months earlier.

In addition, many companies provide an accounting of retirement benefits only on an annual basis. The amount in a pension fund, profit-sharing plan or other type of benefit program could significantly differ from one part of a year to the next. By the time your divorce becomes final, a year or two could have passed since your separation, and the retirement fund may have grown by thousands of dollars.

To safeguard your interest, obtain a copy of the benefit brochure issued by your own or your spouse's employer if possible. It's also helpful to have copies of the actual retirement plan itself or a summary of it. (Chapter 14 covers retirement plans in detail. It includes a letter you'll need to send to request information and give notice of your interest in your spouse's retirement benefit plans.) Because so many factors affect your retirement benefits, it is best to consult an attorney, a financial advisor, a pension plan expert or an actuary who can analyze your particular situation. (See Chapter 7 for more information on seeking advice from a professional.)

Check Your Credit File

During a separation, it is a good idea to obtain a copy of your credit report. You are entitled to a free copy if you:

- were denied credit, employment or insurance within the previous 60 days because of something in your credit report
- are unemployed and plan to apply for a job within 60 days
- receive public assistance
- believe your credit file contains errors due to someone's fraud, such as stealing your Social Security number, or
- live in Colorado, Georgia, Maryland, Massachusetts, New Jersey or Vermont and have not requested a copy of your report within the past year.

Otherwise, you will have to pay up to $8 per copy.

To obtain your report, draft a letter, specifying the following:

- full name, including generations (Jr., Sr., III)
- current home address and previous addresses for the past five years (including zip codes)
- telephone number
- date of birth, and
- Social Security number.

Be sure to specify the grounds under which you're requesting your report and attach documents showing your denial of credit, unemployment or whatever. Send your letter to any of the following:

- Experian, National Consumers Assistance Center, P.O. Box 2002, Allen, TX 75013, 888-397-3742. www.experian.com.
- Trans Union, Consumer Disclosure Center, P.O. Box 1000, Chester, PA 19022, 800-888-4213. www.transunion.com
- Equifax, P.O. Box 740241, Atlanta, GA 30374, 800-685-1111. www.equifax.com

Your credit report will provide you with valuable information about your outstanding debts. In addition, you will have the chance to make corrections should there be any errors in your report. The credit bureau will enclose information on how to dispute incorrect information in your credit file.

3. Income and Income Taxes

Under the laws of many states, the income that you earn after the date of separation is yours and yours alone. Therefore, you are solely responsible for the taxes due on this income. Also, the day you choose to separate may influence your decision to file your income taxes jointly or separately. (See Chapter 11.)

4. Investments and Business Assets

Many states value assets at the date of the divorce, not the date of separation. This means that if one spouse moves out of the house and the assets appreciate between that date and the date the divorce becomes final, the spouses will share in the appreciation. The valuation of investments and business assets should be double-checked, however, as the rules do vary from state to state.

Example: *Having assets valued from the date of divorce instead of the date of separation cost Harry a bundle. On the date of separation, his extensive portfolio was valued at $5 million. By the date of the divorce, his holdings had almost doubled because of the stock market boom during the period between separation and divorce. So instead of having to split $5 million with his soon-to-be-ex-wife, Celeste, he had to share the full $10 million.*

5. Alimony

You may not realize it, but your separation date could have an effect on alimony. In many states, a nonworking, dependent or lower-wage-earning spouse is presumed to be in need of alimony for a longer period of time after the end of a long-term marriage (usually one lasting at least ten years from the date of marriage to the date of separation). If you're a few months shy of the ten-year (or the time length mandated by your state) presumptive period for alimony, you may want to stay around to avoid jeopardizing those future payments.

Social Security Benefits After Divorce

If you were married for at least ten years, you are entitled to Social Security benefits based on your ex-spouse's contributions. These benefits become available after you have been divorced for at least two years. You are entitled to these benefits regardless of whether your ex-spouse claims benefits. Your receipt of benefits will not reduce the benefits payable to your former spouse.

A few additional facts:

- Benefits are based on your ex-spouse's total contributions, not just those made during your marriage.

- If you were married (and divorced) twice and both marriages lasted more than ten years, you can claim benefits through the ex-spouse with the larger Social Security account.

- If you remarry and do not divorce your second spouse, you cannot claim benefits based on your first spouse's account.

- If you receive disabled divorced widow's or widower's benefits, your benefits will continue if you remarry when you are age 50 or older.

Because each worker's Social Security file is confidential, you may not be able to find out the status of your spouse's benefits. You can try to get this information by asking your spouse or by contacting the local or national office of the Social Security Administration (SSA). Call 800-772-1213 to get a "Request for Earnings and Benefits Estimate Statement" (Form SSA-7004). You can also visit the SSA website at www.ssa.gov. The site includes downloadable copies of many publications and forms, including form SSA-7004. Once you have the form, complete it and send it back to the SSA.

If these methods fail, you will probably need a lawyer's help to get information about your spouse's benefits. (See Chapter 12, Section B, for information on working with lawyers. For more on different types of retirement benefits, see Chapter 14.)

Before You Move

Before you move out of the family home, be sure to make copies of those documents referred to in the *Financial Facts Checklist* in Chapter 8. Even if you don't have your spouse's cooperation in this project, it is important that you get the copies. If you must resort to the legal process of discovery (see Chapter 12), your legal bill may run sky high—and there is no guarantee that you will get all the information you may ultimately need.

You should also do an inventory of all shared or individual property. Take photographs or make a videotape to document the condition of property at stake in your divorce. (For more information on dealing with property, see Chapter 6, Section A6.)

B. Questions to Ask Your Attorney

As you can see, you'll need to carefully calculate your legal and financial positions before separating. Because the legal definition of the separation date varies from state to state, however, we cannot explain the nuances of your state's law. We can provide you with this list of important questions for you to ask your attorney or research at your local law library.

1. Who should move out of the house? Can I be forced to move?

2. In our state, what defines the date of separation? Is it when my spouse:

   - moves out?

   - files for divorce?

   - declares the marriage is over?

3. What other legal or financial ramifications of the date of separation should I know about?

4. Which debts—incurred after the date of separation but before the divorce becomes final—is each spouse responsible for?

5. What date is used—separation date, date of final negotiations or date closest to the final divorce—to calculate the value of assets?

6. Can the court award alimony to a spouse indefinitely? If not, when is it likely for the court to terminate spousal support? Does the court consider the length of the marriage in awarding spousal support?

7. What is the usual length of an alimony award in our state?

8. Who should make payments on joint debts during the divorce?

9. Do I have the right to reimbursement for payments I make on joint obligations during the divorce?

10. Can I get divorced before our property is fully divided?

■

CHAPTER

6

Closing the Books: What Do We Do With Joint Accounts?

Your spouse may not want to ruin you—but his or her actions can still leave you at risk.

When you and your mate are in the midst of splitting up, you come face to face with a hard fact we've stated before: When you are connected to another person financially, you are at risk. Does that mean you need to rush out in a panic and close all your joint accounts? Not necessarily—it is never wise to act in panic, and only in a handful of divorces do spouses deliberately destroy each other financially. But even if your spouse doesn't purposefully ruin your financial life, he or she can do things that leave you vulnerable.

One way to gauge how much financial damage your spouse could inflict is to measure the level of hostility between you. For example, if you're no longer on speaking terms—or you speak only about the children—you will probably want to act quickly to separate your financial lives.

Even if your divorce is "friendly," don't count on that goodwill to determine what you should do about joint accounts. Look at your situation objectively. Apply your own common sense and instincts. You should be moving toward eliminating the financial obligations you share with the person you are divorcing. Because income is often reduced—and expenses increased—by a divorce, it may not be possible to cut all connections. Nevertheless, you can still reduce your risks.

A. Joint Account Checklist

The material that follows should alert you to common trouble spots.

1. Credit Cards

Before closing joint credit card accounts, be sure you have established credit in your own name, based on your own income. Department stores, for instance, may open an individual account for you when you close a joint one. You may be tempted to include your ex-spouse's income when applying for separate credit. Don't do it. Because you won't be able to use your ex's income to repay your bills, this practice borders on fraud.

If you don't qualify for credit based on your income, you can apply for a secured credit card. Many banks will give you a credit card if you secure it by opening a savings account. Your credit limit equals a percentage of the amount you deposit into your account. Depending on the bank, you'll be required to deposit as little as a few hundred dollars or as much as a few thousand. Many secured credit cards have a conversion option. This option lets you convert the secured card into a regular credit card (one not tied to a savings account) after a certain time period, if you use the card responsibly.

To find the names of banks issuing secured credit cards, call local banks or check the Internet. Perhaps the most comprehensive website on available credit cards is maintained by the Ram Research Group at www.ramresearch.com. Whatever you do, don't call a "900" or even an "800" number service that claims "instant credit—no questions asked."

Once you have established your own credit, write simple letters to close any jointly held credit cards or revolving loan accounts. Even if a credit card account hasn't been used for years, close it to prevent future usage without your knowledge or authorization. Such letters may not fully protect you from obligation for your spouse's later-incurred debts, but they put the burden on the creditors to take action.

Your credit reports should give you all the information you need to complete the letter suggested below. (See Chapter 5 for information on how to get a copy of your credit report.) Call the lender (a toll-free number is usually on the back of your statement) to confirm the address. Then fill in the creditor's name and address, your account number, your Social Security number and your signature. Send all letters to creditors by certified mail, return receipt requested, and keep copies for your files.

Sample Letter for Closing Joint Accounts

Date:

To:

Re: Account number _____

          Card member_____(your name)

          Social Security number _____[   ]

Dear_____:

This letter is to inform your company that the above-referenced account is to be closed, effective immediately. At this time, my (husband/wife), (name of spouse), and I are seeking a divorce.

Please be aware, if (spouse's name) should happen to be a primary signer on this account, (he/she) does not have my permission to reestablish this card at any time using my name and/or credit. In other words, I am requesting a hard close, not a soft close. Please advise me immediately of any outstanding charges on this account.

If you are unable to close this account with only my authorization, you are instructed to terminate my relationship with this credit card account immediately. In such a case, any debt incurred after the date of this letter shall be the responsibility of (spouse).

In addition, please notify the three major credit bureaus that this account has been "closed by consumer," and kindly send me written confirmation once these transactions have been completed.

Thank you in advance for your help and for the opportunity of doing business with you.

Sincerely,

(Your name)

Most of the time you will have little trouble terminating joint accounts. On occasion, however, a creditor may demand that you pay off the balance first. If you can afford to pay the bill, do so. That's better than leaving the account open and allowing your spouse to run up more debts.

If you can't pay off the entire balance, you can still ask that the account be made inactive while you make payments. This strategy prohibits further charges from being made on the account. Once the balance is paid, the creditor should close the account completely. Most customer service representatives will take care of your request. If you can't make satisfactory arrangements through a customer service representative, however, ask to speak to a supervisor, and continue up the chain of command. Explain that you are going through a divorce and that you are closing out your joint accounts. Remember to put all communications with credit card companies in writing, keep copies and document your payments.

Be aware that if, during your separation, your spouse uses a joint credit card account (before you get a chance to close it) to charge basic items such as food or clothes, you might be responsible for the payments. (See Chapter 5, Section A1.)

2. Equity Credit Lines

A frequently overlooked area of joint financial liability involves equity lines of credit. An equity credit line is an open-ended loan made by a lending institution—usually a bank, savings and loan or thrift company—against the equity in your home. The lender gets a secured interest in your home, and if you don't repay the loan, the lending institution can force the sale of your house.

Some equity credit lines supply a checkbook and can be used just like a joint checking account. Whichever spouse has the checkbook has access to the money.

If you and your spouse have an equity credit line, pay a visit to your lender. Take a letter with you requesting that the account be closed or frozen because of your divorce. If you have a checkbook, be sure to request that no additional checks be issued. By leaving an equity line of credit open during the divorce, you risk losing your home.

Similar to an equity line of credit is a margin account, offered by stock brokerage firms. To close the account, follow the same procedure as with your bank, asking in writing that the account be frozen. Your goal is to keep your spouse from withdrawing money, trading stocks or taking profits. While you may want to shut down the account now, you'll probably have to wait until you are closer to a settlement before closing it completely.

Beware of fraudulent loans. If your spouse claims to have borrowed money during your marriage from friends or relatives, proceed with caution. It may be a scheme to snatch joint assets. Here's how it works: One spouse falsely claims to have borrowed money during the marriage, unbeknownst to the other spouse, from a close friend or relative. The false loan is then paid back from joint assets. The friend or relative who receives the money then returns it surreptitiously once the divorce is final, and voilà! What was once a joint asset now belongs only to one spouse. The way to prevent this is to stay involved in financial matters during the marriage. Specifically, review records showing the flow of money in and out, and check income tax returns to determine if interest is being paid on loans to relatives.

3. Joint Checking, Savings and Other Deposit Accounts

As with joint credit cards, you may not want to close joint checking or saving accounts unless you have an account in your own name, or will open one immediately. If you don't close a joint account, however, you run the risk that your spouse could come in and empty it without your knowledge.

You have a few options:

- Ask the bank to freeze the account and not allow either you or your spouse to move money in or out without both of your signatures.

- Take out half the money in the account and place it into your individual account.

- Close the account and place all the money into a dual-signature account. You'll probably need an agreement with your spouse to use this option.

⚠ If your spouse takes all the money from your joint accounts, your settlement—or a court—will probably provide for your reimbursement. That repayment, however, could be months or years away. Until then, you have to deal with losing your share of a joint account. If you have nothing in a personal savings or checking account, you may have to borrow money to cover the shortfall.

If You Are Broke

If you're out of money, you're probably safe in withdrawing one-half of the cash in joint accounts. (If you have any doubts, ask an attorney.) Of course, there are also the old standby methods of holding a garage sale or calling Mom and Dad. You could also ask for temporary alimony. (See Chapter 9, Section D.)

---

4. Safe-Deposit Boxes

Just as one spouse can remove all money from a joint checking account, so too can a spouse take all of the items out of a joint safe-deposit box. Unfortunately, safe-deposit boxes are one of those items in which "whoever gets there first" is the operative rule. Try to take possession of both keys to the safe-deposit box if at all possible. If your spouse empties the box before you do, you may have little chance of reclaiming the contents.

You might possibly protect yourself if you can get to the box prior to the divorce and write an inventory of the contents and take photos of the items. Then have the bank officer sign the list documenting your inventory. If your spouse removes anything later, you'll have some proof of what was taken.

One of the only ways to legally protect yourself is to get a restraining order from the court and give a copy to the bank. The order would prevent either spouse from having access to the box until you reach a settlement or the court removes the restraining order.

5. Joint Investments and Other Holdings

Make a list of any investments or other joint assets you can think of. Immediately call your broker, your discount brokerage house and any other financial institutions involved. Tell them that no assets or money should be moved or transferred without the knowledge and approval of both you and your spouse. Be sure to tell the broker to make a note to the "online" file on the computer. That way, when your spouse speaks to anyone else at the firm, the computer will show that the account has been frozen. Also, if the account has check writing or credit card privileges, specify whether the freeze applies to those transactions. Follow up the call with a letter identifying the person with whom you spoke, the date and time of the call and a summary of the conversation.

When it comes to joint investments, you will have to move quickly. Many stock transactions are handled over the phone and, increasingly, electronically through e-mail or the Internet. Your spouse may be the one who normally deals with the broker or discount brokerage house. He or she could make one phone call and, in a matter of minutes, have all of your joint holdings sold and the money transferred out of the account. If you call first to freeze the accounts, you stand a good chance of protecting your interests.

Separating in Cyberspace

As the Internet grows increasingly sophisticated, more investors are conducting their transactions electronically.

When it comes to divorce, electronic trading operates essentially in the same manner as traditional trading via phones and live brokers. If a spouse sends an e-mail message that accounts be frozen, then the trading firm should honor that request.

Problems can also arise because one spouse often takes responsibility for electronic trading and could buy or sell investments without the knowledge of the other spouse. In some cases, a spouse could punch numbers on the phone or computer pad to sell or buy investments in a matter of minutes. As with any urgent financial matter, contact the brokerage firm immediately if you suspect a spouse of making damaging financial moves.

Sample Letter to Broker

Rodney Washington
Bull and Bear Investment Company
3400 Financial Square, Suite 1740
Boston, MA 02000

November 27, 20xx

Dear Mr. Washington:

This letter is to inform you that my spouse and I are in the process of divorce. Please freeze our account, #12345-67890, so that no transactions occur until further notice. Please make a note to this effect on the firm's "online" file on the computer. This freeze is to be effective immediately, and this letter confirms my instructions to you by telephone on November 24, 20xx.

These instructions apply to the assets in our account [except for or including] the check writing and/or the credit card privileges we currently have with this account.

Yours truly,

Lenore Kwong

6. Shared Property and Special Collections

While your furniture, appliances and knickknacks around the house may not be as valuable as other assets and investments, this property can cause more irritation and antagonism than almost anything else. Emotions flare up when you reach for a favorite tool only to find it missing or look for your mother's antique brooch and discover it is gone.

To avoid future problems, do an inventory of your home and possessions similar to the kind you would conduct for insurance purposes. Obviously, it will be simpler to do such an inventory while you are still living in the family home and have access to your property—so do it before you move out.

List the contents of each room and photograph or videotape the area for documentation. Your ultimate goal as part of your divorce is to divide these items as fairly as possible. Few couples split the small items exactly 50-50, but you still want to have your property appraised so your division is not horribly one-sided. You can get simple estimates of household property values by asking furniture or appliance dealers and auctioneers to visit your home and give you written estimates. Any coin, gold or other collection should be appraised by a reputable dealer. Realize that these items should be valued at the amount the dealer is willing to pay—not the retail value.

While these values are useful as a starting point, in reality, collections and property are only worth what you can sell them for. If you are valuing property on your own, use "garage sale" values— that is, if you saw your furniture, microwave or other property at a garage sale, how much would you really pay for it? The person who will not be getting the household items may only remember the original price tag, not the current value, so you have to insist on using the garage sale price.

In the meantime, jointly owned household property should not be disposed of unless both spouses agree, as neither one owns an item outright until the settlement. You only own your personal, separate property. Your children's property, such as furniture or toys, should be given to the children and not divided in the divorce settlement.

7. Joint Tenancy

Many couples hold property, especially real property, in joint tenancy. Joint tenancy's major advantage is that when one joint owner dies, the remaining owner or owners automatically inherit the deceased's portion of the property without having to go through the long, expensive probate process. If you don't want your spouse to automatically inherit your share, then change your joint tenancy ownership to tenancy in common.

With tenancy in common, you own equal shares, but upon your death your share goes to whomever you've named in your will or other estate planning document. If you die without a will or other estate plan, your property passes under the laws of your state. Usually the property is divided between the spouse and/or children, if any; if there is no spouse and no children, it goes to the parents or siblings.

The best way to convert property from joint tenancy to tenancy in common is to secure your spouse's agreement and then together execute a deed in which you make this change. For example, a couple could transfer their house "from Herbert and Donna Walker as joint tenants to Herbert and Donna Walker as tenants in common." You can obtain a blank deed from a title insurance or real estate office. In California, homeowners can use *Deeds for California Real Estate*, by Mary Randolph (Nolo).

If you cannot find a blank deed, you could simply draft a statement saying, "Herbert and Donna Walker hereby transfer their real property located at 4555 Ellison Boulevard, Fargo, North Dakota, from Herbert and Donna Walker as joint tenants to Herbert and Donna Walker as tenants in common." Be sure you both sign the statement before a notary public. Then record the deed or statement in the office where your original house deed is recorded.

If your spouse will not consent to the change, you can complete the deed or statement yourself. Write, "Donna Walker hereby transfers her interest in the real property located at 4555 Ellison Boulevard, Fargo, North Dakota, from Donna Walker joint tenant to Donna Walker tenant in common." Any one person can unilaterally terminate his or her interest in a joint tenancy. Again, sign it before a notary and record it in the office where your original house deed is recorded.

⚠️ By closing accounts or serving your spouse with a restraining order, recognize that you are "upping the ante" and increasing the degree of conflict in your divorce. You (and any professional advisors you use) must assess the risks and the consequences, because sooner or later, you will meet your spouse at the negotiating table.

Financial First Aid for Divorce Emergencies

If a stranger stole your wallet with all the credit cards inside, you'd probably have more protection than if your spouse wipes out your joint accounts. Almost nothing can stop one spouse from closing a joint account without the knowledge of the other. During a divorce, it can come down to who gets there first—to the bank account, the computer files, the brokerage office or the safe-deposit box.

If you are concerned that your spouse might empty out a joint account or otherwise take assets to which you are entitled, you may need to obtain a temporary restraining order prohibiting the removal, sale, transfer or other use of the property. Not only can restraining orders be placed against your spouse, but they can also be served on third parties, such as bank managers and others with control over your assets.

Restraining orders are also used to bar a violent or abusive spouse or parent from having contact with the other spouse or children. Domestic violence organizations can help you obtain that kind of restraining order. See the Appendix for more help.

B. Questions to Ask Your Attorney

⚠️ Closing accounts isn't always a straightforward procedure and can vary from state to state. Below is a list of important questions for you to ask your attorney or research at your local law library.

1. Do any state laws prohibit me from withdrawing one-half of the cash in our joint accounts or borrowing money on joint accounts?

2. Can I unilaterally change property from joint tenancy to tenancy in common, or must I have my spouse's consent?

3. Would it be advisable to close my joint accounts and move the funds to an account solely in my name or into a joint account requiring both signatures on the checks?

4. Do any state laws prohibit me from canceling or changing beneficiaries on my life or medical insurance policies during divorce? ■

CHAPTER

7

Getting Help: To Whom Can I Turn?

During divorce, you're going through a time of transition unlike any other in your life. Everything is changing. No matter how capable you are, you'll need help to get through this transition.

Even if you have little money and few resources, it's important to get support. Check with local libraries, churches, community organizations, law schools, colleges or government agencies for low-cost services. In some areas, divorce specialists and centers can advise you for a small fee.

The kind of help you seek will depend on what you need. For some, a personal counselor or therapist is crucial; others want only a temporary advisor to handle financial details. As your divorce progresses, you may also need to call on a variety of specialists ranging from attorneys to real estate agents, credit counselors to appraisers. Because your future is at stake, don't cheat yourself; get the best you can afford. Comparison shop and check references before signing contracts for outside services.

A. Questions to Consider When Seeking Outside Help

While you need to ask different, specific questions of each service provider you consult, the following four questions are useful for dealing with professionals in general.

1. Is the Person Competent and Suited to Handle My Specific Case?

Obviously, you want to work with someone who does a good job and can be trusted. Beyond those basic qualities, it's essential to determine if the person's training and services match your needs. In other words, you don't hire a bookkeeper if your situation calls for an accountant to make complex calculations or compute taxes. By the same token, an experienced divorce attorney is better than a lawyer who specializes in business transactions. Interview potential consultants on the phone, or use introductory sessions to outline your case and find out exactly what to expect, before you hire anyone.

If you accept a free session with a lawyer or other professional, realize that you may be pressured into hiring that person. You may be sold a service that you do not want or need. To avoid such problems, clearly state that you are only gathering information in the initial session and do not intend to make a hiring decision until after you have had a chance to sort through the information you receive. Remember, too, the adage that if something sounds too good to be true, it probably is. Be wary of any lawyer who seems to promise you the world, making guarantees that you can get anything you want in your divorce. There are no guarantees.

2. How Is This Professional Paid?

How a professional is paid—by the hour, on a retainer or through commissions—inevitably affects you. This is a statement of fact, not a matter of philosophy or morals. If you will be paying by the hour, you must understand how that time will be billed. Does the professional bill in 10-minute, 15-minute or longer intervals? Are you going to be charged for time on the phone? Does the clock begin to "run" the minute you walk in the door? Find out.

When people work on commission, their livelihood depends on selling you something. Again, there's nothing wrong with that—you just need to recognize that reality and act accordingly. For

instance, when you call for information about insurance coverage, the agent may try to sell you a new policy or different kind of coverage. Only you can decide whether or not it's appropriate to make such a purchase. Because of the emotional strain of divorce, take extra time to make decisions, or insist on getting a second opinion before you buy anything.

3. What's the Best Use of This Professional's Services?

Like many people going through a divorce, you may sometimes feel that you don't know where to turn. As personal and financial pressures mount, you could go to the wrong people for the wrong services. Trying to use your lawyer as a therapist or your banker as a tax consultant is an exercise in frustration. Think about your needs first and be sure you are using each professional's expertise appropriately.

Recognize the limits of each advisor you contact. Your local real estate agent, for example, may not be able to appraise the value of commercial property or a vacation house located in a different city. If necessary, ask for referrals to specialists, and keep asking questions until you find the right person to answer them. You can save time and money by gathering much of the data the professional will need, especially financial information. Chapter 8 details the kind of information you'll need.

4. Am I Evaluating This Professional Objectively?

It's fine to ask friends and associates for referrals, but do not assume that a professional referred by someone you trust is the right one for you or for your case. You will still want to ask questions to determine whether this person is knowledgeable, capable and a good match for you personally.

Similarly, do not feel compelled to use your sister just because she is an attorney or your uncle just because he is an accountant. While these relatives may have your best interests in mind and be very trustworthy, they may miss creative solutions or the big picture because they are too close to your situation. Objectivity is important.

B. Selecting Professionals to Assist You

Besides providing quality service, a good professional should explain potential risks in your situation and offer realistic appraisals of results and consequences. (Of course, the more risks the professional finds, the more money he or she stands to earn.) Keep that in mind as you review these descriptions of professionals who can help you during divorce. (For handy reference, you can enter names, addresses and phone numbers of your professional advisors in Section G of the Appendix.)

1. Lawyers

For assisting during a divorce, lawyers charge hourly rates. These fees vary widely across the country. Be sure to find one that fits your wallet. Be aware, too, that most lawyers require that you pay an up-front retainer before they do any work, sometimes amounting to thousands of dollars. As the lawyer does work for you, the bill is paid out of your retainer.

When the lawyer uses up the retainer, she'll either bill you directly or ask for another lump sum from which to draw. If you hire a lawyer who requests a retainer, be sure that you get monthly statements showing the precise work done, the amount billed, the amount deducted from your retainer and the amount left over. If there's a balance remaining at the end of the case (or if you change lawyers), you're entitled to get that money back.

If it's at all possible, you should pay your own attorney's fees. Financial negotiations and lines of authority remain clear when each party pays for his or her own legal representative. If there is no way for you to afford an attorney, in some states, a judge can order the wealthier spouse to pay all or part of the other spouse's attorney's fees during the divorce.

What to Look for in a Lawyer

Choosing the right attorney is one of the most important decisions you will make. The right lawyer can help you achieve financial security as well as ease the strain of the divorce process. But the wrong lawyer can add to your woes and possibly cause you to lose your rightful assets and perhaps even custody of your children.

When selecting an attorney, make sure your schedules are compatible. If they're not, you will have difficulties together. Because your lawyer is working on more than one case at a time, he or she may not be able to take your phone calls—but should return them. You must also return phone calls from your attorney and respond to any correspondence promptly to keep your case moving along.

Take the time and make the effort to choose a lawyer who is strong and experienced yet sensitive to your needs. You need to resist the urge to quickly choose a lawyer just because a friend or relative says "so-and-so is good." Instead, interview at least three lawyers and compare them using the following criteria:

- Knowledge and experience in family law. An attorney who's practiced five years or more and devotes all or most of his practice to matrimonial law would be ideal. In addition, ask how much courtroom experience the attorney has, how many contested custody cases he has handled and whether he's given lectures or written articles on divorce (often a sign of in-depth knowledge). Does he belong to the Academy of Matrimonial Lawyers, a professional group that certifies experts?

- Interest in your case. Does the lawyer seem interested and excited, or bored and preoccupied? A divorce case tests any lawyer's zest for facts and details. You want someone who seems energized and up to the challenge.

- Availability of a team. Does the attorney have the assistance of other lawyers and paralegals? Particularly in a complex case, the lawyer may need backup. You might ask how many others in the firm handle divorce cases and if you can meet with them as well. Similarly, because divorce cases often involve other fields of law—such as real estate, taxes, trusts and the like—you should ask if the firm has other attorney resources available for consultation if needed.

- Coherent strategy. All legal cases involve a plan of action that's based on goals on which the lawyer and client concur. After you explain your situation, ask the prospective attorney: What results can I reasonably expect? How will we achieve those results? How will we decide whether to try the case or settle? If we do try the case, how much will that cost?

- Rapport. Ask yourself: What's my "gut feeling" about this person? Charm is no substitute for competence. But you are going to be spending lots of time with your attorney, so you'll need a certain comfort level. Look for a lawyer who is pleasant but also confident and assertive.

In short, you want a lawyer who is going to solve problems, not create them. To get such an able advocate means you need to choose well, not necessarily quickly or cheaply. Take your time and be thorough. Make sure you understand the attorney's fees and billing practices, and have them set forth in a retainer agreement.

For further help in finding a lawyer, see the Appendix.

When you meet with an attorney, ask specific questions about fees and services. Be sure you feel comfortable communicating with your potential lawyer, and check on how often this person will be available to you. Ask about billing practices, too.

In some states, such as California, consider hiring a certified family law attorney. These specialists must pass an examination that tests their specific knowledge of divorce law. Most keep current on developments in divorce law by attending continuing legal education programs. They may know more about divorce law—including support, custody and property division questions—than nonspecialists, but they may charge more as well.

Whether or not your lawyer is a specialist in divorce, you should expect him to:

- provide you with a clear understanding of how you will be billed and what costs to expect, including retainer, court costs, expert witness fees and other expenses

- provide you with copies of everything that crosses his desk related to your case

- maintain detailed time records and send you accurate and understandable bills

- return your phone calls promptly

- explain your rights and how he will go about securing them for you

- keep you up to date on settlement negotiations, and

- do his best to settle your case out of court and, if that is not possible, prepare your case—and you—for trial.

Tips on Working With Your Lawyer

Remember, communication is a two-way street. Just as your attorney should provide you information, you must provide complete and honest information to your attorney. This includes filling out requested forms and gathering requested documents. (This is covered in detail in Chapter 8.) If your attorney has incomplete or inaccurate information, the advice you receive may be inappropriate for your particular circumstances.

Do not be concerned if your attorney is friendly with the opposing counsel. In fact, this often works to your advantage. Even if the attorneys are friends, they will each work for their client's interest. Attorneys who cooperate with each other are better able to negotiate and settle out of court, which will result in lower legal fees. In addition, if the attorneys are enemies and drawn into an emotional fight, the end result will be higher fees and a lower quality of representation for you. An attorney in such a situation will not be able to focus clearly and objectively on the facts of your case.

Expect your lawyer to be pleasant but not to act as your de facto therapist. The lawyer's job is to guide you through the legal maze, not to listen to how your marriage might have turned out better if only you or your spouse had done this or that. If, as is often the case, you're suffering emotionally because of the breakup, you *should* see a therapist (see Section B10, below). Therapists usually don't charge as much as lawyers, and they're much better equipped for hand-holding.

---

2.   Mediators

A private mediator is a neutral third person who assists both parties in resolving their differences and reaching agreement on some or all of the issues involved in the divorce, including child custody and child support, spousal support and all aspects of property. Choose a mediator who has the experience and skills to deal with both the issues in your case and the personality differences.

Mediators charge hourly or daily rates. Mediators who are also lawyers usually charge what lawyers charge, while mediators who are therapists, psychologists, social workers or clergy members charge less. If the mediator is an attorney experienced in family law matters, do not expect to pay less than the hourly rate of your own lawyer. In fact, you could pay more, but keep in mind that the mediator is doing the work of two attorneys. Generally, the spouses share the mediator's fees proportionately, depending on the relative wealth of each of them. Sometimes the spouses split the fees evenly.

When you use mediation, you don't have the opportunity to use formal "discovery" techniques to learn about your spouse's finances. If your spouse is unwilling to fully and voluntarily disclose information, provide documents and answer all questions concerning the issues, you must then decide if mediation is a viable alternative for you.

To locate a mediator, ask friends and professional colleagues for a referral. The court clerk at your local family or domestic relations court may also be able to provide you with names of private mediators in your area. You can also contact the Association for Conflict Resolution for a list of practitioners in your state. ACR is at 1527 New Hampshire Ave. NW, Washington, DC 20036; 202-667-9700 (phone); 202-265-1968 (fax); acr@acresolution.org (email); or www.acresolution.org. As a last resort, let your fingers do the walking in the Yellow Pages.

A mediator acts as an *impartial third party* to help you and your spouse resolve conflicts. By contrast, lawyers are *advocates* for their client's position. Consequently, your individual interests will not be represented in the same manner in a mediation as they would be if you had someone advocating your position. Mediators represent the *marital* interest, not that of either spouse. Do not expect a mediator to take sides.

When working with a mediator, you must be precise about what you want to achieve in the sessions. While many mediators will not meet privately with one spouse, you may want to inquire whether you could have a private session if necessary to clarify your personal goals or to discuss strategies if you are feeling intimidated by your spouse.

When to Use—Or Not Use—Mediation

It is critical to question whether mediation is appropriate before entering into that process. Candid answers to the following questions can help you decide:

- Is each party able to stand up for himself or herself? If so, mediation may be the preferred route.

- Is each person in the process there under his or her "own steam"? If so, consider mediation.

- Is the intensity of the emotional charge between the two parties so strong that one or both are disabled by it? If so, hiring an attorney is advisable.

- Is there a history of violence or emotional abuse by one spouse? If so, hiring an attorney is advisable.

- Is each person able to track the progress of the mediation? If so, mediation may be the way to go.

- Do both people have access to all financial records? If so, mediation may make sense.

You can find more information on deciding whether to mediate, and what to expect if you do mediate, in *Using Divorce Mediation,* by Katherine E. Stoner (Nolo).

The following was written by Gary Friedman, author of *A Guide to Divorce Mediation: How to Reach a Fair, Legal Settlement at a Fraction of the Cost* (Workman Publishing).

"Central to determining mediation's appropriateness is whether or not the parties can deal fairly with one another.

Differences in the parties' openness to the process, the tendency of one party to dominate the other and inequalities in ability (or willingness) to deal with the subject matter must all be examined. Before jumping into mediation, ask yourself several questions:

- Are we both open to reaching a result that is fair to the other?

- Are we able to communicate clearly with each other? Can we each express ourselves and hear the other?

- Can we each identify what is important to us as a realistic and solid base for making choices? Can we each express that?

- Is either of us unwilling to seek outside support or unable to use it effectively when it is needed?

The decision whether or not to mediate should be an informed one, and one that can be reconsidered. Either party's hesitation should be taken seriously; both must be willing for the process to be meaningful. A decision not to mediate or to stop the mediation does not mean that adversary litigation is the sole choice. You can bring in a co-mediator, use a type of mediation more protective of the parties or work with lawyers committed to collaborating with their clients."

Used properly, mediation can be less costly than a prolonged legal battle. To finalize your settlement, however, you may still need to hire a lawyer or typing service. Often, a mediator will draw up a "memorandum of understanding," which outlines your agreement. Then, you could spend a short amount of time with a lawyer or typing service representative who can file the papers to make the agreements legally binding.

For more tips on mediation, we suggest *How to Mediate Your Dispute*, by Peter Lovenheim (Nolo).

3.   Arbitrators

Arbitrators differ from attorneys, who represent the interests of one spouse, and from mediators, who represent the interests of both. Instead, arbitrators (often retired judges) hear a case and make decisions regarding disputed issues, which are then incorporated into a court judgment.

Arbitrators charge hourly or daily rates. Typically, these fees are $100 or more per hour than a top-paid attorney receives. However, arbitration is usually far less expensive than going to trial with an attorney, because fewer hours usually are involved.

Arbitration can be a far better option than going to court. It can be most useful in resolving certain issues on which you cannot agree, such as what a business is worth. Each side presents its case, and the arbitrator decides. Arbitration is not about negotiation and, in fact, may come after all negotiating efforts have stalled. You may want to consider this relatively quick and effective way to reach a decision.

An arbitrator is a private judge. The best way to find one is by asking your professional advisors—attorney, CPA, financial advisor or insurance agent—for a referral.

4.   Financial Planners

As attorneys begin to recognize how complex and critical financial planning is to the decisions their clients make during divorce, they are turning more and more to financial planners to provide advice and recommendations on dividing assets.

A financial planner can be useful as you prepare for your financial future as a single person. A planner may be able to help you identify potential risks in your settlement agreement and the tax consequences of decisions you are contemplating. Planners can also review your net worth and cash flow statements as well as your retirement benefits, investment portfolio and business holdings.

When it comes to compensation, there are three types of financial planners. Fee-only planners charge as much as several thousand dollars to develop a full financial plan addressing every aspect of your finances or offer consultations on your specific questions for a fee based on an hourly rate.

Commission-only planners derive all of their income from 3%–5% sales commissions on the investments they sell you. While they may give good advice, if they earn the majority of their income selling products, they may have a conflict of interest that can bias their recommendations.

Lastly, there are financial planners who are compensated by a combination of fee and commission, and who may also have a conflict of interest when they advise you to buy certain products.

To find a financial planner, ask for a referral from an accountant, banker or attorney you trust. You can also contact the Financial Planning Association at 800-322-4237, or visit their website at www.fpanet.org.

To be certain you are dealing with a reputable professional, check references and credentials. Planners who have undergone a rigorous program offered through the College for Financial Planning in Denver earn the title of Certified Financial Planner (CFP). Chartered Financial Consultant (ChFC) is another credential to look for. It's given to financial planners who pass a series of courses at The American College, located in Bryn Mawr, PA.

In hiring a financial planner, look for someone who can analyze your case and the financial impact of divorce—not someone whose primary focus is on selling investments. You also want someone who can communicate with your attorney, because the financial implications of your divorce will no doubt have an impact on the legal consequences. Your planner should help you identify and assess risks so you can protect yourself. Few of us manage our finances as well as we could, but you will find it to your benefit if you choose a planner who is willing to tell you what you would rather not hear.

How Financial Planners Can Help With Your Divorce

As you go through your divorce, a financial planner can help you:

- set long- and short-term goals

- develop an action plan to reach those goals

- identify cash flow needs, sources of income and expenses

- put yourself on a budget

- evaluate current investments in terms of risks and objectives

- determine which assets are most appropriate for you to keep

- develop an investment portfolio for your needs and goals

- learn the costs and tax consequences of keeping or not keeping the house

- determine whether or not the proceeds from a retirement plan should be rolled over to an IRA or Roth IRA

- determine whether to take an immediate or a deferred distribution from a retirement plan

- evaluate whether insurance coverage is appropriate and cost-effective

- decide how to invest for education funding, and

- make estate planning decisions.

5.   Stockbrokers and Money Managers

Stockbrokers receive commissions or sales charges, which are paid by the client—usually 1% to 5% of the amount of money invested in stocks, bonds, mutual funds or annuities. Money managers, on the other hand, receive a fee for the service they provide, which is designing and managing investment portfolios. They charge a percentage on the value of the money they manage—usually 1% to 1.5% on accounts of $200,000 to $1,000,000 and 1% to 3% on smaller accounts.

Stockbrokers tend to focus on individual stock, bond, mutual fund and insurance transactions. Money managers look at the overall performance of an investment portfolio and evaluate how it meets your short-term and long-term needs for growth, income and safety.

In gathering information on your financial condition, you may have to contact your stockbroker for copies of brokerage accounts or other items. Again, as with other professionals who work on commission, recognize that your stockbroker may try to sell you products when you call for financial information.

6.   Accountants

Accountants can provide a variety of services ranging from auditing a business to assessing employee benefits packages. Accountants charge by the hour or per project. A certified public accountant (CPA) can work as a tax consultant—but don't assume that all CPAs can provide personal tax services. If you have income tax concerns, you may want to start by consulting an enrolled agent (EA), a tax specialist qualified to practice before the IRS. If you think a spouse is hiding assets or covering up essential financial facts, you may want to hire a forensic accountant. These specialists can trace marital property, evaluate financial reports and value businesses.

To find out about enrolled agents, and to find one in your area, you can contact the National Association of Enrolled Agents at 301-212-9608 or www.naea.org.

7.   Bankers

Your bank and banker can prove quite useful in helping you with various financial issues of divorce, such as canceling or opening lines of credit, establishing new accounts or getting loans. Do not expect a banker, however, to advise you on investments or other complex issues outside his or her realm of expertise. Also, while bankers work on salaries, they often function as salespeople for their own institutions, promote their own products or sell mutual funds with a commission. Your banker may advise you to park your money in a certificate of deposit even though your long-term goals might be better served by investing in stocks or mutual funds. Get information from several different sources or consult with your financial planner before making a long-term decision.

8.   Insurance Agents

Insurance is one way to protect yourself from risks, and during divorce it's important to review your coverage. Contact your insurance agent to double-check your policies for life, health, disability, property and business. Also check the cash and surrender values of the policy—they may be different from the amount stated in your contract because the actual rate of interest paid may differ from the rate of interest assumed when the policy was originally bought. You might also be charged a fee if the policy is cashed in.

Divorce is a good time to check the cash value of any life insurance policies because this value represents marital property to be divided. In addition, cashing in the policy can provide emergency cash if necessary; but be aware that the surrender value you get may be lower than the cash value. When you divide the family cars, be sure to check your auto insurance to make sure you are paying only to insure yourself (and perhaps your driving-age children) on the car(s) you keep.

Insurance agents are paid commissions. The commissions are paid by the insurance company, but the company prices its policies to include the commission. Ultimately, the customer pays the commission, but will not see this charge on the bill.

If you do not have an insurance agent, shop around and talk to several to find one with whom you feel comfortable. Be aware that insurance agents hold sales positions and may ask you to buy a new policy or expand an old one when you call for information. Resist their pressures and be sure you absolutely need any new insurance you purchase.

9.   Real Estate Agents

When a real estate agent is involved in the sale of a home, that agent usually receives a commission from the money the seller receives for the house, even if the agent has been working with the buyer. An agent who simply appraises a house usually will do so for free, in hopes of getting your business later when you sell.

Because your house may be the most valuable asset in your divorce settlement, you will want to get an accurate appraisal of its current market value. Try to get estimates from several real estate agents or from a certified appraiser so you can negotiate from a knowledgeable position. The best agents to ask are those familiar with the neighborhood. If you used an agent when you bought the house, that person is often one of the best suited to appraise the property now.

Certified appraisers are covered in Chapter 13. You can get some referrals from real estate agents, escrow companies and lending institutions.

10. Therapists

In the stress of divorce, a therapist or counselor can be a valuable resource for helping resolve personal issues. To find someone, ask friends for referrals, or contact a local mental health association, church or family service agency.

Therapists charge by the hour (the "50-minute" hour). Keep in mind, especially if money is tight, that your medical insurance may reimburse you for all or part of your therapy sessions.

As with any professional, it's important to check credentials, but also make sure the therapist's approach feels appropriate to you. Don't hire a Freudian who does long-term psychoanalysis if you want short-term counseling to help you get through the divorce process. If you can't afford one-on-one therapy, you may be able to find support and encouragement through a self-help group, a community service agency or a program sponsored by a religious group.

11. Credit Counselors

Credit advisors can help you negotiate with your creditors and set up systems to manage your finances. These agencies generally receive most of their funding from major creditors such as department stores, credit card companies and banks.

Use the services of credit counselors who are affiliated with nonprofit organizations such as the United Way, a local "Y" or a church- or synagogue-run association. A few other nonprofit credit counselors operate nationwide. The best are Myvesta (formerly Debt Counselors of America), www.myvesta.org, and the National Foundation for Credit Counseling, www.nfcc.org. As nonprofits, these organizations generally charge nothing or a nominal fee for setting up a repayment plan.

To use a nonprofit credit advisor to help you pay your debts, you must either have some disposable income or be willing to sell some of your property. A credit advisor contacts your creditors to let them know that you've sought assistance and need more time to pay. Based on your income and debts, the advisor, with your creditors, decides on how much you pay. You then make one or two direct payments each month to the agency, which in turn pays your creditors. A credit advisor can often get wage garnishments revoked and interest and late charges dropped. These agencies also help people make monthly budgets.

12. Typing or Paralegal Services

Typing and paralegal services cannot give legal advice or represent you on legal matters, but they can offer services at low cost. If you want help in preparing your divorce papers, these services may be able to help you. Typing and paralegal services charge per project (for typing forms).

In selecting a typing service, you must separate the good (honest and competent) from the bad (dishonest and/or incompetent). Good services will provide you with a written contract that describes the services they plan to provide, states the total price you will be charged and explains their complaint procedure and refund policy.

Unlike attorneys, paralegals are neither state-licensed nor rated by their peers or professional associations.

Here are some things to look for when choosing a typing or paralegal service:

- *An established or recommended service.* Few services stay in business unless they provide honest and competent services. A recommendation from a social service agency, friend or lawyer is probably a good bet.

- *Reasonable fees.* The fee should be based on the amount of work a task requires, the specialized nature of the task and reasonable overhead. For example, if the task is straightforward and takes just 30 minutes of typing, the fee should reflect the rate charged by basic typing services with similar overhead—about $10 a page or $20 an hour.

- *Access to quality self-help publications.* Good typing services provide ready access to reliable self-help materials, either for free or at a reasonable price.

- *Trained staff.* One indication of whether or not people are committed to providing good service is whether or not they have undertaken skills training. Appropriate training is available through independent paralegal associations and continuing education seminars for financial planners.

13. Actuaries

If a pension or retirement plan is at stake in your divorce, you may need the services of an actuary, a specialized financial professional. For details, including fees charged, see Chapter 14, Section C2.

14. Business Appraisers

To determine the financial value of any business—including a sole proprietorship or professional practice—a business appraiser conducts a detailed analysis.

Call the IRS and request a copy of Internal Revenue Rulings 59-60 and 83-120 if you or your spouse operates a business or is a professional—a doctor, lawyer, accountant, psychotherapist and the like—with a private practice in the form of a closely held corporation. You will want to know the value of the business or practice. IRS 59-60 deals with methods of valuing closely held corporations; 83-120 concerns valuation of stock.

Are Fees Paid to Professionals Tax Deductible?

You can deduct from your income taxes certain fees paid to professionals. Not many fees are deductible, but especially during times of divorce, every bit can help. Here are the rules:

- If you receive alimony, you can deduct all attorney fees you pay to secure or collect that alimony. If your spouse is paying your legal fees, the fees are not deductible. Nor are fees paid to lawyers by an alimony payer.

- All fees paid to any professional—including attorneys, accountants, financial planners and stockbrokers—for advice on tax consequences arising from a divorce are deductible from your income taxes.

If you plan to deduct fees, your advisor must itemize your billing showing exactly how much you were charged for the advice regarding alimony collection or tax issues.

Be sure to ask your lawyer, financial planner and/or accountant about tax-deductible fees to be certain you've covered them all.

15. Private Investigators

Private investigators, or private detectives, can sometimes be helpful in a divorce by exposing fraud or locating missing funds or other assets. Contrary to the "gumshoe" image spawned by countless movies and TV shows, private detectives are much more likely to wield a database than a pistol. Computers allow them to obtain massive amounts of information from probate records, motor vehicle registrations, credit reports, association membership lists and other sources. Some specialize in finance.

There are no formal education requirements for most private detectives, but many have gained experience in the military or law-enforcement jobs or by working for insurance or collections companies or in the security industry. Most states and the District of Columbia require that private investigators be licensed, and a growing number of states specify training requirements. California, for example, requires 6,000 hours of investigative experience, a background check and a qualifying score on a written exam, or 4,000 hours and a college or law degree.

A good investigator is curious, aggressive, persistent, assertive and a good communicator. A skilled private detective is able to think on her feet and has strong interviewing or interrogation skills. Most bill their clients on an hourly basis and may ask for reimbursement of expenses. ■

Financial Fact-Finding: What Must I Know and When Must I Know It?

Most often in marriage, one partner takes care of the paperwork and possibly the financial decision making. This is practical when you're still together, but a potential disaster during divorce.

No one can make proper financial decisions without adequate information. How can you tell whether to keep the family home if you do not know what it costs to maintain it? On what will you base requests for alimony or child support if you are in the dark about living expenses? Both you and your spouse will need to document your financial life as you go through the divorce. Now, in the early stages, is the best time to start.

If you left the bookkeeping to your partner, you may feel as though you are starting from scratch. It's important not to panic. Take control by finding out as much as you can about the finances of your marriage. And realize that you *will* live through this part of your divorce.

Linda, a 35-year-old mother of two, recalled that when she first separated from her husband, she was petrified at the thought of confronting her financial life. As she kept at it, however, the job became easier. "Now I can look at all of these complicated papers and forms and not feel scared," she reported.

 If you were the family bookkeeper, you will be in much better shape than your spouse who did not participate in managing the finances. You can move on to Section C and begin verifying the financial information you will need during your divorce. Otherwise, continue reading.

Whatever role you played previously, by the time the divorce is over, you will probably know more about the details of your financial life than you ever cared to. You gain this knowledge by going through these three steps:

1. *Information gathering.* This is the step in which you find information and sort files, receipts, bill statements and other papers.

2. *Information analysis.* After sorting your papers, you'll want to review your files, appraisals and valuations. It's also important to calculate taxes and other costs either by yourself or with an accountant or financial advisor.

3. *Decision making.* Once you analyze what you own and owe and what it costs to live, you can begin to decide what to do with your property in the divorce.

Start investigating your financial position now. Do not wait until you are at the bargaining table for the final settlement to determine the worth of your house or the value of your spouse's retirement benefits. When you enter the negotiations, you want to have as much up-to-date information as you can.

In this beginning stage of the divorce process, focus on information gathering only. Even if you do not understand all of it, do not get sidetracked from your financial fact-finding mission. Later on, you can concentrate on decision making. For now, your time is best spent on documenting your economic situation. Staying focused may seem hard, but it gets easier as you go along. Besides, it will help you:

- save time and money, especially once you hire an attorney

- distinguish your separate property from the marital assets

- negotiate a settlement from a position of strength, and

- begin building a foundation for a secure financial future.

A. Advice to the Terminally Disorganized

Ideally, your books and accounts are up to date and in order. More likely, however, you will have to hunt for records and receipts. You are not alone. Few people are as on top of their personal finances as they would like to be—or pretend to be.

Fortunately, you have a number of options in finding what you need. Tax returns, for instance, are gold mines of information in a divorce. The *Financial Facts Checklist* at the end of this chapter will give you other clues for finding financial data. But before you get there, here are some ideas to get you started:

Tax returns. If you do not currently have your tax returns for the past three to five years, you can get copies from the IRS. Contact the IRS at 800-829-1040 or www.irs.gov to request or download Form 4506. Complete the form and send it back. You should get copies of your returns within about 45 days.

The IRS generally sends your tax information to the "Address of Record" on your previous return. If you've moved or are concerned about arousing your spouse's anger or suspicion, ask that the forms be sent to your office, your attorney, a friend or a post office box. Once you have copies of the tax returns, you can review them with a trusted accountant or financial planner who can show you how to find basic financial information on the forms.

Loan applications and account statements. Check recent copies of credit or loan applications, canceled checks and bank, brokerage and credit union statements for information on assets or debts.

Insurance policies. Look for the names of the beneficiaries on any insurance policies. Determine if the insurance is term or whole life. If it is whole life, find out the cash value.

Estate plans. You may find a wealth of information about property you and your spouse own by reviewing wills, trusts and other estate planning documents.

Retirement plans. Keep track of work-related pension or savings plans.

Financial professionals. Make a list of accountants, lawyers and other financial advisors whom you and/or your spouse have been using.

Credit reports. You can get a copy of your credit report periodically from one of the major credit bureaus. (See Chapter 5, Section A.)

Title reports. Visit your county land records office and conduct a title search, or have an escrow company do one for you, if you suspect there might be liens against your home or other real estate. (See Chapter 13, Section C3, for details on liens.)

If you know you'll have trouble staying organized once you begin getting your paperwork together, you can hire a local bookkeeping service. You might also consider the services of a professional organizer. Modern life has gotten so complicated that there is now a national association of professional organizers. Local groups may be listed in the phone book Yellow Pages or classified advertisements in the newspaper. Before hiring a professional organizer, make sure the person listens to you and asks what you want, instead of telling you what you need.

No matter what approach you take in organizing your documents, keep it simple. You can buy an inexpensive three-ring binder to hold your various papers. As your stack of information grows, create categories of documents by using the divider tabs that come with the binder. The *Net Worth* and *Cash Flow* statements in Chapter 12 will give you an idea of the kinds of divisions you can make.

When you begin to feel overwhelmed, remember that you are not just shuffling papers to get through your divorce. You are doing the groundwork for your financial decision making and security for many years to come. And that is worth the effort it takes to become informed and organized about your paperwork.

B. If You Think Your Spouse May Be Hiding Assets

Unfortunately, divorce can be the occasion for a game of financial "cat and mouse" in which one spouse hides assets or makes other unethical moves.

In some cases, the gaps in the financial information you get from your spouse occur because of honest mistakes. Many people are not detail-oriented when it comes to personal finances, and in the stress of divorce, may forget some specifics.

On the other hand, some spouses purposely conceal the value of a business or switch funds into secret accounts. If the judge finds out, he may declare that the spouse who hides assets is guilty of "economic misconduct." This misconduct is likely to affect the final settlement—the misbehaving spouse will probably get less than his or her full share.

Winning Big?

One California woman learned the hard way how seriously judges take the duty to disclose assets to the other party. In 1996, Denise Rossi won a $1.3-million lottery jackpot and 11 days later filed for divorce from her husband of 25 years. She kept her lottery winnings secret from her husband during the divorce proceedings. Two years later, he inadvertently learned of her windfall when he received a misdirected piece of mail. In 1999, a Superior Court judge ordered that the entire jackpot be given to the husband after determining that the wife violated state disclosure laws and acted out of malice or fraud. News reports indicate that the wife filed for bankruptcy in early 2000.

If you have any reason to believe your spouse is being less than candid with you about income or other assets, you will have to do a little detective work on your own. You may need to examine old income tax returns to spot discrepancies.

If you're still not convinced, consider hiring a special type of certified public accountant called a forensic accountant. These specialists will comb through your records and can usually create an accurate picture of your spouse's financial position. Their services, however, can be expensive. You must weigh the cost of hiring a forensic accountant against the dollar amount at stake in your divorce.

The legal process of "discovery" can be used to force a reluctant spouse to turn over records and statements. Discovery is a formal information gathering process used in lawsuits. Spouses (usually through lawyers) send papers to each other asking that questions be answered or documents turned over.

Another procedure used in discovery is taking depositions—that is, orally asking questions. Be warned, however, that discovery is usually time-consuming and costly, and may ultimately turn up nothing of importance. Therefore, gather information informally if possible. (See Chapter 7, Section B1, for guidelines on working with lawyers.)

![warning icon] No matter how you feel about your soon-to-be-ex-spouse, you may have a legal obligation to behave responsibly toward him or her as long as you remain married. California law states that spouses have a fiduciary responsibility to each other. This obligation is similar to the kind of responsibility real estate agents have toward the people they represent in home sales or to that between the trustee of a trust fund and the benefi-

ciary of the fund. This duty means that each spouse must handle the family finances in a "prudent" manner and must make all information available to the other.

C. Don't Forget the "Easy-to-Forget" Assets

Many assets divided during the divorce are not difficult to account for: the house, cars, retirement plans and stocks. For other assets, you may have to search a little if your spouse is trying to hide them as discussed in Section B, above. Still other assets are in plain view, but you may overlook them nevertheless. While these "easy-to-forget" assets may not be worth a great deal of money, they can turn out to be valuable when you and your spouse are negotiating over who gets what in your divorce settlement. This could include such things as country club member-

---

Searching for Hidden Assets

This checklist was adapted from one created by Ginita Wall, a CPA and Certified Financial Planner in San Diego, CA. This list includes common ways in which a spouse may undervalue or disguise marital assets. Be advised, however, that you may have difficulty finding some items or getting the proof you need to show they exist. As mentioned, a forensic accountant or formal discovery procedures may help.

- Collusion with an employer to delay bonuses, stock options or raises until after the divorce. You might find this information by taking the deposition of your spouse's boss or payroll supervisor, but more likely you'll need a forensic accountant.

- Salary paid to a nonexistent employee. The checks will be voided after divorce. Again, you might find this information by taking the deposition of your spouse's boss or payroll supervisor, but you'll probably need a forensic accountant.

- Money paid from the business to someone close—such as a father, mother, girlfriend or boyfriend—for services that were in fact never rendered. The money will no doubt be given back to your spouse after the divorce is final.

- A custodial account set up in the name of a child, using the child's Social Security number.

- Delay in signing long-term business contracts until after the divorce. Although this may seem like smart planning, if the intent is to lower the value of the business, it is considered hiding assets.

- Skimming cash from a business he or she owns.

- Antiques, artwork, hobby equipment, gun collections and tools that are overlooked or undervalued. Look for lush furnishings, paintings or collector-level carpets at the office, reflecting income that is unreported on tax returns and financial statements. Lifestyle costs will exceed income, so document any of the cash expenses you know your spouse has incurred.

- Debt repayment to a friend for a phony debt.

- Expenses paid for a girlfriend or boyfriend such as gifts, travel, rent or tuition for college or special classes.

- Cash kept in the form of traveler's checks and money orders. You may be able to find these by tracing bank account deposits and withdrawals.

ships; points for hotel, airline or credit card programs; or equity in an auto lease.

Here are some other commonly overlooked assets and some suggestions for how to handle them.

Stock options. The right to purchase the employer's stock at a bargain price some time in the future may have significant value. Usually, the spouse who owns the stock options keeps them in exchange for an asset the other spouse wants to keep. Alternatively, you can agree to exercise the option jointly in the future if the company's buy-sell agreement permits this. (See Chapter 16 for more on stock options.)

Tax refunds. If you file a joint tax return, any tax refund check will be in both names. Your divorce agreement should clearly state how the refund will be split. (See Chapter 11.)

Property taxes. Property taxes are paid in arrears—that is, they are paid for a time period that has already passed. Therefore, the spouse who accepts the house (or other property) for which property taxes will be due in the future may be entitled to a reimbursement from the other spouse for his or her share of those taxes.

Prepaid insurance. Because all insurance is paid for in advance, including life, disability and casualty insurance, consider these prepayments when you are valuing and dividing property.

Vacation pay. The value of accumulated vacation hours should be based on the spouse's pay rate. If the employed spouse will be compensated now or later for unused sick pay, it may also be valued.

Frequent flyer points. To split these points, have free tickets issued in the other spouse's name, or determine the monetary value of the travel benefits and compensate the other spouse accordingly (see sidebar, "Who Gets the Miles?").

Season tickets. For some couples, season tickets for a hot sports team can be practically priceless. Whether you have tickets for the 50-yard line or a box at the opera, be sure you know their financial value and whether they can be replaced or replicated. Otherwise, you could find yourself losing an asset you cherish—or fighting for something that's not worth the effort.

Timeshares. A resort timeshare is often worth less than the amount still owed on it. In a case such

Who Gets the Miles?

Some 70 million Americans belong to frequent flyer programs. With the average active member logging 12,000 miles yearly, the number of banked miles is growing by 400 billion per year. In addition to the usual credits from airline flights, car rentals and hotel visits, miles are offered for use with certain credit cards and other purchases.

Often one spouse accumulates most of the couple's frequent flyer miles through business travel, though they may be used for the couple's joint vacations. Thus, the miles may become an issue in divorce, with one spouse asserting that because he or she shared in the miles while married, they should be split upon dissolution of the marriage.

Some divorce and estate lawyers place a value on air miles—two cents apiece—that approximates what the airlines charge when they sell miles to their corporate partners. Thus, 500,000 miles could be worth $10,000.

But valuation often is more complicated than that. For example, one spouse may be a present or former airline employee who as a retiree will be entitled to fly free. How can that privilege be valued and divided? That would depend on the number of years until retirement, the average present cost of total flights and the presumed inflation rate between now and retirement.

Further complicating the issue of frequent flyer miles is that some airlines do not permit division of this asset. If a significant number of frequent flyer points (more than 25,000) are at issue in your divorce, you or your attorney should review the airline's latest frequent flyer program statement. Be sure to specify in any agreement or court order the points being transferred and a deadline for the transfer before the expiration date of the points. Similar steps should be taken for other bonus plans, such as those sponsored by hotels, credit card issuers, banks, rental car companies and department stores.

Here is how to contact the larger frequent flyer programs:

- American Airlines Advantage: 800-882-8880
- Continental Airlines One Pass: 713-952-1630
- Delta SkyMiles: 800-325-3999
- Midwest Express Frequent Flyer: 800-452-2022
- Northwest-KLM WorldPerks: 800-447-3757
- United Airlines Mileage Plus: 800-241-6522
- US Airways Dividend Miles: 800-872-4738

as this, you must decide whether one of you will accept it at a lesser value or you will continue to own it jointly, sell it or let it go into foreclosure.

Professional dues and magazine subscriptions. Discounts are frequently offered for two- and three-year memberships in professional associations or for subscriptions to academic journals or other magazines. A spouse preparing for divorce may make substantial prepayments using money from marital funds in order to avoid using separate funds in the future. The amounts spent may not be much, but every bit helps when dividing it all up.

D. The W-2 and the Tax Return

Your financial fact-finding process should include an examination of your own and your spouse's W-2 form, as well as your marital tax return or the returns you and your spouse file separately. There are several good reasons. First, it is never too soon to educate yourself on your finances, and the W-2 and the tax return are two primary indicators. In addition, these documents provide information about just how much income is available for alimony and child support payments (see Chapter

18). Finally, if you think it's possible your spouse might be concealing assets (see Section B, above), the information contained there may point you toward sources you were not aware of.

Early every year, employers are required by law to issue a W-2 to each employee for the tax (calendar) year that has just ended. The employee attaches copies of the W-2 when filing his or her federal and state tax returns.

The W-2 form and the information included may change from year to year. For comprehensive information and instructions on the W-2 form, go to the IRS website www.irs.gov and, under "Forms and Publications," type in "W-2."

Of the numbered boxes on the W-2, the most important for this discussion are:

- *Box 1: Wages, tips and other compensation.* This is where the total of straight wages earned during the year appears. Also included are some employee business-expense reimbursements, moving-expense reimbursements and employer contributions

a Control number		OMB No. 1545-0008	Safe, accurate, FAST! Use IRS e-file	Visit the IRS Web Site at **www.irs.gov**.
b Employer identification number			1 Wages, tips, other compensation	2 Federal income tax withheld
c Employer's name, address, and ZIP code			3 Social security wages	4 Social security tax withheld
			5 Medicare wages and tips	6 Medicare tax withheld
			7 Social security tips	8 Allocated tips
d Employee's social security number			9 Advance EIC payment	10 Dependent care benefits
e Employee's first name and initial Last name			11 Nonqualified plans	12a See instructions for box 12
			13 Statutory employee ☐ Retirement plan ☐ Third-party sick pay ☐	12b
			14 Other	12c
				12d
f Employee's address and ZIP code				

15 State Employer's state ID number	16 State wages, tips, etc.	17 State income tax	18 Local wages, tips, etc.	19 Local income tax	20 Locality name

Form **W-2** **Wage and Tax Statement**   **2002**   Department of the Treasury- Internal Revenue Service

Copy B To Be Filed with Employee's FEDERAL Tax Return.   (Rev. February 2002)
This information is being furnished to the Internal Revenue Service.

to certain fringe benefits, such as stock option compensation (for more on stock options, see Chapter 16). However, Box 1 does not include wages that the employee has deferred under certain employer-sponsored retirement plans, such as contributions to a 401(k) plan or a simple IRA (see Chapter 14).

- *Box 5: Medicare wages and tips.* This is usually a larger number than Social Security wages. Medicare wages are gross wages and are not reduced by contributions to salary deferral and other tax-deferred employee benefit plans. Generally, all income reported in Box 5 is considered gross wages, and it is used in calculating child and spousal support.

- *Box 11: Nonqualified plans.* Money that the taxpayer has received from certain retirement plans and certain deferred-compensation plans appears here.

As for income tax returns, the format of the forms varies. Sources of funds may be marital income or separate income, and a joint return may reflect marital property, separate property or both.

There are several items on a tax return and its supplementary schedules that are especially important to look for:

- *Schedule A: Itemized Deductions.* This schedule may include several types of deductions that can figure into the earning-power equation for support. When you read the schedules filed by you and your spouse, look for entries that reveal items such as:

Medical and dental expenses. A taxpayer may claim a deduction only for expenses that exceed 7.5% of adjusted gross income. If there is a large number here, it may indicate that medical expenses will be an important part of a supported spouse's needs or that a supporting spouse may be unable to pay.

Real estate taxes. An entry here indicates home ownership or investment property. Holdings you didn't know about may be reflected here.

Home mortgage interest. An entry here

suggests a family residence or possibly a vacation home. If home mortgage interest is being paid, request a copy of the note. Whether the note is for fixed or variable interest could affect support calculations. Also check whether the property has been refinanced.

- *Schedule B: Interest and Ordinary Dividends.* The entries on this schedule reflect interest from banks, money market accounts, brokerage accounts and the like, as well as dividends paid by corporations to stockholders. These amounts are generally considered income, and thus they are available for child and spousal support. On this schedule, you'll see entries for:

Interest earned. This indicates the size of the current balance of invested funds. Thus, this may be helpful in assessing disclosure statements in other aspects of the divorce process. Whether the interest is taxable or tax-free will affect the support calculation.

Dividends. These are funds paid by securities. An entry here indicates that one or both spouses hold corporate stock or other securities. But many securities do not pay dividends, and those that don't may not be reflected on the tax return.

- *Schedule C: Profit or Loss From Business.* Unless you can come to an agreement between yourselves, the job of placing a dollar value on a business owned by the spouses at divorce is best done by a forensic accountant or a business appraiser. But the annual tax return can reveal clues about the earning power of a sole proprietorship or a sole practice.

Be forewarned, however—you won't necessarily get easy, clear information from a business tax return. As recent scandals involving Fortune 500 companies have shown, business accounting can be an inexact science, with much room for fudging. A businessperson can manipulate figures by delaying the deposit of checks; overstating travel, meals and entertainment ostensibly related to business; putting nonworking friends or relatives on the payroll to inflate "expenses"; buying personal items with business money; or writing off automobile expenses. If you suspect such practices, you may wish to hire a forensic accountant to do a detailed cash flow analysis and to value the business.

If you decide to wade into the world of business accounting, there are a few things you need to know. Businesses use different accounting methods. Some operate on a *cash basis:* They report to the IRS only cash income received, not money that their customers owe them, and they deduct expenses actually paid during the year. Others work on an *accrual basis:* They report income when it is earned, not necessarily received, and they deduct expenses when incurred, not necessarily when paid. Understanding the type of accounting method is essential to determining a business's profit or loss and, thus, its cash flow for purposes of support.

- *Schedule D: Capital Gains and Losses.* On this schedule, the taxpayer notes the sale or exchange of a capital asset, which is an asset owned and used personally or kept as an investment. Almost everything you own, including your house, household furnishings, car, jewelry and personal collections, is a capital asset. If an item is a capital asset, its sale generates a capital gain. If you exercise a stock option, that's also capital gains income. (For more on capital gains and losses, see Chapter 11 and Chapter 13. For stock options, see Chapter 16.)

Many capital gains don't count as income for support purposes. The determining factor may be whether the gain is considered a one-time gain or a recurring gain. For example, if the periodic sale of chunks of land from a large parcel has been funding the lifestyle of the parties and there's a reasonable expectation that this pattern will continue, the sale proceeds may be considered income. In such a case, the tax effect of the capital gains portion of income may

have a significant impact on the after-tax amounts available to both the supporting and the supported spouse.

Most state courts have said that income realized from the exercise of stock options is income available for child support. One Ohio court specifically held that the value of unexercised stock options (their increase in value from the date they were granted to the date they could have been exercised) is gross income for child support purposes.

- *Schedule E: Real Estate, Royalties, Partnerships, Trusts.* In Schedule E, the taxpayer lists income derived from the sources mentioned. Depending on what's listed, the items here may be the source of significant cash flow that may be used in calculating support. In particular, this schedule may show:

Rental revenue. Rental property could be a significant source of cash flow. Think about more than just the monthly rent when evaluating this figure for cash flow purposes. For example, if rental property is leased to a business owned by one or both of the spouses, does it rent at market rates? When was it acquired, and how much is owed on it? Was it ever refinanced? If a taxpayer is paying debt service, there will be less cash available for support.

S corporation and partnership income. S corporations and partnerships do not pay federal income tax. All taxable income, whether distributed or not, must be reported individually by the shareholders and partners based on their ownership percentage and is reflected on what's called a K-1 form. If an S corporation or a partnership is involved, get a copy of the corporate or partnership income tax return, together with a K-1, to understand significant details about what constitutes income and assets.

- *Form 1099-MISC.* This lists miscellaneous income, such as payments made to non-employees (for example, consultants or independent contractors) and interest and dividend income reinvested but not actually received. If the income is for services rendered, you may find it on the Schedule C form.

How long should you keep tax returns?

The short answer: Forever.

As the only official record of your earnings history, the tax return may be your most important financial document, period. It is crucial not only in a divorce but also for other financial purposes, such as setting your level of Social Security benefits.

Some advisors suggest you keep all tax returns for three years. That's just plain bad advice. Our strong recommendation: *Never* throw them away.

E. What About the Gifts You Gave Me?

It's sad but true that some of the most heated arguments during a divorce center on gifts—whether the gifts are an art collection and silverware, or the bread machine and Tupperware. Determining how to attribute financial gifts from family members, such as money used toward the down payment on the house or to buy a car, can also cause a great deal of friction during the divorce.

As a general rule, property acquired by gift or inheritance is the separate property of the spouse who receives it. This rule usually holds true if the property is given to the other spouse, or titled in the other spouse's name. But it may not always be the case. For instance, in a situation involving one of our clients, the husband transferred real estate holdings to his wife to protect himself against creditors. He was dismayed when she filed for divorce, sold the real estate and refused to give him any of the proceeds. She claimed the property was a gift, and the proceeds were entirely hers. He claimed the property still belonged entirely to him. The courts disagreed with both spouses and split the proceeds between them.

F. Financial Facts Checklist

The following list contains most of the items you will want to gather, whether you are doing your divorce yourself or working with an attorney or other legal or financial professionals. We recommend getting this information together yourself—you'll save time and money and gain a sense of control over your divorce.

Most of this information should be in your files at home or your office, or possibly in a safe-deposit box. If you don't have a clue about where to find a particular item, watch the mail as it arrives. You may be able to glean the names of insurance companies, banks, brokerage houses and other institutions, which you can contact to get information. As noted in Section A of this chapter, you can get copies of past tax returns from the IRS. Your insurance agent should be able to answer questions on policies, and the personnel or benefits office of your (or your spouse's) employer can shed some light on retirement benefits. For information on real estate, contact the agent who sold you the house or the company that holds the mortgage.

Instructions: Financial Facts Checklist

Put a check (✓) in the blanks corresponding to items you have. Enter an **X** for items you and your spouse don't have. You'll probably have to leave some spaces blank and enter a ✓ or an **X** as you conduct additional financial fact-finding. Some of the terms in the chart may be unfamiliar to you. Don't worry. You will understand them better as you continue reading this book. For now, use the list to jog your memory—or your accountant's—about what documents to look for.

G. Questions to Ask Your Attorney

1. Is there any hint that my spouse is hiding income? If so, how can we seek to expose that?

2. What documents do I need to prove our real income?

3. What liability do I have if I find our real income is greater than the income we reported on our tax returns?

4. Are there any other obvious sources of income on my spouse's tax return?

Financial Facts Checklist

	Tax returns (past five years)				
		U.S.:			
		State:			
	Pre- and/or postnuptial agreements				
		husband			
		wife			
	Previous divorce documents, including property settlement, alimony and child support orders				
		husband			
		wife			
	Wills				
		husband			
		wife			
	Trust documents				
		husband			
		wife			
	Pay stubs (from Jan. 1 of current year)				
		husband			
		wife			
	Bank records				
		savings accounts		checking accounts	
			in whose name:		in whose name:
			account number:		account number:
			balance:		balance:
			latest statement		latest statement
			deposit slips		cancelled checks
					deposit slips
		children's custodial accounts		certificates of deposit	
	Other accounts (including all accounts closed within past two years)				
		annuities		cash management accounts	
			in whose name:		in whose name:
			account number:		account number:
			interest/dividends:		interest/dividends:
			balance:		balance:
		brokerage accounts		credit union accounts	
			in whose name:		in whose name:
			account number:		account number:
			interest/dividends:		interest/dividends:
			balance:		balance:
		credit card account		credit card account	
			in whose name:		in whose name:
			account number:		account number:
			balance:		balance:
		credit card account			
			in whose name:		
			account number:		
			balance:		

		commodities accounts		mutual funds	
		in whose name:		in whose name:	
		account number:		account number:	
		interest/dividends:		interest/dividends:	
		balance:		balance:	

Tax-free investments

		in whose name:
		account number:
		interest/dividends:
		balance:

Insurance policies (either spouse)

		life		motor vehicles
		homeowners' or renters'		personal umbrella
		liability		disability
		health		
			parents	
			children	

Employee/group insurance benefits (either spouse)

		medical		life
		disability		

Other employee benefits

		auto allowances		expense account
		sick pay		stock options
		travel benefits		salary bonuses
			frequent flyer miles	deferred compensation
			rental car bonus points	military/VA benefits
			hotel bonus points	workers compensation claim/award
		severance pay		vacation pay

Retirement plans

		money purchase plans		401(k) plans
		ESOPs (Employee Stock Ownership Plan)		TSAs (Tax-Sheltered Annuities)
		Keoghs		profit-sharing
		thrift plans		defined benefit plans
		IRAs or SEP-IRAs		Roth IRA
		SIMPLEs		

Financial statements

		net worth—balance sheet or assets/liabilities statements	
		cash flow or income/expense statement	
		statements or documents regarding collections—gold, coins, stamps, etc.	
		inheritances (include copy of will or other verification of amount received)	
		gifts received	anticipated inheritances/gifts
		personal injury awards	litigation claims
		prior court judgments	loan applications
		personal loans payable	personal loans receivable

debts				
	list of outstanding debts on date of separation			
		husband		
		wife		
		joint		
ticket/subscription rights to sports/cultural events				
memberships in country clubs, fraternal orders, social/charitable groups				

Real estate records

current value of home(s)	original mortgage(s)
original purchase price	last monthly statement
property tax statements	escrow closing statements
deeds	appraisals
bills for home improvements	

Safe-deposit box

location/number/key	inventory and/or copies of contents

Documents identifying other property, such as:

patents	copyrights
royalties	license agreements

Miscellaneous personal property, such as:

boat	airplane
camper	motorcycle
other motor vehicles	jewelry
furs	other

Information on businesses

filing papers	current list of owners
percentage of ownership	officer/director positions held by spouse/self
tax returns	retirement plan documents
bank statements	loan applications
financial statements (last five years)	business agreements (partnership, buy-sell, etc.)
credit card records	appointment diaries
documents on business-owned real estate (deeds, appraisals, leases, etc.)	
accounts payable/receivable	

Household furnishings (attach itemized list)

Miscellaneous personal documents

passport
power of attorney
resume (for self and spouse)
appointment diaries
bills for living expenses (child care, phone, electric, Internet access, cleaning, yard work, laundry, etc.)
check stubs for other payments, such as disability income, unemployment compensation or Social Security benefits

Any other document that will help establish

net worth		income	
	husband		husband
	wife		wife
	joint		joint

Facing the Future:
What Must I Plan For?

If you're thinking about a divorce or beginning one, the last place you may want to look is to the future. At this stage, you might see only problems ahead. Nevertheless, you need to begin changing your outlook from "we" to "me"—from being part of a couple to being on your own.

It's helpful at an early stage to set basic goals for yourself. In most goal-setting exercises, you're asked to think about where you'd like to be in a few years—an effective approach for some people. In counseling divorcing clients, however, we've found it helpful to turn the question around. If you have trouble looking at the future, answer this:

*Where **don't** you want to be in the next five years?*

Speaking financially, few of us want to be in debt, burdened with property we can't sell or working two jobs just to survive. Yet that could happen to you if you drift through a divorce without planning ahead. By thinking about the kinds of financial problems you'd like to avoid, you can narrow your focus and clear the way for what you *do* want to accomplish.

As an initial planning exercise, use the columns in the chart that follows to jot down the immediate problems and goals you foresee. (Use the examples to give you ideas about your own needs.)

Once you have a basic idea of where you'd like to go in the future, take a few moments to reexamine where you are now. Use these questions to help you think about your own situation.

A. Major Upcoming Life Events

These events affect what you will and will *not* be able to do with money. For instance, if your teenagers are beginning college in a year, you may need a smaller house and a larger paycheck. You may be completing your own education and will need to budget time and money for a career change or job search. Perhaps you're reaching retirement age and must prepare for living on a reduced income. Whatever your situation, it's better to anticipate major events and prepare for them financially, rather than getting caught off guard when it's time to take care of a major expense.

Where I Do/Don't Want to Be in the Future

In the Next Six Months: *Financial Problems to Avoid*	*Financial Goals to Meet*
Examples: Letting bills become overdue Paying only interest due on credit cards Using credit cards for all purchases Not tracking expenses *Your Problems to Avoid:*	*Examples:* Pay off credit cards, or at least reduce balances by 50% Create a monthly budget calendar to avoid overdue bills Save 5% of income each month in emergency reserve Start monthly investing into XYZ mutual fund *Your Goals:*
In the Next Year: *Financial Problems to Avoid*	*Financial Goals to Meet*
Examples: Not enough money to pay mortgage Being late on mortgage No medical insurance Borrowing from friends or Mom *Your Problems to Avoid:*	*Examples:* Sell house and prepare to buy my own—set aside $20,000 toward down payment Obtain disability insurance policy *Your Goals:*

B. Anticipated Financial Commitments

To whom are you committed, and for how long? Have you agreed to support aging parents or another family member? Is that an indefinite agreement, or does it last for a specific number of years? Will you need to have money available for a business investment? Do you have an upcoming balloon payment? Again, the answers to questions such as these determine what's possible for your financial future.

Now think about what's happening in your life and make a list of Major Upcoming Life Events and Anticipated Financial Commitments. By getting this information down on paper, you will not only clarify your financial needs but may also reduce fears about the future. (Again, use the examples to get you started.) This exercise will serve as a guide as you make financial decisions in your divorce.

Finally, review the lists you've just made and mark your top three priorities in order from one to three. These are the next major issues that will demand your attention and time. We recommend tackling only three items at a time because once you begin to work on them, your financial condition is likely to change, and you may have new priorities. You can repeat this exercise any time you feel stuck about deciding "what to do next" in your divorce.

C. Major Goals That Will Cost Money

We all have goals, such as to lose weight, be popular and exercise more. Here, we're listing important life goals that may affect your finances—and vice versa. So think about what's important for you to accomplish and will cost money to do. This might involve getting more education, improving your business or your employability or fulfilling an aspiration that's key to your happiness and well-being.

List those goals and estimate their corresponding costs.

What's Happening in My Life

Major Upcoming Life Events	Anticipated Financial Commitments
Examples: Daughter beginning college in two years Move to new home in three years Job change in spring because of recent layoffs Son's wedding next June Events in Your Life:	Examples: Pay for Dad's health care New car—$300/month Remodel kitchen—$15,000 Your Commitments:

Major Goal	*Expected Price Tag*
Educational:	
Examples: Earn M.B.A. degree	$20,000 over two years
Example: Earn certificate in computer programming	$3,500 over six months
Your Educational Goals:	
Job:	
Example: Acquire contractor's license	$2,000
Example: Expand catering business by getting second truck	$18,000
Your Job Goals:	
Other:	
Example: Get certified as scuba diver	$1,000
Example: Go on African safari	$5,000
Your Other Goals:	

D. Where Does the Money Come From?

You've taken a look at what you absolutely *must do* and what you'd *like to do* next in your life. But how are you going to pay for it? Where will the money come from?

During Your Separation, Be Aware of Where Your Money Comes From

While separated, you can get money in the same ways you did while married. Funds are available to you through:

- a job (salary) or business (income)
- borrowing/credit
- selling property or assets
- your spouse—in the form of temporary alimony, or
- your spouse's payments of marital debts to be reimbursed later.

But in this time period—between today and the final settlement—you are in a unique situation. You are setting the stage for the settlement, and you do not want to make financial decisions that could work against you. You must be sure to keep detailed, accurate records.

For instance, a woman who had never worked during her marriage got a low-paying job in a retail store and left her children in the care of her parents when her husband filed for divorce. In the final settlement, she received no alimony because she was already working to support herself—even though she had wanted to go back to school to get training for a better job. Had she borrowed money to live on instead of getting the retail job, she might have been able to make a strong case for alimony.

In another case, the husband dutifully paid the household bills and temporary alimony for the two years that elapsed between the separation and the final settlement. Problems arose, however, because he had made the payments based on an informal arrangement with his spouse and had not documented this arrangement in a court order or in a written agreement. In his final settlement, he received no tax deduction for the alimony he paid out.

As these cases illustrate, you must not only figure out where the money is coming from, but also keep track of where it is going.

If you borrow or use credit cards. Under normal circumstances, financial planners would not recommend that you go into debt. During divorce, however, you may need to borrow money simply to survive. If you must use credit cards, try to find those with the lowest interest rate possible. If you borrow from family or friends, see if they will let you start repaying them when you're back on your feet.

It's crucial for you to document any money spent to support yourself and your children. If you paid for "common necessities of life"—food, shelter, clothing or medical care—you may be able to obtain a reimbursement for half of the costs. (See Chapter 5, Section A1.)

If you sell property or assets. Before selling any jointly owned property without your spouse's knowledge or consent, ask your attorney if you are legally permitted to do so. You will not be able to sell real estate, motor vehicles or other assets with title documents that need both spouses' signatures. If you do sell any joint assets, be sure to set aside one-half of the proceeds for your spouse, or keep clear records of the money you received so that your spouse gets similarly valued property in the settlement.

If you need temporary alimony. If you need help paying the bills while the divorce is pending, you can request that your spouse pay temporary alimony. If your spouse is unwilling to do so voluntarily, you will need to request a hearing before the judge to have the issue resolved.

The judge looks at the needs of the party making the request—particularly that spouse's ability to support himself or herself—and the other spouse's ability to pay the temporary alimony. In a few counties, court officials have issued guidelines for judges to use in setting alimony. (For more information on alimony, see Chapter 18.)

If you will be *paying* alimony, be sure to get your agreement either ordered by a court or in writing. If you don't, you cannot deduct the payments from your income tax. If you will be *receiving* alimony pursuant to a court order or written agreement, you must report that alimony as income on your tax return. (See Chapter 11, Section F.)

Enforcing—and Making Permanent— Temporary Support Agreements

If your temporary alimony agreement is in writing, but has not been ordered by the court, you may want to take that extra step to obtain a court order. Without a court order, you probably won't be able to enforce the agreement if your spouse doesn't pay.

As explained in Chapter 11, Section F, getting a court order is not difficult. If you and your spouse agree to the amount of temporary alimony, you can put your agreement into writing as a "stipulation." Your attorney can then take a few simple steps to get that stipulation turned into a court order. It involves asking the judge to sign the stipulation. You and your spouse should not have to appear in court.

Protecting Against Risks to Life, Health and Property

If you had no choice but to drive through a snowstorm on a curvy road, you would no doubt put chains on the tires and check the antifreeze. In navigating through your divorce, you must also take precautions if you are to survive financially.

Use this chapter to "check the antifreeze"—that is, to make sure you are doing what you can to reduce risks and protect yourself and your property.

A. Insurance

Insurance is designed to protect you from financial disaster. But when you divorce, your coverage itself may be at risk. Because policies can make for boring reading, and almost no one thinks about this subject until it's too late, insurance needs are commonly forgotten during divorce.

To demonstrate the importance of insurance in your life, ask yourself:

If I were in an accident or suddenly became ill, how would I pay my medical expenses?

Of course, being aware of what can happen without insurance and doing something about your situation are two different things. Begin to take action by reviewing the steps below, then follow up on these items.

1.   Health Insurance

Find copies of your current policy. Check with your insurance agent to be certain that you and/or your children are still covered according to the policy terms. Find out how long your current policy will remain in effect and what the costs will be for the next six months to one year.

If you are covered under a company policy, you may need to speak to the personnel office or a special agent who handles the firm's health care. If your family is covered by your spouse's insurance, you may still be able to retain protection even if your spouse tries to remove you.

Parents with custody can get health insurance for their children through the *noncustodial* parent's employment-related insurance program (or other group insurance plan), according to a federal law adopted as part of the Omnibus Reconciliation Act of 1993. The child cannot be denied coverage by the noncustodial parent, that parent's employer or that parent's insurance company for any of the following reasons:

- the child does not live with the noncustodial parent
- the child is not claimed as a dependent on the noncustodial parent's federal income tax return, or
- the child lives outside of the plan's service area.

One challenge that the parent with custody may face is the noncustodial parent's reluctance to turn over money received for reimbursed medical claims. To avoid this problem, the custodial parent can obtain a Qualified Medical Child Support Order, known as a QMCSO.

The QMCSO is a court order that provides for health benefit coverage for the child of the noncustodial parent under that parent's group health plan. When this court order is implemented, it forces the employer of the noncustodial parent to enroll the child in the group plan as an alternate beneficiary. Further, the QMCSO requires that the insurance company reimburse the custodial parent directly for the health care expenses incurred by the custodial parent for the child's benefit. This requirement guarantees that more custodial parents actually receive reimbursement for out-of-pocket contributions for a child's health care expenses. (For more on QMCSOs, see Chapter 18.)

2.   Life Insurance

When you divorce, you need to reconsider who should be named the beneficiary of any life insurance policies. Often, divorcing people forget to change the beneficiary. Then, years later, when one spouse dies, the *ex*-spouse gets all the benefits—even if there is a second spouse or if the deceased spouse wanted someone else, such as the child, to be the beneficiary. Whoever is named in the policy is the person who will receive the benefits.

In some divorce settlement agreements, the spouses may name the beneficiaries of their life insurance policies. In certain cases, the judge might make a similar order. If your settlement agreement or divorce decree says whom the beneficiary will be, but you forget to change the policy, the beneficiaries named in the agreement or decree may be protected when you die. But they may also end up in a messy fight with the insurance company or your former spouse's heirs. Don't rely on the settlement agreement or divorce decree to name the beneficiary.

At the same time, don't automatically remove your spouse from your policy. You may be prohibited from doing so until after your divorce is final. Also, to provide for your children's support and college education, you may want to either establish a trust for this purpose or keep your soon-to-be-ex-spouse as the beneficiary of your policy. This way, your spouse will receive a lump sum of cash to rear your minor-age children if you die before they reach adulthood. (For more on trusts, see *Make Your Own Living Trust*, by Denis Clifford (Nolo).)

Your ex-spouse may insist on being the beneficiary of a life insurance policy if you are paying alimony. That will keep your ex-spouse from losing the stream of income you provide if you die prematurely.

Sometimes in divorce, one spouse may want to name the children as beneficiaries rather than have any money go to the children's other parent. Think carefully before you make such a move. If the children are under 18 when you die, the probate court that oversees the distribution of your assets will require that a guardian be appointed to manage the insurance proceeds—usually in a bank account—until the children reach 18. If the guardian wants to remove money from the account, called a blocked or suspended account, the guardian will need court approval—an expensive, time-consuming and cumbersome procedure. And even when the money is distributed to the children at age 18, keep in mind that young adults are rarely mature enough to handle a vast amount of money and may squander these funds on cars instead of college.

If you are receiving alimony and/or child support, don't overlook the importance of maintaining life insurance on your spouse so that your income stream is protected. Keep existing life insurance in force or add a new policy on the life of the person paying support. The person paying alimony can deduct on his taxes as alimony any insurance premiums he pays if the person receiving the alimony is the owner of the policy (the person who has the right to control or change the policy or the beneficiaries). (See Chapter 18 for more on alimony.)

Look After Your Life Insurance

Would you want your soon-to-be-ex-spouse to benefit from your life insurance? When you divorce, you both must make sure that the disposition of any life insurance policies you own is clearly specified in your agreements. These questions can help you clarify what needs to be done with these policies:

- Who will own the policy if it is transferred?

- To whom may it be transferred?

- Are there any restrictions or conditions of transfer?

- Will the original owner get the policy back at some future time (for example, upon remarriage, termination of spousal/child support or death of the person to whom the policy was transferred)?

- Are there any outstanding policy loans? If yes, who will pay this loan?

- Will the policy owner have the right to designate beneficiaries? If yes, are there any restrictions on who is named a beneficiary? Must the policy owner designate a beneficiary (that is, an irrevocable beneficiary)?

- If so, does the restriction end upon a remarriage, termination of spousal support or a death?

- If the beneficiary is a child, does this designation end when the child support obligation ends?

- If a policy matures during the lifetime of the insured person (as can happen with an annuity or an endowment policy), who will receive the maturity proceeds?

- What other policy rights will be affected by ownership or beneficiary restrictions? (These rights might include cash surrender, policy loans or dividends.)

- Who will pay the premiums, and for how long?

- What happens if premiums are not paid? (While negotiating your settlement, you may want to require the payer spouse to provide evidence of payment to the other spouse at least ten days before the end of the policy's grace period.)

- Does a policy provision state what will happen if a premium is not paid—for example, that it will be paid via an automatic premium loan, paid-up insurance premiums or extended term insurance?

If your settlement agreement or judgment makes changes to the life insurance policy, you must notify the insurance company and complete the necessary forms. Ideally, your agreement should give the spouse who will keep the policy until a certain date to complete the forms; if that spouse does not comply, the agreement should permit the court to complete the forms on that spouse's behalf.

(© Northwestern Mutual Life Insurance Company. Reprinted with permission.)

3. Disability Insurance

Another risk to your income is that you may become disabled—or the ex-spouse who is paying your support may become disabled. If you're dependent on alimony and/or child support, you may want to consider obtaining disability insurance on your paying spouse. Talk to the benefits department at the company at which you or your spouse is employed. Or contact your insurance agent to determine the cost of getting your own coverage for disability.

Especially if you're a single parent, you may hesitate to buy disability insurance due to the expense and your perceived lack of need. Consider the harsher reality your children would face, however, if you became disabled and unable to work.

4. Business Continuation Coverage

Do you or your spouse own your own business? Check to see if you have insurance which is referred to as "key man" coverage. This coverage is designed so that the business can cover its operational costs in the event of the death of the business owner or another "key" person.

B. Property and Estate Protection

While the ultimate fate of your property may be unknown at the moment, you should nevertheless protect your interests by double-checking title documents and reviewing your will, trusts and other materials that dispose of your property at death.

1. Title Documents

In order to divide assets and negotiate your divorce settlement, you must know how title (history of ownership) to those assets is legally recorded, regardless of whether that property is ultimately considered your separate property or part of the marital assets. For real estate, title documents (deeds) are located at the local county records office. If you can't find the deeds at the recorder's office, a title company can help you. Other possibilities: Go to your county's website and look for a copy of a recorded document (expect to pay a fee); ask a real estate agent for a "property profile" that shows how title is held (usually free); or ask your mortgage company for loan documents, including any recorded deeds.

You should take a look at all recorded deeds to make sure your spouse has not unilaterally removed your name from property held jointly. For example, in most states, either spouse can change title held in joint tenancy into tenancy in common.

Joint tenancy property is owned with each joint tenant having a "right of survivorship." This means that if either joint tenant dies, the other owner automatically inherits the deceased's portion, even if a will or other document states otherwise. To sell joint tenancy property, all owners must agree, or the owner who wants to sell must change title from joint tenancy to a different form of ownership, called tenancy in common, and then sell his share. Tenancy in common does not have the right of survivorship. Either owner can leave—or sell—his share to whomever he wants. (For more on joint tenancy property, see Chapter 6.)

Keeping Health Care Coverage Through Your Spouse's Employer

If your health insurance is provided through a plan offered by your spouse's employer, and 20 or more people work for that employer, you can continue the health care coverage after the divorce. Under the federal COBRA (Consolidated Omnibus Budget Reform Act) law, divorced spouses of employed medical plan participants can pay for their own coverage for up to 36 months after the divorce. Under the law, the premiums you're charged for the COBRA coverage may not exceed 102% of what the employer pays to cover you. But you should check the costs of other health plans before deciding to get COBRA coverage through your spouse's employer. (For more information, contact your local office of the federal Department of Labor and ask for a copy of the booklet entitled "Continuing Health Care Coverage" or check the department's website, www.dol.gov.)

Your spouse's employer must inform you of your right to continue the coverage when your divorce becomes final. Don't leave it to your ex-spouse to notify the employer of that date. You should contact your ex-spouse's employer (probably the human resources department) and request the continued health care coverage as soon as your divorce is final.

Remember, the maximum length of time you can continue the coverage is 36 months. If you are healthy, start looking into individual coverage immediately. It may cost less than the continued group coverage. (Ask if the provider of your continued coverage offers conversion to individual coverage. Be aware that such plans are usually expensive and limited in benefits.) Also, if you get a new job that provides group health insurance or if you remarry and your new spouse's employer offers group coverage, your continued coverage will usually be terminated.

Keep in mind that if you don't obtain new insurance before the end of the 36-month COBRA period, you risk getting ill and becoming uninsurable.

Even if the employer has fewer than 20 employees, state law may require it to provide COBRA-type benefits. For more information, contact your state Department of Labor, the personnel office at your spouse's job or your attorney or financial advisor.

Title documents for other types of propert—for example, car registration forms and bank account and investment statements—are located in different places. To protect yourself from having your spouse unilaterally change title, you may need to write to the Department of Motor Vehicles, bank or stockbroker to ask that no title changes take place until the divorce is settled.

2. Wills, Trusts and Other Estate Planning Documents

If you've made a will or living trust or taken other measures to determine what will happen to your property after your death, your divorce most likely alters those plans dramatically.

In many states, a final divorce automatically revokes part or all of your will. It's common for divorce to cancel all parts of your will that leave property to your ex-spouse; in some states, the entire will is wiped out. In any case, you should make a new will.

If you die before your divorce is final, your spouse may be entitled to a share or all of your property—even if your will leaves everything to other beneficiaries. To be certain about the distribution of your property, you can consult a Nolo estate planning publication (see resource list at the end of this chapter) or an attorney. Take steps to ensure that your property is distributed according to your wishes.

If you don't have a will and haven't arranged to transfer your property by other means (for example, joint tenancy or a living trust), at your death your property will be distributed according to state law. Usually this means your spouse and children will get your property. If you're divorced and have no children, your property will probably go to your parents, siblings and siblings' children.

Planning for Your Children

If you have children, it's especially important to also have an estate plan. At the least, consider:

- who will physically care for your children if you can't

- how they will be supported if you're not around, and

- who will manage the property you leave them if they are under 18.

In your will, you can name someone to be the personal guardian of your children and have physical custody. And you can name the same person, or someone else, to manage the property your children inherit from you. As for figuring out how to support the children after your death, you may want to consider term life insurance, which provides a preset amount of money if you die while the policy is in force. It's a relatively cheap way to provide quick cash for beneficiaries.

C. Questions to Ask Your Attorney

1. Can I change the beneficiary of my life insurance from my spouse to my children during the divorce? How and when can I do that?

2. Can the divorce settlement include a provision for life insurance on the person who provides support to protect the support order or alimony?

3. As additional alimony, can the settlement include a provision for health insurance? Disability insurance?

Nolo's Estate Planning Tools

 Nolo publishes several books and software products on wills, living trusts and avoiding probate:

- *Plan Your Estate,* by Denis Clifford & Cora Jordan, is a comprehensive estate planning book, covering everything from basic estate planning (wills and living trusts) to sophisticated tax-saving strategies (AB trusts and much more).

- WillMaker interactive software lets you make a sophisticated will. For example, with WillMaker you can choose among three ways to provide property management for children should you die before they are competent to handle property themselves. In addition, WillMaker allows you to express your last wishes for your funeral and burial and contains both a healthcare directive (living will) and durable power of attorney for finances valid in your state.

- Living Trust Maker software lets you create a revocable living trust to avoid probate. The program creates an individual trust or a trust for a married couple.

- *Nolo's Simple Will Book*, by Denis Clifford, provides step-by-step instructions and forms to create a detailed will. Its will is similar in scope and sophistication to WillMaker's. The book comes with a disk, which you can use with any standard word processing program to make drafting and printing out the will easy.

- *8 Ways to Avoid Probate*, by Mary Randolph, explains important and often overlooked ways to avoid probate, an often lengthy process of certifying a will. It is now possible to avoid probate for many kinds of property without creating a living trust. If you suspect you should be paying attention to probate avoidance, but dread thinking about it, start with this small but thorough book.

- *Make Your Own Living Trust*, by Denis Clifford, explains in plain English how to create a trust yourself, without hiring a lawyer. It contains all the forms you need to create your own living trust with step-by-step instructions for filling them out.

- *9 Ways to Avoid Estate Taxes*, by Mary Randolph, tells you what you need to conserve as much of your estate as possible for family or other beneficiaries. Written in easy-to-read, plain English, the book presents the nine major methods people can use to avoid or reduce federal estate taxes.

Taxes: How Do I File and Pay?

When you're divorcing, you can't wait until just before
April 15 to think about your taxes.

While you do not have to confront every small detail in your tax papers when you're in the midst of a separation, you can take basic precautions that will save you money and prevent hassles later.

For instance, suppose you assume that you and your divorcing spouse will file income taxes jointly. At tax time, however, you discover your spouse has already filed separately. How will you pay the IRS for taxes you did not expect to owe? Better to

grapple with the filing question now than to make costly assumptions that can easily be wrong.

The following guidelines will help you address the income tax questions that are most important at this stage of your divorce. As you move through the rest of the divorce process (and this book), you will face more complicated tax issues regarding your property. For now, stick to the basics.

A. Get a Rough Estimate of Your Tax Bill

You don't want any nasty surprises next April 15. To avoid problems, make a rough calculation of your federal and state taxes or ask your accountant or tax preparer to help you. Figure the amount you would pay if you filed separately and the amount you would pay if you filed with your spouse. Even if you haven't done all the paperwork necessary to find the exact amount, it's useful to get a tax estimate. The estimate will at least give you a guide for deciding how to file. You'll also be able to use the information if you eventually try to convince your spouse to file jointly.

If possible, discuss the decision on tax filing with your spouse, lawyer, accountant or tax advisor. Your goal is to reach an agreement about filing and then document that agreement in writing.

If you don't have access to tax information. One spouse often does most of the bookkeeping for a family. If your spouse played that role and does not want to give you the information, you may have to get a court order or use legal discovery (evidence gathering) techniques. (See Chapter 8, Section B.) For either, you'll probably need the help of an attorney. Consult the Appendix for resources. Before obtaining legal help, however, be sure to point out to your spouse that the legal bills of both of you will rise because of his or her attempts to withhold information.

You can also contact your accountant for copies of previous returns, or ask the Internal Revenue Service for Form 4506. By completing the form and returning it to the IRS, you should be able to get the tax returns you need, but only if you signed the return when it was filed. The easiest way to get forms from the IRS is to visit the website at www.irs.gov. From this address, you can link to state tax forms, tax tables and publications. Also, you can search for divorce or other divorce-related tax topics by a word search.

The IRS has several publications that can help you if you're going through divorce with an uncooperative spouse. The most important are:

- Publication 17, Your Federal Income Tax for Individuals

- Publication 501, Exemptions, Standard Deduction, and Filing Information

- Publication 504, Divorced or Separated Individuals

- Publication 505, Tax Withholding and Estimated Tax

- Publication 552, Recordkeeping for Individuals, and

- Publication 555, Community Property. If you live in the community property states of Arizona, California, Idaho, Louisiana, Nevada, New Mexico, Texas, Washington or Wisconsin, many federal tax rules are applied differently than in the other states, which are called equitable distribution states.

If you have to wait for copies of previous returns and financial information, you can work with a tax accountant to estimate the amount you will owe the IRS. You can find out about deductions in several ways. Banks and lenders can tell you how much interest has been paid on a mortgage, and charities can give you the dollar amount you or your spouse may have donated. Call your spouse's employer to verify his or her salary and check copies of any loan applications you have. In Chapter 12, you will prepare *Net Worth* and *Cash Flow* statements, which can help clarify your tax situation.

B. What Status Can Be Used When Filing Tax Returns?

One of the most important decisions you will need to make is whether to file a joint return with your spouse or to file separately. The table below summarizes the types of filing status available to you and the requirements for each.

Filing Status	*Requirements*
Married filing jointly	You must be married up to and including last day of tax year (December 31) even if you are living apart.
Married filing separately	You must be married up to and including last day of tax year.
Head of household	If you are single: • you must provide more than half of the costs of maintaining your household, and • your household must be the principal home of at least one dependent. If you are married and have lived physically apart prior to July 1 of the tax year: • you must file a separate return • you must maintain your home and have your child, stepchild or other dependent living there for more than half the tax year (temporary absences such as vacations, time in school and time when a child is absent under a custody agreement do not count as time spent away) • you must be able to claim the child as a dependent or release that claim (provide your spouse with a waiver—see Form 8332), and • you must furnish more than half the cost of maintaining the household during the tax year. (In figuring that cost, include clothing, education, medical treatment, mortgage principal payments, vacations, life insurance, transportation and the value of services performed in the household by the taxpayer. Exclude property taxes, mortgage interest, rent, repairs, utilities, home insurance and food eaten in the home.)
Single	You must be unmarried, legally separated or have your marriage annulled as of the last day of tax year and be ineligible for head of household status.

C. When in Doubt, File Separately

If you and your spouse are unable to agree on how to handle your taxes, file separately. Generally, you can amend two separate returns (yours and your spouse's) and file jointly. You cannot, however, amend a joint return after the due date for that return in order to file separately. If you initially file separately, you have only three years to amend your returns and file jointly. Although filing separately may actually cost more in dollars, it could save you a great deal of grief.

You will, of course, want to file separately if it will save on taxes—but you should also file this way if your spouse misrepresents income or expenses. If you file jointly, you could be liable for back taxes, interest and penalties on a joint return. By filing separately, you will lessen your risk and keep your options open. Bear in mind that if you file separately you forfeit the right to certain deductions. These include education credits, child or dependent care expenses in most instances, the earned income credit and interest paid on student loans.

Except in community property states, if you file a separate return, you generally report only your own income, exemptions, credits and deductions. If your spouse had no income, you can claim an exemption for your spouse. If your spouse refuses to provide the information necessary to file a joint return, both spouses should file separate returns.

Special Rules for Single Filers Living in a Community Property State

As explained in Chapter 12, Section A, married couples in Arizona, California, Idaho, Louisiana, Nevada, New Mexico, Texas, Washington and Wisconsin live under community property laws. (Alaska gives married couples the option of identifying property held in trust as community property.)

Although these states' community property laws generally operate in the same way, there are differences among the states. One significant variation is how they treat income from separate property. Arizona, California, Nevada, New Mexico and Washington treat it as separate income. Idaho, Louisiana, Texas and Wisconsin consider it community income even though it comes from separate property. (See "Questions to Ask Your Tax Advisor" at the end of this chapter.)

Broadly, these rules provide that income earned and assets acquired during marriage are owned 50-50, regardless of which spouse actually brought home the paycheck. Before filing a separate tax return in a community property state, check with a tax advisor. You will probably have to report one-half of the combined community income and be permitted to take one-half of the joint deductions, in addition to reporting your separate income and claiming your deductions. As straightforward as this sounds, it's not always clear whether a deduction (expense) is community or separate. It basically depends on whose money was used to pay it and the character of the debt. If you paid an expense out of community funds, you must divide it equally and report half of it on each spouse's return.

Community property laws also affect exemptions for dependents. When community income supports a dependent child, the exemption may be claimed by one spouse or the other; it cannot be divided. If you have two or more dependent children, however, you can divide the exemptions (each claiming a child), but you cannot divide any single exemption in half. If you both try to take the exemption, the IRS will assume that each of you provided exactly half of the support and won't permit either of you to claim the exemption.

Avoiding Liability for Your Spouse's Dishonesty With the IRS

The IRS Restructuring and Reform Act of 1998 provides relief from joint liability when a spouse incorrectly reports items on a jointly filed tax return. The three kinds of relief and the factors influencing them are shown below. Innocent Spouse Relief is for all joint filers. It relieves you of all or a portion of the responsibility for paying tax, interest and penalties if your spouse did something wrong on your joint tax return. The Separate Liability Election permits you to limit your liability for any deficiency to the amount that would be allocated to you if you had filed a separate return. Rules for Equitable Relief give the IRS discretion to relieve you of liability when you cannot qualify for relief under the rules for Innocent Spouse Relief or the Separate Liability Election.

If you believe you may qualify for relief, go to the IRS website, www.irs.gov. The material there includes a section called "Spousal Tax Relief Eligibility Explorer." From the IRS home page, under the "Contents" heading, click on "Innocent Spouses"; from there, under the "Topics" heading, click on "Eligibility Explorer." The Explorer will guide you through the qualifying factors one question at a time and, if you appear to qualify for the relief, will download the appropriate application forms. Before filling out the forms, however, consult your tax advisor.

Factors:	Rules for Innocent Spouse Relief:	Rules for Separate Liability Election:	Rules for Equitable Relief:
Type of Liability	• You must have filed a joint return that has an understatement of tax due to an erroneous item of your spouse.	• You must have filed a joint return that has an understatement of tax due, in part, to an item of your spouse.	• You must have filed a return that has either an understatement or underpayment of tax.
Marital Status	• No requirements.	• You must be no longer married, be legally separated or have not lived with your spouse in the same house for an entire year before you file for relief.	• No requirements.
Knowledge	• You must establish that at the time you signed the joint return you did not know, and had no reason to know, that there was an understatement of tax.	• If the IRS establishes that you actually knew of the item giving rise to the understatement, then you are not entitled to make the election to the extent of actual knowledge.	• No requirements.
Other Qualifications	• None.	• None.	• You do not qualify for innocent spouse relief or separation of liability.
Unfairness	• Not applicable.	• Not applicable.	• The IRS must determine that it would be unfair to hold you liable for the underpayment or understatement of tax taking into account all the facts and circumstances.
Refunds	• Yes, your request can generate a refund.	• No, your request cannot generate a refund.	• Yes, for amounts paid between July 22, 1998 and April 15, 1999, and for amounts paid pursuant to an installment agreement after the date the request for relief is made.

A Note on Tax Rates

Reduced tax rates on ordinary income are a centerpiece of the federal Taxpayer Relief Act of 2001. But the cuts are phased in gradually, and the full effect won't be felt until 2006.

For example, the highest individual rate, which had been 39.6%, decreased to 39.1% in 2001, falls further to 38.6% in 2002 and on down until it reaches 35% in 2006. Similarly, the 28% tax rate eventually will become 25%, and a new 10% bracket will be added, though the 15% bracket will be unchanged. (Capital gains rates aren't changed and will continue to be attractive compared with all but the lowest of the new tax rates on ordinary income.)

This presents a problem for this book because most tax rate figures we specify will be obsolete by the time you read them. So, in the interests of sanity and clarity, we have stuck with the 2000 rates—generally 39.6%, 28% and 15%—in our examples throughout the book. But the same planning principles will apply, and you can choose mentally to reduce slightly many of the tax rates mentioned.

D. What to Know If You File Jointly

Filing a joint return is often to your economic advantage. A married taxpayer can claim the child and dependent care credit and the earned income credit (for low-income taxpayers) only on a joint return. In addition, certain deductions—such as the dependency exemption for a spouse and the deduction for a spousal IRA contribution—can be taken only on a joint return.

In deciding whether or not to file a joint return, you will want to calculate—or talk to your tax advisor about—how each of these factors will affect your tax bill:

- your tax rate
- any deductions or credits you may lose
- tax losses from partnerships or business losses
- tax benefits available by filing a joint return as compared to filing separately, and
- your liability for your spouse's dishonesty in reporting income and taking deductions when you file a joint return. (See sidebar, below.)

Liability on Joint Tax Returns

If you file a joint return, each spouse is liable for 100% of the taxes due on the return as well as any penalties and interest assessed on that return. Unless you qualify as an "innocent spouse" (see the table "Avoiding Liability for Your Spouse's Dishonesty With the IRS," above), you are generally liable for any unpaid taxes, even after your divorce is final. (In some cases, if you sign a joint return under duress or your spouse forges your name, the IRS will not consider you jointly liable.)

If you believe your spouse is not being honest in reporting income or claiming deductions and credits, file a separate return—even if it is to your economic disadvantage. If it turns out that your spouse was being honest in his reporting, you can always amend your returns and file jointly within three years of the original due dates. You cannot, however, amend a joint return and file separate returns. See the table above, "Avoiding Liability for Your Spouse's Dishonesty With the IRS."

The federal government increasingly gets involved in collecting past-due child support and alimony payments. If the IRS withheld a tax refund on your joint return because your spouse has fallen behind in child support or alimony payments, you may qualify as an "injured" spouse and be able to recover your share of that refund. There's an easy process for doing this. Simply download the Injured Spouse form from the IRS website, www.irs.gov. Complete the form and return it to the IRS.

Additional factors to consider include such issues as your responsibility when signing a joint return and liabilities you could incur if your spouse signs your name to a return or refuses to sign the return.

1. Your Responsibility When Signing a Joint Return

According to the IRS, you may not ignore the information on any income tax return you sign. Legally, you must examine the return and make certain that any transaction of which you are aware is properly reported.

2. What If Your Spouse Refuses to Sign a Joint Return?

If a spouse refuses to file a joint return and instead files separately, the other spouse must also file a separate return.

The spouse can file a joint return using only his/her name if the other spouse:

- refuses to file a joint return
- doesn't file a separate one
- had no income or earnings, and
- always filed a joint return in the past.

This works only if it is clear that the couple intended to file a joint return. If the refusing spouse won't sign because he or she feels the prepared return is fraudulent, the other spouse cannot file a joint return without the refusing spouse's signature.

3. Other Concerns When Filing a Joint or Separate Return

You may have several other concerns regarding your spouse and the IRS, such as:

a. What If Your Spouse Settles a Tax Bill With the IRS?

Suppose one spouse makes an agreement (called an offer in compromise) to pay the IRS less than the actual taxes due, plus interest and penalties, on a jointly filed return. That does not prevent the IRS from collecting money from the other spouse for the balance due. If the ex-spouse who is not covered in the settlement remarries, that person's new spouse also could be subject to unforeseen tax liabilities.

For instance, in one case, a widow had reached a settlement with the IRS to take care of the significant tax liabilities that were attributable to her deceased husband. When she remarried, she had not finished paying the amount mandated by the settlement. She also transferred the property received from her first husband to her new husband. The IRS sought to collect the balance of the settlement from the second husband, who tried to argue that he should not be responsible for the payments because he did not participate in the original agreement. The court found, however, that because the property had been transferred to him, he was effectively a party to the agreement and therefore had to pay up. (Although this example involved a widow, the same principle would apply had she been divorced and transferred her divorce settlement property to her new husband.)

b. Will an Indemnity Clause in a Divorce Agreement Protect You From the IRS?

An indemnity clause is a section in a marital settlement or separation agreement in which one spouse agrees to pay the tax liability and to hold the other spouse harmless. This clause, however, offers no protection from the IRS. In fact, except in unusual circumstances, the IRS can grab a joint taxpayer's property even after it has been divided in divorce to satisfy a joint tax debt.

c. What If Your Marriage Is Annulled?

If your marriage is legally annulled, the IRS takes the position that it never existed. If you filed joint tax returns during your marriage, you will have to file corrected returns (as a single person) for the prior three years. You must do this even if you had no separate income to declare.

E. Dividing the Joint Tax Liability— Or the Refund

Once you have prepared a joint income tax return, you will discover that you owe additional taxes or are due a refund. To avoid animosity and misunderstandings, you and your spouse must find a fair way to share the tax liability or divide the refund.

Of course, you need not do all of this work by yourself; a tax preparer can make these calculations for you. No matter who does the math, plug the numbers into the formula below. To do so, you must first figure out what you each would have owed (or would have received as a refund) if you had filed separately.

Example: How to Calculate Your Share of a Refund on a Joint Tax Return

	Example	You
1. Your individual separate tax liability (*married filing separately*)	$3,000.00	_____
2. Your spouse's individual separate tax liability (*married filing separately*)	$7,000.00	_____
3. Total separate tax liability [Step 1 + Step 2]	$10,000.00	_____
4. Joint tax liability on return (*married filing jointly*)	$6,000.00	_____
5. Your share of the total tax liability [Step 1 ÷ Step 3]	.30	_____
6. Your spouse's share of the total tax liability [Step 2 ÷ Step 3]	.70	_____
7. Your share of joint tax liability [Step 4 x Step 5]	$1,800.00	_____
8. Your spouse's share of joint tax liability [Step 4 x Step 6]	$4,200.00	_____
9. Total tax payments made by couple	$12,000.00	_____
10. Total tax payment made by you [in Step 9]	$3,000.00	_____
11. Your share of the refund [Step 10 – Step 7]	$1,200.00	_____

Step 1. Prepare a separate tax return for yourself using the "married filing separately" status to find the amount you would owe individually if you and your spouse filed alone.

Step 2. Prepare a separate tax return for your spouse using the "married filing separately" status to find the amount your spouse would owe individually if you and your spouse filed alone.

Step 3. Add together each spouse's individual separate tax liability to determine the total amount of your separate tax liabilities.

Step 4. Prepare a joint tax return using the "married filing jointly" status to determine your total joint tax liability.

Step 5. Determine the percentage of the total taxes you owe by dividing your individual separate tax liability by the total separate tax liability.

Step 6. Determine the percentage of the total taxes your spouse owes by dividing your spouse's individual separate tax liability by the total separate tax liability.

Step 7. Determine the amount of the total taxes you owe by multiplying your joint tax liability by the percentage of the total taxes you owe.

Step 8. Determine the amount of the total taxes your spouse owes by multiplying your joint tax liability by the percentage of the total taxes your spouse owes.

Step 9. Calculate the total tax payments made by each spouse by adding all federal tax withheld as shown on the W-2 forms and all estimated tax payments made. If this amount is less than the amount in Step 4, more money must be paid to the IRS; if this amount is more than the amount in Step 4, the IRS will send you a refund.

If you owe more to the IRS:

Step 10. Subtract the total amount of tax payments made by each spouse (Step 9) from each spouse's separate share of the joint tax liability (Step 5).

Step 11. Send a check to the IRS for the amount due. The spouse who pays the IRS is entitled to be reimbursed from the other spouse, who must make up the difference between what he or she has already paid individually (through withholding or estimated tax payments) and that spouse's share of the amount the couple still owes the IRS.

If you are entitled to a refund:

Step 10. Determine the amount of the total tax payment that should be refunded to each spouse by subtracting each spouse's individual share of the joint tax liability (Steps 7 and 8) from the amount each spouse has already paid to the IRS (through withholding or estimated tax payments).

Step 11. The spouse who receives the refund from the IRS must reimburse the other spouse for his or her share of the refund as determined in Step 10.

If you and your spouse anticipate receiving a tax refund on your joint return, don't forget that this money is likely to be considered marital property. That means it will be assigned or divided between the spouses as part of the property division upon divorce. For more on dividing up property, see Chapter 12.

F. Tax Issues Involving Temporary Alimony or Child Support

Often in divorce negotiations or mediation, spouses reach informal agreements about temporary alimony or child support payments. But sometimes they neglect to get the agreement in writing or to get a court order outlining the agreement. Do not make this mistake. (Read Chapter 18 before entering into any agreement to pay or receive alimony or child support.)

Getting a court order is not difficult. If you and your spouse agree on the amount of temporary alimony and/or child support, you can put your agreement in writing as a "stipulation." Your attorney can then take the simple steps needed to get that stipulation turned into a court order. It involves asking a judge to sign the stipulation. You and your spouse should not have to appear in court.

If you're paying alimony, you may resent it—but at least there is one bright spot. Alimony, including temporary alimony, is tax deductible to the payer. For alimony to be deductible, however, the court must order it or the parties must agree to it in writing. If you pay alimony or temporary alimony based on an informal, oral agreement, you cannot deduct those payments on your tax return.

For alimony to be deductible, the payer and the recipient of alimony cannot file a joint return.

If you're the recipient of alimony, it is income you must report on your tax return. And beware: Alimony payments made after the legal obligation to pay alimony ends—that is, voluntary payments—are not tax deductible to the payer, but they could be taxable income to the former spouse who received the payments.

Child support, unlike alimony, is neither deductible for the parent paying it nor taxable as income to the parent receiving it. However, regardless of whether you and your spouse are living apart, you will want to make arrangements for child support so that your children are adequately cared for. For more on child support agreements, see Chapter 18.

G. Get Your Tax Agreement in Writing

Whatever you and your spouse decide to do about taxes, be sure to get the agreement in writing. Have it notarized or possibly even reviewed by an attorney. Be certain, too, to check with an accountant or a financial planner for advice on the tax implications of your divorce.

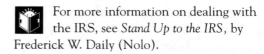 For more information on dealing with the IRS, see *Stand Up to the IRS*, by Frederick W. Daily (Nolo).

H. Questions to Ask Your Tax Advisor

1. In my state, is income from separate property considered separate or marital income?

2. What income from separate property is considered to be separate property?

3. If my spouse and I ran a business while we were married, under what circumstances must I report the income and deductions on my own tax return now?

4. Is the income I earned after we separated but before the divorce becomes final considered separate or marital income? ■

CHAPTER

12

Property and Expenses: Who Owns and Who Owes What?

What—exactly—is at stake in your divorce? To answer that question, you must get a handle on your property and living expenses.

In this chapter, you define which property is legally yours and which assets you may have to struggle for in the tug-of-war of divorce. You will also develop a much-needed picture of your cash flow. And you will learn about the use of legal discovery procedures if you have any trouble getting the information you need. The financial fact-finding you did in Chapter 8 (you *did* do it, didn't you?) will be immensely helpful here.

By completing the tasks that follow, you will lay the foundation for the analysis and decision making that must be done to reach your final settlement.

Think of this stage as developing your database or stocking your pantry with the items you will need throughout the divorce process.

The four basic issues you must address at this point are:

- Who owns what—marital property and the laws of your state.

- Who knows what—using legal discovery.

- Net worth—what do you own and what do you owe?

- Cash flow—where does the money go?

A. Who Owns What—Marital Property and the Laws of Your State

Before you begin to negotiate your divorce settlement, you must know what property you own alone—as opposed to what property is owned separately by your spouse or by the two of you together. Keep in mind that the rules that follow are general. To get the specifics on the property laws of your state, you will have to consult your lawyer or do some legal research.

Read this section for an overview of ownership. Once you have determined which of your property is separate and which is marital, you will list this information in the *Net Worth Statement* in Section C, below.

1. Jointly Owned Property

The property that couples accumulate during marriage is called, straighforwardly enough, marital property. Depending on which state you live in, however, marital property will take different forms.

Community Property: Arizona, California, Idaho, Louisiana, Nevada, New Mexico, Texas, Washington and Wisconsin. (Alaska also gives married couples the option of identifying property held in trust as community property.) In community property states, all earnings during marriage and all property acquired with those earnings are considered community property owned jointly by the couple. Even if one spouse earned a salary during the marriage while the other one kept house, those earnings are community property. Separate property in these states—that is, not "community"—consists for the most part of money and property that the individual spouses owned before marriage, as well as gifts and inheritances that one spouse receives during marriage (see Section A2, below).

At divorce, community property is divided equally (in half) between the spouses. A spouse who contributed separate money to an item bought with community funds—for instance, a wife who contributed her $5,000 inheritance toward a $20,000 down payment for the family home—may be entitled to reimbursement for that contribution.

Conversely, a spouse who added community property money to a separate property item belonging to the other may be reimbursed.

In most community property states, a court has the discretion to divide the property equitably (fairly), if dividing the property in half would result in unfairness to one party. Additionally, in some community property states, a spouse whom the court considers at fault in ending the marriage may be awarded less than 50% of the community property. (These exceptions do not apply in California.)

Equitable Distribution of Property: All Other States. In the District of Columbia and 41 states that follow equitable distribution principles, assets and earnings accumulated during marriage are divided equitably (fairly) at divorce. In theory, equitable means equal, or nearly so. In practice, however, equitable often means that as much as 2/3 of the property goes to the higher wage earner and as little as 1/3 goes to the lower (or non-) wage earner—unless the court believes it is fairer to award one or the other spouse more. In some equitable distribution states, if a spouse obtains a fault divorce, the "guilty" spouse may receive less than a full share of the marital property upon divorce.

2. Separately Owned Property

In all states, a married person can treat certain types of earnings and assets as separate property. At divorce, this separate property is not divided under the state's property distribution laws, but rather is kept by the spouse who owns it.

In community property states, the following is considered separate property:

- property accumulated before marriage
- property accumulated during marriage with premarital earnings (such as income from a pension that vested before marriage) or with the proceeds of the sale of premarital property
- gifts given to only one spouse
- inheritances, and

- property acquired after permanent separation.

In the equitable distribution states, separate property includes:

- property accumulated by a spouse before marriage

- gifts given to only one spouse, and

- inheritances.

In addition, some equitable distribution states consider wages kept separate from other marital property to be separate property.

Separate Is Separate Unless It's Mixed

In both community property and equitable distribution states, the separate property of a spouse generally remains separate property. However, if it's mixed with marital property or the other spouse's separate property, you may not be able to keep your separate property separate, unless you can trace the origin of your separate property and how it was commingled.

B. Who Knows What—Using Legal Discovery

As described in Chapter 8, there are several ways to gather financial information. Doing it yourself not only keeps down your lawyer's bill but also educates you about your family's finances and prepares you to negotiate from a position of strength.

If you can't find the information yourself, however, and all efforts to collect it informally fail, you can have your lawyer conduct "discovery." Discovery is the term for formal procedures used to obtain information during a lawsuit. As with all matters in your divorce, remember that the attorney works for you. You should be the one making the decisions about how extensive discovery procedures should be.

If you've never seen the checkbook and have signed the tax returns for years without reviewing them, then your lawyer may have to do a lot of

digging to create a picture of your financial life. Likewise, if you have participated in budgeting and bookkeeping, but your spouse owns a cash-and-carry business that you suspect is being used to hide assets, discovery may be worth every penny you spend.

On the other hand, if you and your spouse have few assets and you have a pretty good idea of what you're both worth, then using discovery to ferret out more information may simply be a waste of money.

Think financially and act legally—remember that truism in divorce. Apply that maxim to discovery procedures and you should be fine.

In a divorce, the common discovery devices likely to be used include:

Deposition (or examination before trial). A deposition is a proceeding in which a witness or party must answer questions orally under oath before a court reporter. In divorces, many lawyers want to take the deposition of the other spouse in order to ask about potential hidden assets.

Interrogatories. Interrogatories are written questions sent by one party to the other to be answered in writing under oath. Interrogatories are often used to ask a spouse to list all bank accounts, investment accounts and other assets ever held by that spouse.

Request (or notice) for production of documents. This is a request to a party to hand over certain defined documents. In divorce cases, spouses often request from each other bank statements, tax returns, pay stubs and other documents showing earnings, assets and debts.

Request (or notice) for inspection. This is a request by a spouse to look at items and documents in the possession or control of the other spouse. Items commonly inspected are original financial documents, houses and cars. In divorces, the request often comes up regarding house appraisals. For example, Bill and Bernice are divorcing. The court ordered Bill out of the family home to allow Bernice to stay with the children. They cannot agree on the value of the house, and Bernice won't give Bill's appraiser access in order to evaluate it. Bill must request an inspection.

Subpoena and subpoena duces tecum. A subpoena is an order telling a witness to appear at a deposition (or at trial). A subpoena duces tecum is an order to provide certain documents to a specific party. These devices are commonly used to get documents or testimony directly from banks, insurance companies, stockbrokers and the like.

C. Net Worth—What Do You Own and What Do You Owe?

Generally, we divide our marital net worth at divorce. Subtracting what you owe from what you own reveals that net worth. It is important to know that net worth number because if you go to trial, the judge will attempt to see that you each end up with your fair share, depending on the laws of your state. But it's also important for you to know specifically—item by item—what there is to divide. If, as is usually the case, you (perhaps with the help of attorneys or a mediator) are able to negotiate a property settlement and avoid a court battle, you'll want to know exactly who owns what and how much it's worth. Only by knowing that can you negotiate the fairest deal.

The *Assets and Liabilities Worksheet* in this chapter will help you figure this out. It will also help you complete the *Marital Balance Sheet* in Chapter 19 that will set out your joint property, the equity in it and its before-tax value. Your home, for example, might have a fair market value of $400,000. But if the loan is $250,000, you have just $150,000 in equity. Further, you or your spouse may have contributed from separate property unequal amounts of cash for the down payment. That kind of information must be tabulated if you are to have a realistic view of what true assets there are to divide.

While it may seem laborious to compile all these facts and figures, your effort will pay off in succeeding chapters. We will refer back to these lists often. Patience and attention to detail now will be rewarded later.

Debts incurred during a marriage are usually considered joint debts—that is, during the marriage, both spouses are legally responsible for them. When a couple divorces, however, responsibility for marital debts is allocated in accordance with the property division laws of the state.

This usually means that the debts are divided equally or equitably (fairly, though not in half), especially when they were incurred for food, shelter, clothing and medical care (called necessities). The court also considers who is better able to pay the debts (the spouse with the higher income and/or lower living expenses). If a couple has many debts but also has a great deal of property, the spouse better able to pay the debts may be ordered to assume the payments and also to receive a larger share of the property.

To figure out your net worth, use the worksheets on the following pages. If you can't fill in everything in each category, don't worry. Gather as much information as you can. If you eventually hire someone to help you, you'll still be far ahead and will have saved money by gathering some of the information yourself.

Do You Hate Filling Out Forms?

Almost no one enjoys the task of writing information into small blanks on financial forms. In your divorce, however, you must get your financial facts straight. Any attorney or other professional you consult will want the information you are documenting in your *Net Worth* and *Cash Flow* statements. Most important, you will be organizing the information you must have to make the best decisions in your divorce.

Get help or meet with others who are dealing with the same issues so you can assist each other when the work gets tedious. You are not completing these forms as a mere exercise—you are using them to lay the groundwork for your new financial life.

Make copies of these forms so you can use them throughout your divorce and make changes as events change. Also, keep copies of the documents you consulted to fill out the forms.

Instructions: Net Worth Statement
Assessing Assets

To determine your net worth, you need only estimate the current value (last column) of each asset you own. Complete the other columns if the information is available. List all marital property—not just the property in which you have an interest. These columns will help you understand as much as possible about your assets so you can make informed decisions when it comes time to divide your marital property.

As you fill in the information, subtotal the amounts in the last (far right) column for various asset categories (such as real estate or personal property). You will then transfer these subtotals to the *Net Worth: Balance Sheet Summary*, which follows.

Column 1: Title or owner. List the owner of each item of property, and how ownership is listed on any title document. You or your spouse may have an ownership interest in an item of property even if title is in only one spouse's name. This could happen if marital money or labor went toward the purchase of, payments on or improvements to the property. Several types of property—such as houses, cars and stocks—come with title documents (the house deed, car registration and stock certificate). When property is owned jointly, these title documents specify exactly how "title is held"—meaning how the property is owned. The possible ways to hold title to property are:

- *Joint tenancy.* Co-owners of joint tenancy property own the property in equal shares. When two or more persons own property as joint tenants, and one owner dies, the remaining owner(s) automatically inherits the share owned by the deceased person. This is termed the "right of survivorship." For example, if a husband and wife own their house as joint tenants and the wife dies, the husband ends up owning the entire house, even if the wife attempted to give away her half of the house in her will.

In most states, a joint tenant can terminate a joint tenancy and change title to tenancy in common at any time, even without a spouse's knowledge. The easiest way to do this is to write up a deed stating something like the following:

Leslie Matthews transfers her one-half share of the home at 1312 Lincoln Drive from Leslie Matthews joint tenant to Leslie Matthews tenant in common.

When such a change is made, the right to survivorship no longer holds.

- *Tenancy by the entirety.* Tenancy by the entirety is a way married couples can hold title to property in some non-community property states. Tenancy by the entirety is very similar to joint tenancy; upon the death of one of the spouses, the property automatically passes to the surviving spouse, regardless of contrary provisions in the will. Unlike joint tenancy, however, one person cannot unilaterally sever the tenancy by the entirety. After divorce, former spouses cannot hold title as tenancy by the entirety. Instead, it changes to tenancy in common (just below) unless you specify joint tenancy.

- *Tenancy in common.* Tenancy in common is a way for any two or more people to hold title to property together. Each co-owner has an "undivided interest" in the property, which means that no owner holds a particular part of the property and all co-owners have the right to use all the property. Each owner is free to sell or give away his interest. On his death, his interest passes through his will or by the automatic inheritance laws if he had no will. Divorcing spouses who plan to own property after they split usually hold the property as tenants in common.

Occasionally, ex-spouses will hold property in joint tenancy.

- *Community property.* Couples in community property states can take title as community property. Community property is divided equally at the end of their marriage. Property owned jointly after divorce cannot be held as community property.

- *Separate title.* Sometimes title will be in only one person's name, even if both spouses own the property. The property will be divided between the husband and wife if the spouse whose name is not on the title document can otherwise prove an ownership interest. For example, if the house is in the wife's name only, but the canceled checks for the mortgage payments are written on the husband's separate account, the property will be divided.

Column 2: Source of asset. Specify where the money to purchase the asset came from. Be sure to note whether the source is separate or marital property or income, and keep copies of all records that show the disposition of separate property.

Column 3: Date of purchase. Put the date you bought items or received a gift or inheritance. For items bought over time—such as shares of the same stock—list all dates and the number of shares bought each time. Use a separate sheet of paper if necessary to record information on these assets.

Column 4: Current balance or market value. For deposit accounts and similar investments, list the balance from your last statement. Keep copies of each statement.

Market value means what you could sell the item for now, not your purchase price or replacement cost. For valuable assets, such as art, jewelry, collections, antiques, furs, china and silver, list the wholesale value. To determine these values, you might go to pawnshops, antique stores, jewelers, art galleries, auctioneers or sterling silver replacement firms; you might also visit eBay at www.eBay.com to find sale prices on the Web. For automobiles, use the *Kelley Blue Book* value. (Check out their website,

www.kbb.com.) For household furniture, furnishings and personal effects, give your best estimate of their garage sale value.

Column 5: Debt. How much do you still owe on this item?

Column 6: Equity or legal value. Equity is the actual value of the item after the debt is paid off. Subtract debt from current balance/market value to get this figure.

Instructions: Net Worth Statement Calculating Liabilities

The other half of determining your net worth is listing your liabilities (that is, what you owe). The Balance Due in the last column on the worksheet shows what you currently owe in each liability category. But you should also fill in the information asked in the other columns because it will be useful in working on your *Cash Flow Statement* and in evaluating assets in your settlement negotiations.

Column 1: Original loan amount. Enter the amount you originally borrowed. Don't include interest. On your credit cards, put the amount of your purchases or cash advances.

Column 2: Date made. Put the date the debt was incurred. For credit cards, note the various dates you charged items.

Column 3: Interest rates on loans. List all interest rates. If the rate is variable (as many mortgages and credit cards are), list the present rate and note that it is variable.

Column 4: Term of loan. How many years do you have to repay the loan or debt?

Column 5: Monthly payment. List the amount you actually pay each month.

Column 6: Balance due. Enter how much it would cost to pay off the loan in full. Check with the lender or creditor to determine the loan payoff amount. This balance is your current liability. The subtotal for each liability will be the amount you transfer to the *Net Worth: Balance Sheet Summary* chart, which follows.

ASSETS AND LIABILITIES WORKSHEET

ASSETS	Title H/W/Jt/Cmn	Source Sep/Marital	Date of Purchase/Acquisition	Current Balance or Market Value	Debt	Equity or Legal Value
CASH & CASH EQUIVALENTS						
Cash						
CDs						
CDs						
Checking						
Checking						
Savings						
Credit Union						
Money Market Funds						
Money Market Funds						
Money Market Funds						
Other Liquid Assets						
SUBTOTAL, CASH & CASH EQUIVALENTS	$					
MARKETABLE ASSETS & INVESTMENTS						
Life Insurance (cash values)						
Life Insurance (whole life policies)						
Stocks						
Bonds						
Mutual Funds						
Loans/Accounts Receivable						
General Partnerships						
Limited Partnerships						
Liens and Judgments Due You						
Mortgages and Notes Receivable						
Contract Rights						
SUBTOTAL, MARKETABLE ASSETS & INVESTMENTS	$					

ASSETS AND LIABILITIES WORKSHEET (Continued)

ASSETS	Title H/W/Jt/Cmn	Source Sep/Marital	Date of Purchase/Acquisition	Current Balance or Market Value	Debt	Equity or Legal Value
RETIREMENT PLAN ASSETS						
Keogh or Self-Employment Plan						
IRA						
IRA						
Roth IRA						
Employee Stock Ownership Plan						
Pension/Profit Sharing - 401(K)						
Annuity Plan						
SUBTOTAL, RETIREMENT PLAN ASSETS	$					
REAL ESTATE						
Residence						
Vacation Home						
Income Property						
Unimproved Real Property/Lots						
SUBTOTAL, REAL ESTATE	$					
BUSINESS INTERESTS						
Closely Held Private Stock						
Sole Proprietor						
Other Business Assets						
SUBTOTAL, BUSINESS INTERESTS	$					
PERSONAL PROPERTY						
Vehicle						
Vehicle/Motor Home						
Motorcycle/Off-Road Vehicle						
Home Furnishings (inc. art, antiques, silver, heirlooms)						
Jewelry/Furs						
Collections/Coins/Stamps						
Boat/Plane						
Horses/Other Livestock						
Other (specify)						
SUBTOTAL, PERSONAL PROPERTY	$					

ASSETS & LIABILITIES WORKSHEET (Continued)

LIABILITIES	Original Amt.	Date Made Incurred	Interest Rate	Loan Term	Monthly Payment	Balance Due
MORTGAGES/LOANS						
Mortgage						
Mortgage						
Equity Loans						
SUBTOTAL, MORTGAGE/LOANS	$					
VEHICLE LOANS						
Loan						
Loan						
SUBTOTAL, VEHICLE LOANS	$					
OTHER LOANS (Be sure to note if loans are secured by an asset)						
Bank Loan						
Bank Loan						
Loan Against Retirement Plan						
Private Loan						
Loan Against Brokerage Account						
Student Loans						
Student Loans						
SUBTOTAL, OTHER LOANS	$					
CREDIT ACCOUNTS						
Credit/Charge Account						
Credit/Charge Account						
Credit/Charge Account						
Credit/Charge Account						
SUBTOTAL, CREDIT ACCOUNTS	$					
MISCELLANEOUS DEBTS						
Claims						
Unsettled Damages						
Liens & Judgments Owed						
Leases						
Taxes Owed						
SUBTOTAL, MISCELLANEOUS DEBTS	$					

NET WORTH: BALANCE SHEET SUMMARY

Instructions: Enter the subtotal for each Asset and Liability category from the last (far right) column of the asset and liability worksheets. Add those figures to get total Assets and Liabilities. To find your net worth, subtract Total Liabilities from Total Assets.

<u>Summary of Assets:</u>

CASH AND CASH EQUIVALENTS $ _____

MARKETABLE ASSETS/INVESTMENTS   _____

RETIREMENT PLANS   _____

REAL ESTATE   _____

BUSINESS INTERESTS   _____

PERSONAL PROPERTY   _____

<u>Total Assets:</u> $ _____

<u>Summary of Liabilities:</u>

MORTGAGES/LOANS $ _____

VEHICLE LOANS   _____

OTHER LOANS   _____

CREDIT ACCOUNTS   _____

MISCELLANEOUS DEBTS   _____

<u>Total Liabilities:</u> $ _____

NET WORTH (assets minus liabilities)

$ _____

D. The Difference Between Assets and Income

You've just inventoried your assets and how much they're worth. In the next section, you'll be examining your income—the continuing stream of money that enables you to pay your expenses.

Does the difference between assets and income matter much? After all, in the end they're both your money, right? Well, when you're divorcing, the distinction is crucial. *Assets* are what get divided in the course of your divorce settlement. *Income* is what a court primarily looks at in determining how much alimony and child support you're entitled to, or how much you have to pay.

Some items are considered both income and assets. And both terms cover more things than you might think. Now is the time to get as accurate an idea as possible about what your income and assets both are.

You can begin to define "income" by using the IRS's rules—if you have to pay taxes on it when filing your returns, it's income. The government generally taxes you on your salary and wages, including tips, commissions, bonuses, vacation pay, sick leave and compensatory time, as well as distributions from retirement, deferred compensation plans and income from investments. You also owe taxes on income paid for lost wages and salary, such as severance pay, workers' compensation, unemployment insurance, disability insurance and some disability pensions.

But for purposes of determining alimony and child support, income isn't just what the IRS says it is. A judge will consider virtually every possible source of funds in calculating the amount. (For more on the legal, financial and emotional realities of alimony and child support, see Chapter 18.)

As for assets, certain ones are obvious: cash, house, car, bank accounts, etc. But others are more obscure and easy to miss. (See Chapter 8, Section C for a rundown of "easy-to-forget" assets.)

"Sources of Compensation" lists various types of compensation and assets—the items of value you're likely to be dealing with when ending a marriage. The table indicates whether each one is treated as income for purposes of determining child and spousal support, or whether it is considered marital property that may be divided when the marriage ends. As you know, sometimes an item can be classed as both.

Sources of Compensation

Source	Income for Support Purposes?	Asset Subject to Division?
Capital gains from sale of assets	Yes	Yes
Social Security benefits	Yes	No
Veterans' benefits	Yes	No
Military personnel fringe benefits, such as overseas housing allowance	Yes	No
Gifts	Generally no	No
Prizes	Possibly	Usually yes, if won during marriage
Educational grants and loans	No, at least in some states	No
Income of new spouse or partner	No, in most states	No
Reimbursement for employment expenses	Yes, to the extent it reduces cost of living	No
Personal loans from corporations	Yes	Yes
Retained earnings of private corporation	Yes	Yes
Depreciation on equipment	Yes	Equipment is treated as property
Depletion allowance from oil and gas interests	Yes	Interests are treated as property
Personal expenses paid by a business	Yes	Payment increases value of marital business
Voluntary contributions to pension, retirement and savings plans	Yes	Yes
Voluntary debt reduction	Yes	Yes
Stock options	Yes, whether exercised or not, as long as they are exercisable and have increased in value	Yes
Accrued vacation time or sick time payable in cash	Yes	Yes

E. Cash Flow—Where Does the Money Go?

Cash flow is your income and outgo of money. Realize that regardless of how your settlement winds up, a divorce forces *two* households to exist—at least for a while—on the same income that had supported only *one*. So you need to know as precisely as possible what it costs you to live. And, of course, you must take the needs and expenses of any children into account.

The cash flow worksheets on the next few pages outline the income and outgo of your money—day-to-day living expenses and sources of income. While filling out the worksheets, be realistic. And do not worry if you do not have enough information for every line. Do the best you can.

Instructions: Cash Flow Statement
Adding Up Income

Income generally comes from three sources:

- earned salary or wages from your job as an employee

- earnings from your own business as a self-employed individual, or

- miscellaneous other sources, such as job bonuses, interest earned from investments and income from a disability insurance policy.

Record all sources of income for you and your spouse, completing only those categories that apply. For investments from marital property such as interest income, rental property and notes and trust deeds, divide the monthly income by two and enter half in your column and half in your spouse's column.

If an investment or asset is not owned 50-50, enter the appropriate percentages that apply. For instance, suppose a second house that produces rental income was bought partially with one spouse's separate property and partially with marital property (the income earned during marriage). In that case, the split might be 75-25 instead of 50-50.

If either you or your spouse holds more than one job or owns a self-run business, total your income on a separate sheet of paper and enter the total on this worksheet.

How Much Do Children Cost?

You now have a good idea of your estimated annual expenses. But what proportion of that goes for raising your kids? Knowing that figure could be important as you negotiate child support.

So you need to estimate how much you spend on your kids. To find that sum, do the following simple calculation:

Total monthly expenses $_____

Subtract total child care expenses $_____

Subtotal = $_____

Now multiply that subtotal by the percentage of your household that's composed of children. (For example, if you have two children living with you, that's 2 out of 3 or 2/3; if three out of four residents are children, that's 3/4, and so on.)

(Subtotal) _____ X (fraction representing children) _____ = _____

That's the children's pro rata share of non-child care expenses. Now add back in the amount of child care expenses.

Child Care Expenses = $_____

And your total is the child care expenses plus the children's pro rata share of other expenses.

Total estimated child care expenses = $_____

Instructions: Cash Flow Statement
Estimating Expenses

Designed to create a realistic picture of your cash flow, this worksheet is divided into fifteen categories, such as residence, child care, installment debt, transportation, insurance and other expenses.

To determine your current expenses, record the actual amount you spent for the past month for each item that applies. Multiply this monthly average by 12 and enter the amount at the bottom of the page. Don't forget to include once-a-year expenses such as insurance premiums or real estate taxes. Finally, estimate how much of each expense is allocated for your children, and enter it in the box at the end of this chapter.

Listing Credit Card Expenses

To get a clear picture of your spending, list your various credit card expenditures under appropriate categories. For example, if your Visa bill is $198, with $120 spent for clothes and $78 for meals out, and you pay the bill off in full each month, enter the $120 under clothes and $78 under food expenses. If, however, you carry a balance on your credit card bill—for example, the bill totals $4,000 now and you make monthly payments of $300—enter the amount of the monthly payment under installment debt, and do not list the payment under the specific expense category.

Be aware that certain payments could be listed under more than one category. For example, a car payment could be considered a loan payment under the Installment Debt category, but may also be listed under the Transportation category. To help develop a picture of where your money actually goes, expense items are specified whenever possible—as with the car payment. When you complete the worksheet, double-check it to be sure you have not listed the same expenses under more than one category.

Income and expenses must be considered together. If you're spending too much, you've got to reduce those expenses or increase your income. Otherwise, you'll find yourself facing serious debt problems.

F. Questions to Ask Your Attorney

1. In my state, does the way title is held determine the disposition of property at divorce? Does it determine whether property is characterized as "marital" or "separate"?

2. Does interest, income or appreciation on separate property belong to "me" or to "us"?

3. What happens if that asset loses money?

4. Are debts in my spouse's name separate property or marital property?

5. Am I liable for my spouse's credit card debt even though I did not sign the credit application?

CASH FLOW: INCOME AND EXPENSES

INCOME	Self		Spouse	
	Per Pay Period	Per Month	Per Pay Period	Per Month
A. SALARY & WAGES — Pay period is: [ ] weekly [ ] biweekly [ ] monthly				
Gross income (including commissions, allowances and overtime):				
Subtract: Federal & State Taxes				
FICA-Social Security				
Other: medical or other insurance, pension, stock plans, union dues…				
NET INCOME FROM SALARY & WAGES				
B. SELF-EMPLOYMENT				
Gross Income				
Subtract: Federal & State Taxes				
Self-Employment Taxes				
NET INCOME FROM SELF-EMPLOYMENT				
C. OTHER SOURCES				
Bonuses				
Commissions				
Dividends				
Interest income				
Rental property				
Royalties				
Notes and trust deeds				
Annuities, pensions/401(k)				
Alimony				
Child support				
Social Security				
Income tax refund				
Other (Misc.) *				
Subtract: Any deductions				
NET INCOME FROM OTHER SOURCES				
TOTAL NET MONTHLY INCOME FROM ALL SOURCES				
ESTIMATED NET ANNUAL INCOME (net monthly income x 12)				

* Include income from trusts, disability, unemployment insurance, welfare and other public assistance programs.

CASH FLOW: INCOME AND EXPENSES (Continued)

MONTHLY EXPENSES	Husband	Wife
RESIDENCE (family home and vacation home, if applicable)		
rent/mortgage		
property taxes		
house insurance		
savings for repairs		
maintenance, general repairs & painting		
lawn/garden service		
supplies		
pool care		
housecleaning		
pest control		
HOA fees		
other, specify:		
Total Maintenance		
TOTAL RESIDENCE EXPENSES		
MEDICAL AND DENTAL CARE (expenses not covered by insurance; include children)		
doctors		
hospital		
counseling/psychiatrist		
prescriptions		
optometrist/eyecare		
dentist/orthodontist		
lab costs		
vitamins		
other, specify:		
TOTAL MEDICAL/DENTAL EXPENSES		

CASH FLOW: INCOME AND EXPENSES (Continued)

MONTHLY EXPENSES	Husband	Wife
CHILD CARE EXPENSES		
babysitter/daycare		
nursery school		
lessons (art, sports, music, etc.)		
allowances		
school tuition		
school lunches		
school transportation		
school books and supplies		
school uniforms/clothing		
school		
extracurriculars		
other, specify:		
TOTAL CHILD CARE EXPENSES		
FOOD AT HOME/HOUSEHOLD SUPPLIES		
groceries/household supplies		
liquor/wine		
health/diet food		
other, specify:		
TOTAL FOOD AT HOME/HOUSEHOLD SUPPLIES EXPENSES		
FOOD OUTSIDE HOME		
restaurant meals		
socializing outside home		
TOTAL FOOD OUTSIDE HOME EXPENSES		
UTILITIES		
gas and electric		
water		
garbage		
cable TV		
cell phone/car phone		
home phone/ pager		
other, specify:		
TOTAL UTILITIES EXPENSES		

CASH FLOW: INCOME AND EXPENSES (Continued)

MONTHLY EXPENSES	Husband	Wife
LAUNDRY AND CLEANING		
drycleaning and laundry (clothes)		
drycleaning and laundry (rugs, drapes and furniture)		
other, specify:		
TOTAL LAUNDRY AND CLEANING EXPENSES		
CLOTHING		
for yourself		
for children		
TOTAL CLOTHING EXPENSES		
INSURANCE (do not include property insurance from section 1)		
life insurance		
disability insurance		
personal property insurance		
umbrella policy		
other, specify:		
TOTAL INSURANCE EXPENSES		
TRANSPORTATION/AUTO EXPENSES		
gas		
oil/antifreeze		
repairs/tires		
car insurance		
registration/fees		
auto club		
parking		
taxi/train/bus/rentals		
savings for new car		
TOTAL TRANSPORTATION/AUTO EXPENSES		
ENTERTAINMENT EXPENSES		
movies		
videos		
plays		
concerts		
sports events		
gym/club dues		
entertaining/catering		
records/tapes/CDs		
books/magazines/newspapers		
family trips/vacations		
hobby supplies		
other, specify:		
TOTAL MONTHLY ENTERTAINMENT EXPENSES		

CASH FLOW: INCOME AND EXPENSES (Continued)

MONTHLY EXPENSES	Husband	Wife
SCHOOL/ADULT EDUCATION EXPENSES		
tuition/fees/books		
transportation		
lunches		
TOTAL SCHOOL/ADULT EDUCATION EXPENSES		
INSTALLMENT PAYMENTS (Important: Include here only charged items not listed in other expense categories. Also note which party acquired the debt.)		
creditor _____		
creditor _____		
creditor _____		
TOTAL INSTALLMENT PAYMENTS		
INCIDENTALS		
pet care (food/veterinarian)		
gifts (weddings, birthdays, holidays)		
donations and charities		
personal care (hair care/cosmetics manicures/massages)		
stationery (paper/postage/computer supplies)		
tobacco products		
bank service charges		
professional dues		
plants (florist/houseplants)		
storage		
church/synagogue contributions (tithes)		
miscellaneous		
specify _____		
specify _____		
specify _____		
TOTAL INCIDENTALS EXPENSES		
OTHER EXPENSES		
estimated tax/income tax		
tax preparation		
nonreimbursed business expense		
alimony paid		
child support paid		
legal/accounting (nonbusiness)		
savings and investments		
support of relatives not living in your home		
deductible paid for auto accident		
other, specify:		
TOTAL OTHER EXPENSES		

What Will Happen to the House?

*If you're a homeowner, a divorce raises some difficult
questions. Before making a decision, think through all
the available options.*

If you and your spouse don't own a house, skip ahead to Chapter 14. If you do own a house, be sure to read the explanation on changes in the tax law in Section B of this chapter.

A home can represent the commitment to partnership between husband and wife, a place where the children grew up or a refuge from the demands of life. Perhaps your house stands for a connection to the community—or to the future generations of your family to whom you had hoped to bequeath it.

Whatever your house has meant to you, you're threatened with its loss during divorce. But rather than thinking you will "lose" your house, consider at least four basic options available to you:

Option A: *Buy out your spouse's share and either keep it or sell it in the future.*

Option B: *Sell your share of the house to your spouse.*

Option C: *Sell the house together and split the proceeds with your spouse.*

Option D: *Own the house jointly with your spouse and sell it in the future to your spouse or a third person.*

To ease your anxieties, it helps to look at the numbers to find the true value of your home so you can make an informed choice. In the following sections, we explain the financial factors you need to consider before choosing the best option.

⚠ The laws in your state and the circumstances of your particular case may affect your options regarding the house. For example, if you cannot reach an agreement concerning the house, judges may presume that a custodial parent and children will stay in the family home until the children reach maturity. In that case, you would not be able to sell the house and split the proceeds with your spouse (Option C). Rather, the custodial parent would have to buy out the other parent's interest, or you can sell it some time in the future (Option A or D). If you are unsure of your state's laws regarding custody and the right to sell the house, consult with an attorney before completing the calculations in this chapter.

A. Financial Versus Legal Realities

To understand your options better, consider home ownership from both legal and financial perspectives.

Suppose that during your marriage, you and your spouse bought a house using income earned from the marriage. You might assume that if you sell the house, the proceeds will be split 50-50. But the following table compares the legal and financial realities.

Legal Reality	Financial Reality
In the 41 states that follow the principles of equitable distribution, it's quite possible that the proceeds of the house won't be split down the middle. The 41 equitable distribution states are all the states except Arizona, California, Idaho, Louisiana, Nevada, New Mexico, Texas, Washington and Wisconsin. (In Alaska, a married couple can elect to designate property as community property when it is within a trust. See Chapter 12, Section A, for a full discussion.) In equitable distribution states, judges are supposed to divide property "fairly." "Fair" doesn't necessarily mean "equal." In reality, "fair" could mean that one spouse receives a greater share of the proceeds.	If you and your spouse can reach your own settlement without going to court, you can each negotiate the best deal for yourself, rather than have a judge impose one on you. Rarely is anyone happy with the settlement a judge carves out. The judge won't factor in most financial consequences of keeping or giving up certain assets. A negotiated settlement, though not perfect, is usually more palatable.

B. The House—Keep It, Transfer It or Sell It? Now or Later?

If you've been in a house any length of time, you're probably accustomed to paying a set amount each month on your mortgage. Many people going through divorce simply focus on that monthly payment, which often looks lower than anything they would have to pay if they moved into an apartment or bought another home.

But looks are deceiving. A low or moderate monthly payment can keep you from seeing many of the other costs of owning a home. Suppose you do keep the house. Will you be able to cover the cost of insurance, property taxes, repairs, cleaning, painting and the like? What if you decide to sell it in a few years? Are you prepared to cover the costs of sale alone? Can you afford to buy out your partner's share of the house and still have money to live on? Unless you know the true financial costs of keeping a home, you can't answer these questions.

A Tax Break on Capital Gains

The Taxpayer Relief Act of 1997 changed the rules for determining the financial value of the family home. Under the old rules, the house was not always such a great asset to take in a divorce settlement, because any profit realized from its sale could ultimately be eaten up in taxes. But now that equation has changed, and most homes can be sold without incurring capital gains taxes.

The key change made by the 1997 law, for purposes of this discussion, is that capital gains—such as profit from selling the house—are not taxable up to $250,000.

Most capital gains that exceed $250,000 are taxed at a maximum capital gain tax rate of 20%. But for some homeowners, gains between $250,000 and $500,000 are also tax-free. To qualify for the $250,000 exclusion, you must have owned and occupied the residence for two of the five years prior to the sale or exchange of the house.

If you are still married (or are remarried) when you sell the house, you and your spouse will owe no taxes on the first $500,000 of gain if you file a joint tax return and:

- either spouse owned the house two of the last five years

- both spouses used the house two of the last five years, and

- neither spouse used the exclusion during the prior two years.

If you hold on to your house and sell it after remarrying, you may have to pay taxes on gains over $250,000 if, for example, your new spouse doesn't live in the house at least two years, or if your new spouse used the exclusion on the sale of a different house during the previous two years.

C. Steps Toward Settling the House

Option A: Buy out your spouse's share and either keep it or sell it in the future.

This option can hold the most unforeseen financial risks. Therefore, you'll want to take into consideration as many known factors as possible. You must determine if you can afford your monthly housing costs. You also want to estimate how much you can expect to make if you sell the house, and to recognize the tax implications of a future sale. And, you want to compare what you would receive if you and your spouse sold the house now. Of course, if you keep the house for life, you don't need to worry about future sales costs or income taxes.

Option B: Sell your share of the house to your spouse.

To determine whether or not your spouse is making a good offer for your share of the house, you must understand its true financial value.

Option C: Sell the house together and split the proceeds with your spouse.

Before choosing this option, you need to know not only your current housing costs and equity value— you also need to know the costs of selling the house and the amount of profit you will realize after the taxes are paid.

Option D: Continue to own the house jointly with your spouse and sell it in the future to your spouse or a third person.

When a divorcing couple holds on to their house, it's usually because either a custodial parent is staying with the children or the housing market is so weak that the couple doesn't want to sell the house yet. Keep in mind, however, that owning the house together can be emotionally tricky. And make sure you have a written agreement so the out-of-house spouse doesn't lose the $250,000 capital gain exclusion (see "A Tax Break on Capital Gains," above). It is possible also to buy the house from your spouse in the future. But before making such an agreement, ask your tax advisor about the consequences.

Finding the true value of your house will take several calculations. Follow the steps below to answer these questions:

1. What is your total housing cost per month?

2. What is the current fair market value of your house?

3. What is the Legal Equity Value of your house?

4. How much will it cost to sell the house?

5. What is the tax basis for your house?

6. What would be the Financial Value (after-sale/after-tax value) of your house if you sold it with your spouse?

7. What would be the Financial Value (after-sale/after-tax value) of your house if you keep it now and sell in the future?

8. What is your share of the house?

9. What is your best option regarding the house?

10. Can you purchase the house from your spouse?

⚠ You may be tempted to skip certain steps, knowing that you favor one option over the others. Nevertheless, you are strongly advised to work through each step before making a decision. Completing all of the calculations will give you the most comprehensive picture of your financial choices—and can alert you to costs you may have overlooked.

1. What Is Your Total Housing Cost Per Month?

Your mortgage does not represent the entire amount you spend on housing. (And remember, if you refinance the house in order to raise cash to buy out your spouse, you're going to end up with a larger loan and probably bigger monthly payments.) You must also consider costs like your utilities and maintenance to get a true picture of expenses.

Use these steps to find your Net Monthly Housing Costs:

a. List your Monthly Housing Costs.

b. Total your Gross Monthly Housing Costs.

c. Find your Net Monthly Housing Costs by subtracting Tax Savings from your Gross Monthly Housing Costs.

a. List Your Monthly Housing Costs

List the amount you pay each month for the items on the *Monthly Housing Costs* chart that follows. You already have this information on the *Cash Flow Statement* you completed in Chapter 12. If you don't know the monthly cost of an item, or if you don't incur an expense every month, estimate the amount you spend per year and divide by 12. To estimate what you'll spend on significant repairs and maintenance needs, look around the house and note any major work that needs to be done. Check previous invoices to get an idea of what you'd normally spend on these expenses—or call a plumber, electrician or whomever else you may need for an estimate.

Monthly Housing Costs

Item	Example	Your Monthly Costs
Mortgage	$1,200	$ _____
Second mortgage (or equity loan payment)	272	$ _____
Property taxes	188	$ _____
Maintenance		
General repairs & painting	50	$ _____
Lawn/garden service & supplies	50	$ _____
Pool care	60	$ _____
Housecleaning	50	$ _____
Pest control	35	$ _____
Homeowner's Association fees	115	$ _____
Other	0	$ _____
Total Maintenance	360	$ _____
Insurance	42	$ _____
Utilities	100	$ _____
Major repairs	75	$ _____
Total Gross Housing Costs Per Month	$2,237	$ _____

As this chart reveals, the price of owning and maintaining your house is higher than your monthly mortgage alone. Even if certain expenses aren't being incurred now—or haven't been for a while—do not be lulled into thinking they no longer exist.

This chart includes the cost of repairs because those repairs will be your sole responsibility if you opt for keeping the house. You may be able to get your spouse to split repair costs with you when you negotiate the settlement. But because that possibility is still unknown, figure that you will have to come up with the money yourself.

b. Total Your Gross Monthly Housing Costs

Once you have filled in the information on the Monthly Housing Costs chart, add up all of the items in the Your Monthly Costs column. That figure is your Gross Monthly Housing Costs. Write that amount here.

$ _____ *Gross Monthly Housing Costs*

c. Find Your Net Monthly Housing Costs

In considering your monthly housing costs, you should not overlook the tax benefits of home ownership. Under current tax laws, you can deduct your mortgage interest payment and the property taxes you've paid, so your housing costs may be *lower* than the sum of your Gross Monthly Housing Costs. At the end of each year, you'll receive a Form 1099 from the bank or lender who holds your mortgage showing how much in mortgage interest you paid during the year.

If you take out a loan to purchase your spouse's share of the house, interest on that loan won't be deductible unless you use the house as collateral, you are legally liable for repayment and the mortgage or deed of trust is recorded. Thus, interest on an informal loan from parents or friends may not be deductible, unless you give the lender a secured note and record it.

In addition, you may be able to deduct points (prepaid interest) in the year you purchase a home if you take out a mortgage to buy it. However, points are not deductible if you refinance your house to buy out your spouse's interest. Points on loans for home improvements are deductible in the year in which the loan is taken out. If you refinance the mortgage on your house, your deductions for the points are spread out over the life of the new loan. Additionally, any prepayment penalty you incur because you refinance the mortgage is deductible as interest in the year paid. Any points not previously deducted can be deducted as interest in the year of the refinancing.

To calculate your tax savings, follow these instructions:

a. Add the total amount of interest paid on your mortgage during the year to the amount you paid in property taxes.

b. Multiply that number by your tax bracket—we assume a 28% federal tax bracket. (Don't forget your state tax bracket if your state allows a deduction for mortgage interest.)

c. Divide this calculation by 12 to get a monthly average.

d. Subtract the monthly average from your Gross Monthly Housing Costs to get your Net Housing Costs.

Although the result may not be the exact amount you can deduct, you'll get a pretty close estimate for your housing costs. For precise figures, consult your accountant or tax advisor. The example and step-by-step formula that follow will make it easier for you to find your net monthly housing costs.

Example: *Mitch and Candy's house is worth $150,000. Their mortgage is $1,200 per month ($14,400 per year), and they pay $272 a month ($3,264 per year) on a second mortgage. Their annual mortgage payments are $17,664 ($14,400 + $3,264); $14,000 of those payments is interest. They pay property taxes of $2,250 a year. Their federal tax bracket is 28%, giving them an annual Tax Savings of $4,550 or $379 a month. Assume their Gross Monthly Housing Costs equal $2,502.*

Mortgage Interest		$14,000
Property Taxes	+	2,250
Deduction	=	16,250
Tax Bracket	x	.28
Tax Savings	=	4,550
Monthly Tax Savings	÷ 12 =	379

Gross Monthly Housing Costs		$2,502
Monthly Tax Savings	–	379
Net Monthly Housing Costs	=	$2,123

To apply this formula to *your* situation, fill in the blanks below. You will need to know your annual mortgage interest, annual property taxes and tax bracket.

$ _____ *Annual mortgage interest*

To find your mortgage interest, contact your lender and request a calculation of the annual mortgage interest on your loan. Or, ask the lender for the amortization schedule for your loan. On either document, you will see a monthly listing of how much of the mortgage payment repays principal (your debt or balance due) and how much pays interest on the loan.

$ _____ *Annual property taxes*

To find your property taxes, refer to your federal tax returns, call the county tax assessor or call your lender if your property taxes are paid through an escrow account with your lender. You can subtract taxes assessed for street, sidewalk, utility, curb, sewer and other property improvements.

Some high-income taxpayers must reduce their annual mortgage interest and property taxes by the lesser of 3% of their adjusted gross income over a certain amount (in 2002, $137,000 for individual filers and $206,000 for joint filers) or 80% of the amount of the itemized deductions otherwise allowed for the year. (Internal Revenue Code § 68.) Your tax preparer can help you make the calculation.

_____ % *Tax bracket*

To find your tax bracket, check the income tax schedules contained in the IRS tax packet or ask a tax advisor to verify your current tax bracket. Or simply use 28%, the federal tax bracket into which most people fall. Remember to use only your anticipated income as a single person, including any alimony you might receive or pay, as the basis for your tax bracket. And your filing status will be either "single" or "head of household." (For help in figuring out which category to use, see Chapter 11, Section B.)

Now enter those numbers in the Net Monthly Housing Costs chart. Using the formula in the chart, calculate your Net Monthly Housing Costs. You will refer to this number later when making your decision on what to do with the house.

Net Monthly Housing Costs

Annual Mortgage Interest*	=	$ _____
Annual Property Taxes*	+	$ _____
Deduction**	=	$ _____
Tax Bracket	x	$ _____
Tax Savings	=	$ _____
Monthly Tax Savings	÷ 12	
	=	$ _____
Gross Monthly Housing Costs		$ _____
Monthly Tax Savings	–	$ _____
Net Monthly Housing Costs	=	$ _____

$ _____ *Net Monthly Housing Costs*

* Some high-income taxpayers may not be able to fully deduct mortgage interest and property tax payments. See section on annual property taxes, above.

** Remember: Your interest and your interest deduction may be higher if you refinance to get the money to buy your spouse's share of the house. Ask yourself: "Can I afford to keep the house if I include the additional costs of buying out my spouse?"

2. What Is the Current Fair Market Value of Your House?

The current "fair market value" of your house is the amount you can realistically expect to sell it for. You can obtain fair market value estimates from real estate agents free of charge. You might especially want to ask the agent who helped you buy the house originally, or an agent who consistently markets your neighborhood.

You can also get estimates of fair market value from a certified appraiser, but be prepared to pay. For a referral to a certified appraiser, ask your banker or lender or contact the Appraisal Institute at 550 West Van Burean St., Suite 1000, Chicago, IL 60607; 312-335-4100; www.appraisalinstitute.org. If you and your spouse cannot agree on the value of the house, ask your attorney to select an appraiser. This person will testify as to the house's value if the issue is contested in court.

Real estate appraisers generally look at a house from several financial angles and take an average of these values to estimate what it is worth. The two primary views they take are:

- what the market will bear—that is, the sales prices of comparable houses in the area, and

- your house's replacement value (the cost of building materials and the like).

 General real estate sites that may be helpful in determining your home's value:

www.dataquick.com. Offers detailed information to help you compare sales prices for many areas of the country based on information from county recorders' offices and property assessors.

www.realtor.com. Can help you find a home or neighborhood, learn about lenders, make calculations, compile checklists and locate real estate reference materials.

www.realtylocator.com. Provides more than 100,000 real estate links nationwide, including property listings, real estate agents, neighborhood data, real estate news and other information resources.

Once you find the Fair Market Value of your house, write it here:

$ _____ *Fair Market Value*

Think Like a Buyer

Before paying for an appraiser, you might ask a real estate agent who regularly markets your neighborhood to prepare a Comparative Market Analysis. This is typically provided at no charge.

After physically inspecting your house, the agent researches the market for recent sales, how long the property took to sell, currently listed homes, pending sales and expired listings (unsold homes taken off the market.)

Don't hesitate to ask more than one agent to provide you with a CMA. In addition to getting a consensus about what your home is worth, you will also learn about the quality of agents with whom you may do business later.

In valuing your house, think like a buyer, not a seller. Specifically, do not rely on the following as an indicator of a sales price for your home:

- The amount you spent on improvements. (You may have spent more than the home prices in your neighborhood will support.)

- The price you paid for your home. Markets are dynamic; the market value of your home may have gone up or down since you purchased it.

- The assessed value shown on your property tax statement. These values rarely reflect the actual market value.

---

3. What Is the Equity Value of Your House?

The Equity Value of your house is its Fair Market Value (the figure you obtained in step 2) minus whatever debt you have connected to your house. Remember—if a court were to calculate each spouse's share of a house, the court would consider only the amount of equity. That number, however, does not reflect the sale costs or taxes—that is, the financial reality of owning or selling a house.

The debt connected to your house equals what you owe to any lenders (first mortgage, second mortgage or home equity loan or line of credit) plus any liabilities on the house. All liabilities must be paid before any cash disbursements can be made from the sale of a house. Liabilities include income or property tax liens, child support liens, judgment liens (if someone sues you and obtains a judgment, that person can put a lien on your house) or mechanic's or materialman's liens placed by a contractor who did work on your home but who wasn't paid.

Ask your lender for the balance on your mortgages and equity loans. The lender should offer you two figures—a principal balance and a payoff balance. The principal balance is simply the amount of principal remaining to be paid on your loan. The payoff balance is the principal balance plus an additional month's interest and any prepayment charges you must pay to close out the loan. Use the payoff balance in calculating the debt on your house.

You may not be aware of all liens on your property. Tax liens and mechanic's liens, for example, often appear without the owner's knowledge. To find all liens on your house, you'll have to do a title search. You can hire a title insurance company to conduct the search, or you can visit the records office in the county where your deed is recorded. A clerk in that office can show you how to search for any liens on your house.

Possible Debts Against Your House

Mortgage balance	$ _____
Second mortgage balance	$ _____
Equity loan or line of credit balance	$ _____
Property tax lien	$ _____
Income tax lien	$ _____
Child support lien	$ _____
Judgment lien	$ _____
Mechanic's or materialman's lien	$ _____
Other liens	$ _____
Total Current Debt on House	= $ _____

Now subtract the debt on the house from its Fair Market Value to obtain the Equity Value.

Fair Market Value (step 2)	$ _____
Total Current Debt on House (step 3, above)	– $ _____
Equity Value of Your House	= $ _____

4. How Much Will It Cost to Sell the House?

To determine how much money it will take to actually sell your house, you can do a quick ballpark estimate, or you can use the calculations that follow to find a more precise figure. To find a precise figure, you'll have to include not only the costs of sale, but also the amount it will take to fix up the house and prepare it for sale.

a. Quick Ballpark Estimate of Cost of Sale

Take the Fair Market Value figure you determined in step 2. To get a ballpark amount for the sales cost, multiply that amount by .07. Obviously, some sales will yield higher or lower costs of sale, but 7% will do in getting a rough estimate. Enter that number in the "Total Cost of Sale" blank, below.

b. Precise Valuation of Cost of Sale

To obtain a more accurate cost of sale figure, you need to total the following amounts:

$ _____ Agent's commission

This represents the amount a real estate agent charges you for selling a house. Generally, it's set at 6% of the final selling price. The fee can sometimes be negotiated down. Also, if you list your house as a "FSBO"—for sale by owner—you avoid the agent's commission altogether. But be sure to educate yourself about the process before you list your house as a FSBO. You can find information on the topic at www.nolo.com under "Real Estate."

$ _____ *Closing costs*

These costs can include escrow fees, abstract and recording costs, appraisal fees, surveys, title insurance, transfer and stamp taxes, loan charges and miscellaneous expenses. All this can add up to several thousands of dollars. A lender or real estate agent can help you figure the exact amount.

$ _____ *Attorney's fees*

In a few states, you will need to hire an attorney to help you "close" the sale of your house. If you used an attorney when you bought the house, the figure should be similar, though you may need to adjust it upward to account for inflation and the passage of time. Otherwise, ask a real estate agent for an estimate.

$ _____ *Fix-up costs*

Fix-up expenses are not considered when calculating capital gains, but they are a very real expense when selling a home. Estimate here the amount of money you will have to spend to prepare your house for sale. Does it need major repairs or just a paint job? Does the foundation, roof or plumbing need work? Will you need to have the house inspected? Must you get a termite inspection? (If you need help in getting a handle on what repairs are necessary, the American Society of Home Inspectors' website at www.ashi.com provides a list of inspectors near you.)

$ _____ *Total Cost of Sale*

Add these amounts together to get a reasonably close estimate of what it will cost to sell your house.

What Happens When the House Secures a Spouse's Separate Property Debt?

Generally, a spouse should not keep a house that secures the debts of a soon-to-be-former spouse. Before agreeing to keep a house securing your spouse's separate property debt, be certain your spouse has paid all such debts, and request proof of payment.

A California case underscores the point. The husband forged his wife's signature on a quitclaim deed (giving him sole ownership) and then used the house as security while running up additional debts. His creditors got a judgment against him and attached a lien to the house. At the divorce trial, the court ordered the husband to pay the judgment. The wife chose to keep the house and buy out his share. In calculating the value of the house, however, the court did not reduce it by the amount of the lien. Thus, the wife had to pay the husband one-half of the value of the house—and also pay off the lien plus interest.

Moral of this story: Once a lien, always a lien—until the creditor is paid. A creditor's right to payment is not affected by who is ordered to pay the debt in divorce. If you want to keep the house, deduct all liens, plus interest, when calculating the value. If your spouse refuses, don't keep the house.

If you decide to sell the house together, make sure that all separate property debts secured by the house are identified as separate property. Instruct the escrow company to pay debts incurred separately by one spouse out of that spouse's share of the proceeds. For instance, if the net sale proceeds total $100,000 after costs of sale, each spouse is entitled to $50,000. However, if there is a separate property lien of $25,000 against one spouse, the escrow company should issue checks as follows: $50,000 to the spouse without the separate property debt, $25,000 to the spouse with the separate property debt and $25,000 to the creditor.

5.   What Is the Tax Basis for Your House?

The tax basis of an asset is a little-mentioned financial concept no one thinks about until it's time to sell the asset—or until a divorce.

The tax basis is the dollar amount the IRS uses to determine if you've made or lost money on an asset. Essentially, your tax basis is the original purchase price plus the cost of any improvements you have made, minus any tax benefits you have realized. Knowing the tax basis lets you calculate your profit to determine whether or not you'll owe taxes when your house is sold during or after divorce. If the house isn't sold until after the divorce, the person who gets the house gets the tax liability.

To figure your tax basis, enter the appropriate amounts in the blanks below.

$ _____ *Purchase price*

The purchase price should be on the original purchase contract or closing statement—check your home bookkeeping files or a safe deposit box. If you still can't find it, call your lender or the escrow company that processed your purchase.

(Or, if you acquired the house prior to May 6, 1997, check to see if you filed IRS Form 2119 with your tax return. The "Adjusted Basis of the New House" shown on the form is equal to the purchase price plus the Acquisition Costs. If you use Form 2119, you don't need to add in the Acquisition Costs below.)

$ _____ *Acquisition costs*

These are costs associated with the purchase, such as recording fees, title insurance and document fees listed on the escrow statement. Do not include loan principal, interest or "points."

$ _____ *Capital improvements*

Capital improvements are items that add value to your house, such as a new bathroom or den you've added, a security system you've installed or extensive landscaping you've done. The costs of these changes are not fix-up or repair costs. You will need to go through your files to find receipts to document the improvements made to your house.

The following are examples of capital improvements:

- Additions
  - ✓ bedroom
  - ✓ bathroom
  - ✓ deck
  - ✓ garage
  - ✓ porch
  - ✓ patio
  - ✓ storage shed
  - ✓ fireplace
- Lawns and grounds
  - ✓ landscaping
  - ✓ driveway
  - ✓ walkway
  - ✓ fence
  - ✓ retaining wall
  - ✓ sprinkler system
  - ✓ swimming pool
  - ✓ exterior lighting
- Communications
  - ✓ satellite dish
  - ✓ intercom
  - ✓ security system
- Heating and air conditioning
  - ✓ heating system
  - ✓ central air conditioning
  - ✓ furnace
  - ✓ duct work
  - ✓ central humidifier
  - ✓ filtration system
- Electrical
  - ✓ light fixtures
  - ✓ wiring upgrades

- Plumbing
  - ✓ water heater
  - ✓ soft water system
  - ✓ filtration system
- Insulation
  - ✓ attic
  - ✓ walls
  - ✓ floors
  - ✓ pipes and duct work
- Interior improvements
  - ✓ built-in appliances
  - ✓ kitchen modernization
  - ✓ bathroom modernization
  - ✓ flooring
  - ✓ wall-to-wall carpet
- Miscellaneous
  - ✓ storm windows and doors
  - ✓ roof
  - ✓ central vacuum system

$ _____ *Total Improvements*

Tax benefits refer to the rollover of gain (profit) from homes sold up to August 5, 1999 as well as deductions taken for a home office. To find your tax benefits, refer to your tax returns or call your accountant. *For simplicity's sake, you can calculate the tax basis without subtracting any tax benefits.*

Use the figures you entered earlier in this section to find the tax basis of your house.

Purchase Price		$ _____
Acquisition Costs (*Do not include Fix-up Costs*)	+	$ _____
Rollover Tax Benefits	–	$ _____
Capital Improvements	+	$ _____
*Tax Basis of House**	=	$ _____

*If you have Form 2119, you can use the Adjusted Basis for this figure if you add "Improvements."

For Those With Home Office Depreciation After May 6, 1997

Claiming a tax deduction for use of a home office is a growing trend. However, the law allowing you to exclude $250,000 of gain (profit) on the sale of a house does not include the amount attributed to depreciation for home office use. So if you depreciate your house for home office use, the amount of depreciation will be taxed as a capital gain (25%).

The following formula allows you to figure the amount not qualifying for the exclusion:

Total home office depreciation taken since May 6, 1997	= $	_____
x 25% capital gains rate	x .25	
Taxes not qualifying for exclusion	= $	_____

---

6. What Would Be the Financial Value of Your House If You Sold It With Your Spouse?

If you have a profit on the sale of a house, you may exclude up to $250,000 ($500,000 if you file a joint return) of that profit every 24 months. You must consider this exclusion in order to figure out the Financial Value (after-sale/after-tax value) of your house and analyze your future options concerning house purchases and tax deferrals. Remember, too, that you will need to know your capital gains rate to determine the Financial Value of the house. As a general rule, if you were in the 28% tax bracket your capital gains rate is 20%, and if you're in the 15% bracket, your capital gains rate is 10%. (Don't forget that you may owe state taxes as well.)

To find the Financial Value (after-sale/after-tax value) of your house, enter the following information from the previous steps:

$_____ *Fair Market Value (from Step 2)*

$_____ *Current Debt (from Step 3)*

$_____ *Cost of Sale (from Step 4)*

$_____ Fix-up Expenses (from Step 4)

$_____ Tax Basis of the House (Step 5)

$_____ Taxes to Pay from Home Office Use (Step 5)

_____% Capital Gains Rate (including state)

Now take the following steps:

1. Find the Amount Realized by subtracting the Cost of Sale from the Fair Market Value.

2. Find the Gain or Loss on the potential sale by subtracting the Tax Basis from the Amount Realized. If you had a Loss, use zero as the amount of Gain and go directly to Step 5.

3. Find the Taxable Gain by subtracting your Exclusion from the Gain. (Taxable Gain is that portion of Gain exceeding the maximum Gain you can exclude.) The maximum exclusion is $250,000 for individuals and $500,000 for many married couples filing jointly. The Net Gain is the portion of the Gain that will be taxed. If your Net Gain does not exceed the maximum exclusion allowed, go directly to Step 5.

4. Find the taxes on the Taxable Gain by multiplying the Taxable Gain by the Capital Gains rate.

5. Find the Financial Value by subtracting the Current Debt on House, Taxes on Taxable Gain, Cost of Sale, Fix-Up Expenses and Taxes on Home Office Use from the amount realized.

Example:

1. Find the Amount Realized:

	Your House	Example
Fair Market Value	_____	$400,000
Cost of Sale	_____	$ 28,000
Amount Realized	_____	$372,000

2. Find the Gain or Loss

Amount Realized	_____	$372,000
Less Tax Basis	_____	$100,000
Gain (or Loss)	_____	$272,000

3. Find the Taxable Gain

	Your House	Example
Gain	_____	$272,000
Exclusion	_____	$500,000
Taxable Gain	_____	$ 0

4. Find the Taxes on Taxable Gain

Taxable Gain	_____	$0
Capital Gains Rate	_____	x 20%
Taxes on Taxable Gains	_____	$0

5. Find the Financial Value

Amount Realized	_____	$372,000
Current Debt on House	_____	$ 90,000
Taxes on Taxable Gain	_____	$0
Taxes on Home Office Use	_____	$0
Fix-Up Expenses	_____	$ 6,000
Financial Value	_____	$276,000

7. What Would Be the Financial Value of Your House If You Sold It in the Future?

Of all the options you may pursue regarding the house, the choice of selling it in the future can be the most difficult to analyze. Take your time and get help in determining real estate values, if necessary.

No one can predict what will happen in the future to the real estate market or tax laws. But real estate brokers can make calculated guesses about it. Based on the assumption that you would not keep a house that is expected to decrease in value, you can anticipate that the house value will stay the same or, more likely, increase.

But increase by how much?

A technical aid, the Future Value Factor chart, lets you calculate changes in the value of an asset like a house. We've included a Future Value Factor chart in the Appendix. Use it, along with the formula, below, to get an idea of what your house will be worth in the future. But remember that this will be only an estimate.

To use the Future Value Factor chart, you must decide how long you plan to stay in your house (called the Holding Period), and you must select a rate of inflation. Financial planners often figure an annual inflation rate of 3% or 4% when estimating housing values. Depending on the state of the economy and your local housing market, you may be tempted to use an inflation rate higher than 3% or 4%. Certainly many houses increase in value at a rate substantially higher than the inflation rate. Nevertheless, we recommend that you be conservative when speculating on the future value of your house. It's better to expect less and get more than vice versa.

You will see that the Future Value Factor chart lists numbers of years vertically and rates of inflation horizontally. Estimate the number of years you expect to hold onto the house, select an anticipated inflation rate and find where the selected row and column intersect. That will give you the Future Value Factor. For example, if you expect to hold the house another seven years and assume inflation won't go above 4% during that period, your Future Value Factor is 1.3159.

To find the future Financial Value (after-sale/after-tax value), enter the following information for your house:

_____   % Inflation (rate you anticipate)

_____   Holding Period (how many years you plan to keep the house)

_____   Future Value Factor (from Appendix, Section F)

$ _____   Fair Market Value (Step 2)

$ _____   Current Debt on House (Step 3)

$ _____   Cost of Sale (Step 4)

$ _____   Fix-Up Expenses (Step 4)

$ _____   Tax Basis (Step 5)

_____   % Capital Gains Rate (Use the state rate. Virtually all states follow the federal law for exclusion regarding the house, but many have their own capital gains rules.)

$ _____   Taxes to Pay From Home Office Use (see sidebar, "For Those With Home Office Deprecation," above)

Now take the following steps:

1. Find the Future Value Factor (Appendix, Section F) by estimating the Holding Period and the rate of Inflation.

2. Find the Future Sale Value by multiplying the Fair Market Value by the Future Value Factor.

3. Find the Potential Amount Realized by subtracting the Cost of Sale from the Future Sale Value.

4. Find the Potential Gain or Loss on the potential sale of your house by subtracting the Tax Basis from the Amount Realized. If you had a Loss, use zero as the amount of Gain and go directly to Step 7.

5. Find the Potential Taxable Gain by subtracting your Exclusion from the Gain. Taxable Gain is that portion of Gain exceeding the maximum Gain you can exclude. If you are single, the maximum Gain you can exclude is $250,000. (Remember: To qualify for the Exclusion, you must own and reside in the home for two of the last five years prior to sale, and you must not have sold or exchanged a principal residence in the two years prior to the sale.) If your Taxable Gain does not exceed the maximum exclusion allowed you, go directly to Step 7.

6. Find the taxes on the Taxable Gain by multiplying the Taxable Gain by your Capital Gains Rate.

7. Find the Financial Value (after-sale/after-tax value) by subtracting what you expect your debt on the house will be, as well as taxes on Taxable Gain, Cost of Sale, Fix-Up Expenses and Taxes on Home Office Use, from the Amount Realized calculated in Step 3.

Example:

1. Find the Future Value Factor—See Appendix, Section F.

   For the purpose of this example, assume a Holding Period of five years and an Inflation rate of 5%—the Future Value Factor is 1.2763.

2. Find the Future Sale Value

Fair Market Value	$400,000
Future Value Factor	x 1.2763
Future Sale Value	= $510,520

3. Find Potential Amount Realized

Future Sale Value	$510,520
Cost of Sale	− 35,736
Potential Amount Realized	= $474,484

4. Find Potential Gain or Loss

Amount Realized	$474,484
Less Tax Basis	− 100,000
Gain (or Loss)	= $374,784

5. Find the Potential Taxable Gain

Gain	$374,784
Exclusion	− 250,000
Potential Taxable Gain	= $124,784

6. Find the Potential Taxes on Taxable Gain

Taxable Gain	$124,784
Capital Gains Rate	x 20%
Potential Taxes on Taxable Gain	= $24,957

7. Find the Future Financial Value

Amount Realized	$474,784
Anticipated Debt on House	− 90,000
Taxes on Taxable Gain	− 24,957
Taxes on Home Office Use	− 0
Fix-Up Expenses	− 6,000
Potential Financial Value	= $353,827

Now fill in the numbers for your house.

1. Find the Future Value Factor

   Enter number from Appendix, Section F: _____

2. Find the Future Sale Value

Fair Market Value	_____
Future Value Factor	x _____
Future Sale Value	= _____

3. Find Potential Amount Realized

Fair Market Value	_____
Cost of Sale	− _____
Potential Amount Realized	= _____

4. Find Potential Gain or Loss

Amount Realized	_____
Less Tax Basis	− _____
Gain (or Loss)	= _____

5. Find the Potential Taxable Gain

Gain	_____
Exclusion	− _____
Potential Taxable Gain	= $ _____

6. Find the Potential Taxes on Taxable Gain

Taxable Gain	_____
Capital Gains Rate	x 20%
Potential Taxes on Taxable Gain	= _____

7. Find the Future Financial Value

Amount Realized	_____
Anticipated Debt on House	− _____
Taxes on Taxable Gain	− _____
Taxes on Home Office Use	− _____
Fix-Up Expenses	− _____
Potential Financial Value	= _____

8.   What Is Your Share of the House?

You may have expected your marriage to be a 50-50
proposition, and you may believe that your divorce
will be the same—a simple division in which each
person gets half. When it comes to the house,
however, those percentages may not hold up. For
example, you may be entitled to as little as 25% of
the house, or as much as 75%.

In this step, you must determine what share of
the house belongs to you. You will use that amount
in choosing your best option regarding the house
and in negotiating the final settlement. When you
determine the total value of the house under
different scenarios, you need to know your share so
you can figure out how much of that total value you
can expect to receive. For instance, if the total value
of your house is $100,000 and you are each entitled
to 50% of it, you'd get $50,000. But if you were only
a one-fourth owner of that house, you'd be entitled
to $25,000, not $50,000.

The laws of your state and the origin of the
money used to buy your house determine the
amount of your share. Refer to Chapter 12, Section
A, for an overview of marital and separate property.
If one spouse solely owned the house when you
entered the marriage, the other spouse may nevertheless be entitled to a share at divorce. In some
community property states, when the nonowning
spouse or the marital earnings pay for mortgage
payments and improvements (such as additions and
renovations), that action usually gives the nonowner
some ownership interest.

In equitable distribution states, if a house is one
spouse's separate property but the nonowner spouse
uses her *own* separate-property funds to make
improvements to it, the nonowner spouse may
acquire a monetary interest in the improved property. That interest might equal the value of the
improvements or the increase in the property's
overall value.

Once you have determined your estimated
ownership share, enter it here.

_____ % *Separate Property*

_____ % *Marital Property*

Your house can be worth different amounts
under different circumstances, depending on your
ownership share and the option you ultimately
choose. Multiply the percentage of Marital Property
by the Equity or Legal Value and place that figure
on the *Marital Balance Sheet* in Chapter 19, Section
B. Then, using the same process, figure out the
amount of the home that is Separate Property and
place that in *Marital Balance Sheet,* noting that that
separate-property share must be bought out as part
of the ultimate negotiations.

9.   What's Your Best Option Regarding the House?

Now consider your options in light of your calculations in the previous steps. The advantages and disadvantages of each option are recapped below. If you choose Options A or B and do not think you can afford to buy out your spouse's interest, see the suggestions in step 10.

Option A: Buy out your spouse's share and either keep it or sell it in the future.

Advantages: For the sake of children, or stability in your own life, it may serve you to keep the family home. You can take advantage of the IRS exclusion that lets you sell a house and not pay taxes on the first $250,000 of profit.

Disadvantages: When you eventually sell the house, you will be solely responsible for costs of sale and taxes on the profit over $250,000. There is also a chance that the real estate market in your area could crash and that the house could sell for less money in the future.

Is this a viable option for me? _____ Yes _____ No

Option B: Transfer your share of the house to your spouse.

Advantages: You do not have to pay taxes on the money you receive because the IRS does not tax money received as a property buyout during a divorce.

Disadvantages: You may not earn enough on the sale of the house to afford to buy a new one. If your income is not high enough, you may not qualify for financing.

Is this a viable option for me? _____ Yes _____ No

Option C: Sell the house together and split the proceeds with your spouse.

Advantages: You share the cost of sale and the tax liability with your spouse. Also, you can each take advantage of the IRS provision that lets you exclude up to $250,000 of gain on the sale of the house ($500,000 if you've remarried and meet certain conditions; see "A Tax Break on Capital Gains," above).

Disadvantages: You'd be selling the family home, to which you may have strong emotional ties. Further, the amount you receive from the sale of the house may not be enough for you to afford to buy another house, or you may not qualify for financing to buy another home.

Is this a viable option for me? _____ Yes _____ No

⚠ If you sell the house to a third person before your divorce is final, consider filing taxes separately using a "married filing separately" taxpayer status if taxes are due on the sale of the house. Otherwise, you could be responsible for your spouse's liability if your spouse is dishonest with the IRS (see Chapter 11). Alternatively, you could set up an escrow account to cover potential taxes due.

Option D: Own the house jointly with your spouse and sell it in the future to your spouse or a third person.

Advantages: You (and your children) will continue having a familiar place in which to live. You and your spouse will jointly share the eventual costs of sale and taxes. While you're living in the house, your spouse may agree to pay part of the mortgage (in the form of alimony or child support), repair costs or maintenance costs.

Disadvantages: Major misunderstandings between divorced spouses can arise as to responsibility for repairs, maintenance, improvements, taxes and the like. Nonresident spouses often are unable to purchase homes for themselves. As a safeguard, spouses who jointly own a home while one party uses it should make written agreements stating the rules for repairs and other financial contributions. This agreement must provide for the in-the-house spouse to have exclusive use of the premises; otherwise, the out-of-house spouse could lose his or her capital gains tax exclusion of $250,000.

Is this a viable option for me? _____ Yes _____ No

Continued Home Ownership and Estate Planning

If you decide to hold onto your house with your spouse and sell in the future, you will need to plan your estate and possibly acquire adequate life insurance coverage in the event of the other spouse's death.

You should also evaluate how title to the house is held. (See Chapter 12, Section C.) For example, couples who held their property in tenancy by the entirety or as community property will no longer have that option after divorce. In addition, if you held your house in joint tenancy while you were married—an arrangement whereby the other automatically inherits if one owner dies—that joint tenancy may no longer be appropriate. In some states, divorce may automatically sever joint tenancy. Converting ownership to tenancy in common would let you leave your share of the house to whomever you wish when you die (see Chapter 12, Section C).

Carrying life insurance on your former spouse up to the value of her interest in the home provides you with ready cash if that you purchase the home from her estate if she dies before the house is sold. An agreement outlining your rights and responsibilities for co-ownership also can protect you in the event your ex-spouse dies prematurely.

🕐 Regarding the house, the following option is the best one for me:

_____ *Option A: Buy out my spouse's share and either keep it or sell it in the future.*

_____ *Option B: Sell my share of the house to my spouse.*

_____ *Option C: Sell the house together and split the proceeds with my spouse.*

_____ *Option D: Own the house jointly with my spouse and sell it in the future to my spouse or a third person.*

10. How to Purchase the House From a Spouse or Former Spouse

Now that you have chosen an option, you need to face one more financial reality: paying for your choice. Typically, individuals going through divorce do not have sufficient cash to purchase a spouse's interest in the family home. The following suggestions may help you to find a way to finance your best option on the house.

a. Refinance the house and pay proceeds to selling spouse.

Refinancing the home provides a source of cash to buy out the other spouse. If refinancing does not generate enough cash to buy out your spouse, you'll need a loan (called a second mortgage) secured by the house. Interest payments you make on this second mortgage are usually deductible.

Generally, points paid in refinancing a mortgage—percentages paid to the lender—are not deductible. Check with your attorney or tax advisor on this question.

b. Sell the nonresident's interest to a third person.

If you're going through a divorce, a relative or friend may be able to help you acquire your home while getting a tax benefit herself. Your relative or friend would purchase your spouse's interest in the house under what is called "an equity share financing arrangement." You would then co-own the property with that person and probably would pay rent. If you were to sell the property, the two of you would share in any profit.

You and your relative or friend will need an agreement spelling out the rights and responsibilities of each. To be sure the agreement complies with IRS rules and that you will both obtain available tax benefits, see your tax advisor.

c. Sell to a spouse using an installment loan.

Spouses often agree, and some courts order, that the custodial parent live in the family home with minor children. The custodial parent could purchase the home from the other, who accepts a secured installment note with payments over a fixed period of time. An installment note secured by the home allows the buyer to deduct interest and protects the seller in case the buyer defaults.

d. Exchange the family home for a release of alimony.

If an ex-spouse would be entitled to a sizable amount of alimony, consider exchanging it for the house. You will want to discuss this fully with a tax specialist to determine the present and after-tax value of total support payments. Courts may not allow all future support payments to be waived; check with your attorney on this point.

e. Keep the house in exchange for other assets.

Most often, couples trade assets and debts depending on needs and affordability. If you choose this option, see Chapter 19, Section B.

f. Borrow from your retirement plan to finance the buyout.

Consider your retirement plan account as a possible source of financing for a home purchase. By doing so, you may save time and money. The costs of borrowing from a retirement account are usually lower than borrowing from a traditional lender. And because you are borrowing from yourself, loan payments are credited to your retirement account. Plus, loan processing is often quicker than with a traditional lender.

If you do not immediately repay the loan within a reasonable time period, it is considered a distribution from your retirement plan. In addition to having to report the withdrawal as income on your tax return (and pay ordinary income taxes on it), you'll be subject to a 10% IRS early withdrawal penalty unless certain conditions are met. (See Chapter 14 for details on retirement plans.) You can only borrow the money if:

- the loan provides for both principal and interest payments, and
- you agree to repay the money within a "reasonable" time, generally assumed to be five years.

To be able to deduct the mortgage interest paid, the loan must be secured by your residence. You will not be able to deduct the mortgage interest, however, if:

- the loan is secured by your employer's contributions to your retirement plan, or
- you are considered a "key employee" of the company, which means you:
  - ✓ are an officer or the employer
  - ✓ are one of the ten largest owners
  - ✓ own more than 5% of the company during the current year or preceding year, or
  - ✓ own more than 1% of the company and earn more than $150,000 per year.

D. Questions to Ask Your Attorney or Financial Advisor

⚠️ The issue of the house raises several important legal and financial questions. Below are some important questions for you to ask your attorney or research at your local law library, as well as questions for your financial advisor.

Attorney Questions

1. Is a portion of the house considered separate property? How does the court treat a separate property interest in the family home in my state?

2. Am I entitled to a credit for mortgage payments I make while my spouse resides in the family home? Is this credit reduced by the value of tax benefits received from the mortgage interest deduction?

3. What happens if the bank forecloses on this loan?

4. What is my income tax liability, if any, if the title to the house transfers to me and there is a foreclosure?

5. If there is a foreclosure, can the lender get a judgment against me for any difference between the foreclosed value of the house and the mortgage balance that I owe?

6. Should I get divorced before or after the house sells?

7. If we continue to hold the house as joint tenants, does the right of survivorship continue after the divorce?

Financial Advisor Questions

1. What penalties am I subject to for prepayment of our mortgage?

2. Do we have any unamortized points from our existing mortgage?

3. Am I adequately insured?

4. If our house sells and we are still married, should we file a joint tax return?

5. If we own it jointly and then I buy out my spouse's share, how do I report this for tax purposes?

6. Who gets the mortgage interest deduction and the property tax deduction if the title is held as tenants in common? If it's held as joint tenants?

■

Retirement Benefits: Who Gets What?

*Whether your retirement benefits come from
your own job, your spouse's job or plans that you
invested in together, those benefits must be
divided when you divorce.*

 If neither you nor your spouse has a
retirement plan, skip ahead to Chapter 15.

Under the best of circumstances, planning for your
retirement is difficult. You may not have given
much thought to retirement planning. Perhaps you
hoped it would somehow take care of itself. But it
won't. You've got to give some serious consideration
to when you will retire, how much income you'll
need during retirement, the sources for that income

and how you will divide the retirement benefits
with your ex-spouse.

Retirement planning is a relatively new
concept. Generations ago, few people had to worry
about late-life security because most just didn't live
that long. Today, an entire industry has emerged to
provide retirement planning services to aging Baby
Boomers. The pressure to create sound retirement
plans can be intense, and divorce adds another layer
of complexity.

In most states, retirement plans are property to divide at divorce. Naturally, you may be emotionally attached to the retirement benefits that you worked so hard to earn or feel that you are entitled to as part of your commitment to the marriage. Take heart. Retirement benefits can serve as signigficant bargaining chips when spouses trade assets in the final property settlement.

Planning for Your Retirement

No matter how you and your soon-to-be-ex-spouse divide the retirement benefits, it is important now to plan for your own retirement. Here's why and what you will need to do:

- Americans are living longer. You should plan for an income stream through at least age 90.

- The responsibility for providing retirement income is being shifted slowly but surely by employers onto the shoulders of employees. Take advantage of any and all retirement plans available to you now through your employer. Once your credit cards are paid off, contribute more—the maximum allowed if possible.

- You have more investment choices now than ever before in 401(k) plans and self-directed plans. Learn what you need to know about available mutual funds, as well as their objectives and performance, so you can make intelligent decisions.

- If you are not part of the "triple squeeze" generation—supporting an aging parent, putting a child through college and trying to save for your own retirement simultaneously—you may be soon. Be sure to consider these factors as you make your decisions about splitting retirement plans in divorce.

We only introduce the concept of retirement planning in this chapter. For more information, we recommend four excellent resources: *Get a Life: You Don't Need a Million to Retire Well*, by Ralph Warner (Nolo); *IRAs, 401(k)s and Other Retirement Plans: Taking Your Money Out*, and *Creating Your Own Retirement Plan*, both by Twila Slesnick, EA and John Suttle, CPA (Nolo); and *Your Next Fifty Years: A Completely New Way to Look at How, When and If You Should Retire*, by Ginita Wall and Victoria F. Collins (Henry Holt).

A. Understanding Retirement Plans

Little agreement exists on how retirement plans should be categorized, and almost every book and expert on the subject uses a different system. In the pages that follow, we separate plans into several major categories.

The table on the next several pages gives detailed information on many major categories of retirement plans. Once you've determined which plans cover you and your spouse, you can focus on the sections in this chapter that apply to you.

The table also specifies how, under the law, particular plans may be divided at divorce. To divide some types of plans, you must get a special kind of court order called a QDRO (pronounced "quadro")—a Qualified Domestic Relations Order (see Section B, below). Other retirement assets can be divided by a court order or judgment other than a QDRO. And some kinds of retirement assets can't be divided at divorce.

One distinction we make in this chapter is between *defined benefit plans* and *defined contribution plans*. In defined benefit plans, also called pension plans, an employer provides a fixed amount to an employee at retirement, usually in monthly payments that continue until the employee's death. In defined contribution plans, which include 401(k) plans among others, the employee and often the employer contribute money into the employee's retirement account, which grows over time. IRAs, or Individual Retirement Accounts, have similarities to defined contribution plans, although dividing the assets at divorce doesn't require a QDRO.

If you or your spouse has a defined benefit plan, it's difficult to determine just how much the plan is worth today. That's because the plan is designed to pay out in the future, and inflation causes today's dollars to have a different value than they'll have 20 or 30 years from now. It takes an expert, such as an actuary, to find the current value of this kind of plan. That makes dividing the asset a complicated task, as we'll see. It's a lot easier to tell how much a defined contribution plan or an IRA is worth today: As the account grows, the current value is reported to the account holder in regular statements.

Employer-Sponsored Defined Contribution Plans

		Type of Order Necessary to Divide Plan
Salary Savings/401(k)	Employee contributes a portion of salary on a pre-tax basis, which may be matched in full or in part by the employer. The employee may defer up to $11,000 annually, effective January 1, 2002.	QDRO (For more on QDRO, see Section B, below.)
Thrift Plan	Employee contributes a portion of salary on an after-tax basis, which may be matched in full or in part by the employer. Because the employee's contribution is made on an after-tax basis, distributions (payouts) may be partially tax-free.	QDRO
Profit-Sharing Plan	Employer contributes to the employee's account only if company is profitable. Amount of contribution is based on either a fixed or a discretionary formula.	QDRO
Money Purchase Plan	Employer contributes a fixed percentage of salary to employee's account every year. Employer contribution is mandatory, regardless of whether company makes a profit.	QDRO
Employee Stock Ownership Plan (ESOP)	Contributions are a percentage of salary and are used to purchase company stock. The stock is held in trust for the employee, who receives his or her accumulated interest in the plan at termination of employment in the form of stock or cash. The plan provisions define the rights of the employee to exercise any stock options.	QDRO
Tax-Sheltered Annuities (TSAs)	TSAs are a retirement vehicle allowing teachers, public school system employees and employees of nonprofit organizations to contribute a portion of salary into the annuity. If your TSA is through the Teachers Insurance and Annuity Association–College Retirement Equities Fund (TIAA-CREF), you can get detailed information, including account values, on the Web at www.tiaa-cref.com.	QDRO

Employer-Sponsored IRAs

		Type of Order Necessary to Divide Plan
Simplified Employee Pension IRA (SEP-IRA)	SEP-IRAs are retirement plans in the form of individual retirement accounts. The same early withdrawal penalties apply here as apply to traditional IRAs or Roth IRAs. The maximum contribution is 15% of the employee's compensation.	A regular court order or judgment divides these plans.
Salary Reduction-Simplified Employee Pension IRA (SAR-SEP)	These retirement plans were available prior to 1997 and included a salary reduction agreement in which the employee could elect to have a portion of salary contributed to a SEP-IRA on a pre-tax basis.	A regular court order or judgment divides these plans.
Simple IRA (Simplified Incentive Match Plans for Employees)	Some small employers, including self-employed individuals, set up Simple IRAs for the benefit of their employees. The Simple IRA involves a written salary reduction agreement between the employee and employer that allows the employee-participant to reduce compensation and have the employer contribute that amount to a Simple IRA on the employee's behalf. (Employees may elect not to contribute.) The employer makes matching contributions or nonelective contributions. Nonelective contributions are made for each eligible employee, even if the employee does not elect to contribute. The total employee contribution (from salary reduction) allowed for the year 2002 is $7,000 (workers over age 50 are allowed to contribute another $500). Nonelective contributions are limited to 2% of compensation. The matching contribution is the lesser of the employee contribution or 3% of the employee's annual salary. The distribution rules applicable to a traditional IRA also apply to a Simple IRA, except that if the employee withdraws money prematurely within two years after she began participating, the 10% penalty is increased to 25%. In addition, during the first two years of plan participation, a rollover (transfer of funds) can be made only to another Simple IRA plan. A Simple IRA cannot be designated as a Roth IRA.	A regular court order or judgment divides these plans.

Defined Benefit Plans

		Type of Order Necessary to Divide Plan
Business/Corporate Pension	Businesses or corporations offer these defined benefit plans. The maximum annual benefit beginning January 1, 2002 is $160,000.	QDRO

Government-Sponsored Retirement Plans

		Type of Order Necessary to Divide Plan
Government/Military Pension	These defined benefit plans are offered to civil service workers, government employees and military personnel. Veterans can get additional information on their benefits at www.va.gov.	Specific governmental regulations and procedures apply for implementation of a court order to divide these plan benefits between spouses.

Personal Retirement Plans/Personal Annuities

		Type of Order Necessary to Divide Plan
Deferred Annuity	A deferred annuity is an annuity contract in which an insurance company promises to make payments at some future date. Taxes on appreciation are deferred until the money is withdrawn.	A regular court order or judgment divides these plans. Most insurance companies have forms that permit the transfer of ownership.
Traditional IRA	Individuals may accumulate up to $3,000 per year (workers over age 50 are allowed to contribute another $500 per year). Withdrawals before age 59½ are subject to a 10% penalty. The early withdrawal penalty does not apply to a withdrawal necessitated by disability or if the withdrawal is for certain medical insurance premiums, educational expenses or first-time home buyer expenses up to a maximum of $10,000. The account value is untaxed until funds are withdrawn.	A regular court order or judgment divides IRAs.
Roth IRA	Individuals may contribute up to $3,000 per year (workers over age 50 are allowed to contribute another $500 per year). Contributions are not deductible when you make them, but qualified distributions of the contributions and earnings are tax-free when withdrawn. In general, you can take tax-free withdrawals if, after holding the account for five years, you meet certain conditions. You must be at least 59½, disabled or using the money (up to $10,000) toward the purchase of your first home, or you must be the beneficiary of the account. If you do not meet any of these conditions, an early withdrawal penalty will apply.	A regular court order or judgment divides IRAs.

Miscellaneous Retirement Benefits

		Type of Order Necessary to Divide Plan
Nonqualified Deferred Compensation Plan	A small percentage of executives and key upper-level employees have deferred compensation plans. Generally, such a plan provides that a portion of the employee's compensation is deferred until the future. Agreements to participate in the plans are made directly between the employer and the employee, which makes requesting documentation from the employer important. (For more on these plans, see Chapter 16.)	Often the plans do not permit the asset and/or income to be divided, making them legally complicated. In such a case, the court might order the employee spouse to pay the nonemployee spouse when he or she receives the benefit. Because the employee spouse pays taxes when he receives the benefit, the order should include a provision that the employee spouse will deduct the non-employee spouse's share of taxes on the benefit.
Social Security	If you are divorced, you can receive benefits based on your former spouse's earnings if the marriage lasted at least ten years, you are unmarried and the benefit based on your own earnings is not greater than 50% of your former spouse's benefit. You can begin receiving benefits at age 62 if your former spouse is receiving benefits. If your former spouse is at least age 62 and not receiving benefits but can qualify for them, you can still receive benefits if you have been divorced for at least two years and meet the other requirements. To apply for benefits on your former spouse's record, you will need either the spouse's Social Security number or the spouse's date and place of birth and parents' names. Your benefits as an ex-spouse do not reduce or otherwise affect benefits available to your former spouse or your current spouse, if you are remarried. You can find out about Social Security benefits by calling 800-772-1213 or visiting the Social Security Administration online at www.ssa.gov. For more on Social Security, see "Social Security Benefits After Divorce" in Chapter 5.	Social Security benefits are not considered marital property and are not divisible at divorce.

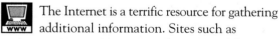 The Internet is a terrific resource for gathering additional information. Sites such as www.morningstar.com, www.yahoo.com and www.financenter.com offer valuable insights into and analysis of many different types of retirement funds. Be sure to check whether your retirement plan has information available online. Many company and government plan sponsors provide up-to-date account values and information through their websites or through automated phone systems.

1. Retirement Plans Are Not Created Equal

Retirement plans vary tremendously. Even if two plans look equal on paper, fine-print plan provisions can make one plan more valuable than another. For instance, one plan may allow for a lump sum payout upon retirement, while another may not. Getting your retirement dollars in a lump sum may provide more flexibility than getting monthly payments in dollars whose value erodes over time or disappears entirely if the plan becomes insolvent in later years.

Retirement plans must comply with federal regulations, but the way they are apportioned at divorce may differ from state to state. One state may define retirement benefits as marital property (an asset to be divided at divorce), while another may rule that benefits are income (and not to be divided). Be sure to ask your lawyer how your state treats retirement benefits upon divorce. (In a worst-case scenario for the employee spouse, a state may regard retirement benefits as both marital property and income, allowing "double dipping" for the non-employee spouse.)

2. Some Plans Promise Better Tax Breaks Than Others

One major attraction of most retirement plans is that you defer paying income taxes on the money that accumulates in the plan. In some plans, though, you must pay income taxes on the money before it's deposited. One task during your divorce will be to determine the tax position of your benefits. Normally, you want to defer paying the taxes until you withdraw the money from the plan and presumably are in a lower income bracket or have a lower annual income.

3. Divorce Leads to Division Decisions

Will you split the retirement money now or later? A present division means you divide the value of the plan now, at divorce. A future division means the plan is divided at retirement or at the point in the employee spouse's career when the benefits would normally be paid out. When and how you divide the plan depends on the type of plan you have, payout provisions, valuation methods and other factors. Your division decision at divorce has a direct impact on your future financial security, so do not make this choice lightly.

Retirement Plan Lingo

Before you start making decisions, familiarize yourself with the terms you are likely to hear when you investigate your retirement plans. You have a better chance of getting answers to your questions if you know what to ask for.

- **Account Balance**. For plans such as IRAs and defined contribution plans, you want to know how much is in the account. This amount may simply be called the balance.

- **Accrued Benefit.** The amount that has been earned (or has accrued) in a retirement plan as of a particular date.

- **Annuity Contracts.** A contract between a life insurance company and the investor or owner of the annuity. Typical provisions include the amount of interest (both the guaranteed minimum and the current), surrender charges (fees for ending the contract prematurely) and penalties and options at retirement.

- **Defined Benefit Plan.** A plan in which the employee's retirement benefit is fixed, based on a specific formula.

- **Defined Contribution Plan.** A plan in which the employee and sometimes the employer contribute to a retirement account, often at regular intervals.

- **Full Plan.** You may or may not need a copy of the full plan, depending on how well the summary plan description (see below) is written. Do not hesitate to ask for the full plan if you have questions or need to check details.

- **Procedures and Model Orders for Division.** Often companies have written procedures for dividing up company retirement plan benefits. Request a copy of these materials.

- **Qualified Plan.** A retirement plan that qualifies for certain benefits described in Section 401 of the U.S. Tax Code. Also known as an ERISA plan because it is governed by the Employee Retirement Income Security Act.

- **Summary Plan Description.** Employers are required to issue a description (annually in most cases) outlining the status and terms of retirement plans. This summary should tell you the amount of benefits (in dollars) that have accumulated in your name or your spouse's.

- **Trust/Custodial Agreement.** A document spelling out specific provisions of the retirement plan and the agreements between the legal owner of the plan, usually the plan administrator (called the "trustee") and the employee (the beneficial owner). Understanding these agreements is particularly important with IRAs because they describe the costs of establishing, maintaining and terminating IRA accounts.

B. Qualified Domestic Relations Orders

QDROs, interim QDROs and other kinds of court orders are used to divide various kinds of retirement plans.

1. QDRO

QDRO stands for Qualified Domestic Relations Order. It is an order from the court to the retirement plan administrator spelling out how the plan's benefits are to be assigned to each party in a divorce. One important consideration with a QDRO is that any assets or items that the order omits, even accidentally, cannot be reinstated.

2. What Constitutes a QDRO

For a document dividing a retirement plan to be considered as a QDRO, it must specify:

- the name and last known mailing address of the employee spouse ("the participant")

- the name and mailing address of the non-employee spouse (the alternate payee)

- the amount or percentage of the participant's benefits that is to be paid to the alternate payee, or the manner in which the amount or percentage is to be determined

- the number of payments or the period to which the order applies, and

- the name of the plan, such as the Walton Company Pension Plan, to which the order applies.

A QDRO cannot:

- require a plan to pay any benefit or option not otherwise provided by the plan

- require a plan to provide benefits that exceed the value of the participant's interest as determined by an actuary

- require the payment of benefits to an alternate payee if those benefits are already payable to

another alternate payee (that is, another ex-spouse) under a previous qualified order, or

- specify who will be responsible for payment of taxes.

Plans subject to QDROs include:

- qualified plans

- defined contribution plans

- defined benefit plans, and

- tax-sheltered annuities (TSAs).

Plans that QDROs do not cover include:

- deferred annuities

- traditional IRAs

- Roth IRAs

- SEP-IRAs

- nonqualified deferred compensation plans (government and church plans)

- plans administered by a plan participant (you or your ex-spouse), and

- plans under which you do not receive benefits from your ex-spouse's retirement plan.

Sometimes an order concerning the retirement plans is in a document called a Domestic Relations Order, Marital Settlement Agreement or Divorce Settlement Agreement. These kinds of orders are not QDROs.

3. Interim QDROs

If you are not ready to divide the retirement plan assets and prepare a QDRO, you can still protect your rights to survivor benefits under your spouse's retirement plan by filing what is called an interim QDRO. Later, when retirement assets are divided, a QDRO may be obtained. Here's what an interim QDRO accomplishes:

- Treats the nonemployee spouse as a surviving spouse. Even if the employee remarries, the former spouse's interest in survivor benefits is paid before the new surviving spouse receives anything.

- Prohibits the employee from electing to receive retirement plan benefits during his lifetime without permission of the former spouse or a court order, except for any minimum required distribution.
- Sets the former spouse's rights at 50% of the community portion of the employee's benefit.

An attorney should be able to advise you on filing an interim QDRO. But don't wait very long to obtain the actual QDRO. A delay can mean a loss of benefits to the nonemployee spouse that he or she would otherwise be entitled to. Be sure the QDRO is accepted by the employee spouse's plan administrator. A divorced ex-spouse without a QDRO does not have the same protection under the plan as he or she had while still married.

Benchmarks to Retirement

Most people think of age 65 as the standard retirement age. Nonetheless, other birthdays are important in preparing for the after-work years. By noting these key ages ahead of time, you may be able to minimize taxes and maximize benefits.

Be sure to review your company's retirement plans. Each plan has its own rules about at which age retirement benefits can begin. In some circumstances you may choose to receive your retirement benefits early, but your monthly benefit will be lower. Your benefits administrator can give you more information on what retirement benefits are available to you and the ages at which you can begin receiving these benefits. Most employers also provide employees with a statement showing an estimate of retirement benefits at early and regular retirement ages. Ages to note include:

55. If you retire, quit or are fired and are age 55 or older, you may receive benefits from an employer-sponsored qualified plan without having to pay a 10% penalty. This exception *does not* apply to either personal or employer-sponsored IRA distributions.

59½. You are allowed to withdraw funds from personal and employer-sponsored IRAs and retirement plans without paying the 10% penalty.

60. Widows and widowers become eligible for Social Security benefits.

62. You may be eligible to receive Social Security benefits, but benefits will be less than if you retire at ge 65.

65. Retirees qualify for Medicare benefits.

67. Full Social Security benefits are available for anyone born in 1960 or later. The actual age at which full Social Security benefits are available depends on the year in which you were born. For those born before 1938, full Social Security benefits are available at age 65. For those born later, the retirement age is between 65 and two months and 67, depending on your birth year.

70. Full Social Security benefits are available, even if you continue to work full time.

70½. You're required to begin taking distributions from IRAs (except Roth IRAs) by April 1 of the year following the calendar year in which you reach age 70½. For other employer-sponsored qualified retirement plans, distributions must begin by April 1 of the year following age 70½ or the year of retirement, whichever is later. If the participant is at least a 5% owner of the business, distributions must begin at age 70½.

C. The Legal Value of Your Retirement Plans

As we've often stressed in this book, the value of an asset as recognized by a court may be vastly different from what the asset is worth outside the courtroom. So it is with retirement plans. Normally, the value of a plan as determined by the court—its "Legal Value"—is the following:

- For defined contribution plans, personal annuities and IRAs, the amount that appears on your statement as the current value of the account, less any loans outstanding.

- For defined benefit plans, what the plan administrator or an actuary tells you it's worth.

You need to know the Legal Value because it is often the only dollar value lawyers and judges will take into consideration. This value represents the amount you and your spouse will argue over if you disagree about the value of the benefits. However, the Legal Value does not account for important financial realities: taxes, early withdrawal penalties, early termination fees and other assessments.

1. Defined Contribution Plans, Personal Annuities and IRAs

If you have a defined contribution plan, personal annuity or IRA, determining the legal value is simple. The plan statement gives the value. If you can't find the information you need, consult the plan administrator or get a copy of the annuity contract.

2. Defined Benefit Plans

If you have a defined benefit plan, you'll need to do some work to find its legal value. Because these plans promise a payment in the future, they are harder to value in the present.

The legal value of a defined benefit plan is the plan's present or actuarial value. The plan administrator or the company may be able to give you this value. Another option, if the two spouses can agree, is to hire an independent third-party actuary to calculate the plan's present value. This should be relatively inexpensive—perhaps $100 to $200. The bill could run higher if your spouse hires his or her own actuary to argue that your actuary's assumptions about the future are wrong, and you find yourself having to call the actuary as an expert witness to testify in a court trial. Disputes can arise because the value of these plans lies in the future and is therefore speculative.

After you get the actuarial value for each plan, you will need to determine what percentage of the plan qualifies as marital property to be divided at divorce.

3. Determining the Marital Portion

To simplify the process of calculating the marital portion of your retirement plan, use the marital interest percentage method (total months of participation while married divided by total months of plan participation.) This method is generally used in dividing defined benefit plans.

The problem with using this method is that it does not accurately value the higher contributions made during the later years of employment. In the early years of plan participation, the contribution is smaller because contribution is based on salary, which is likely to have increased over time. For a more precise calculation, you may need to talk to your CPA, financial planner or pension administrator.

How Can a Pension Worth Hundreds of Thousands Later Be Worth So Little Now?

Actuaries commonly look at several factors when calculating the value of retirement plans. For example, plans often assign benefits based on the highest three years of earnings. But during divorce, current salary is used in the calculation.

Similarly, calculations of the future worth of a plan will differ if a person retires at age 62 rather than age 65. They will also vary with the rate of inflation that's predicted and how the payouts are structured. Some plans include a COLA—cost of living adjustment—that affects the plan's value. And, finally, some actuaries assume a consistent rate of growth—say, 5% of retirement plan investments—and others use a different figure.

For example, take the case of John and Andrea. An actuary tells Andrea that the marital portion of John's plan will pay out about $100,000 during John's retirement but is worth only about $38,000 in today's dollars. So if she and John divide the plan equally at divorce, she will get one-half, or $19,000. If she waits until John retires, she could get $50,000. Andrea, understandably, wants to know why something supposed to be so valuable tomorrow can be worth so little today.

Here's why. John's pension plan shows that he will get $10,000 per year during retirement. He's supposed to retire at age 65 and, according to actuarial tables, live ten years after that. In theory, then, he will receive $100,000.

John, however, is only 45 and won't be retiring for another 20 years. Assuming an inflation rate of 4%, the $10,000 he will be paid in the first year of his retirement is equivalent to $4,564 today. The second year of his retirement (21 years from now) is worth even less.

The *Present Value Factor* chart in the Appendix compares time value with inflation and can help you make a rough estimate of the value of benefits. The left-hand column on that chart represents years, while the percentages across the top of the page are rates of inflation. Following the 20-year line (the number of years after which we assumed John would retire) to the 4% predicted rate of inflation and you find the Present Value Factor of .4564. Multiply $10,000 by .4564 and you get the "value today" of $4,564. You can follow the rest of the 21–30 year lines to see how the rest of the value of John's plan was calculated.

How the Separation Date Can Affect a Retirement Plan's Value

A doctor in California asked the pension plan administrator of his medical group to tell him the value of his plan. The doctor had separated from his wife four years earlier, and they were ready to divide the retirement plan. The administrator valued the plan currently at $225,000. Wanting a second opinion on this obviously valuable asset, the doctor went to an actuary for another valuation of the plan. The actuary valued the plan at only $175,000. Why the difference? Under California law, the marital period of the doctor's retirement plan stopped on the day of separation four years previous. The doctor's wife was entitled to only a portion of the amount that had accrued from their wedding day to the date they separated. By contrast, the plan administrator had calculated the entire value of the plan, including the four-year period that the couple had been separated.

For more on the separation date, see Chapter 5.

D. The Financial Value of Your Retirement Plans

The Financial Value of a retirement plan is almost always lower than its Legal Value. Financial Value encompasses everything from unexpected bonuses (a cash settlement upon divorce) to nasty surprises (a penalty from the IRS).

Although retirement benefits are often years away from being paid out and you may not see the financial return for some time, you nevertheless want to compare all assets on similar terms during your divorce. Just as you may be contemplating a sale of the family home, so, too, must you assume the "sale" (or liquidation) value of a retirement plan. When negotiating the overall settlement, you'll want to be able to compare each asset's Legal Value and Financial Value.

To find the Financial Value of your retirement plans, you'll have to look at income tax consideration as well as charges and penalties. Below is an overview.

Tax Brackets and State Income Taxes

Throughout this book, we assume that you fall into the 28% federal income tax bracket. Because some states tax a percentage of IRA deposits and other retirement plans (Thrift Plans and Employee Stock Ownership Plans), you'll need to ask a tax advisor if you might owe state taxes on your benefits. You won't owe state income taxes in Alaska, Florida, Nevada, South Dakota, Texas, Washington or Wyoming, states that impose no income taxes. (New Hampshire and Tennessee tax only interest income and dividends.)

---

1. Income Tax Considerations

Uncle Sam does not let you simply accrue money for retirement without receiving a share sooner or later. Your job is to find out when taxes on benefits are paid—either before the money goes into the retirement plan or when it comes out during retirement. The plan will contain this information.

Suppose your ex-spouse offers to keep the house but to give you all the retirement plan benefits. Should you take the deal? You cannot answer that question unless you know what income tax you will owe when the benefits begin paying out.

At first glance, your share of the retirement benefits and your share of the house may equal the same dollar amounts. But those amounts probably reflect legal reality only. You may have to pay substantial income taxes when you begin receiving the retirement benefits, while your spouse could take the house and possibly avoid any tax liability.

When dividing plans at divorce, look to keep the plan in which the contributions—or at least some of the contributions—were made with after-tax dollars. When plans are funded with after-tax dollars, part of the money you withdraw at retirement will not be taxed.

Qualified plans—such as defined contribution plans and defined benefit plans—must meet certain IRS regulations for employers to get tax benefits. Tax-Sheltered Annuities (TSAs), although not considered qualified plans, tend to be affected by the same regulations.

In determining the taxability of money contributed to a retirement plan, the IRS asks two questions:

- Did the employer contribute money? If the answer is yes, when you begin collecting your retirement benefits, you'll have to pay taxes on the amount your employer contributed and the interest earned on that contribution.

- Was the contribution made with pre- or after-tax dollars? Retirement plans are sometimes referred to as contributory or noncontributory. Contributory plans are those to which the employee makes a contribution, and employers often make a matching contribution. For instance, some employers chip in 50 cents for every dollar the employee contributes. Some even match the employee contribution dollar for dollar, often to a limited amount, such as $1,000.

The IRS may seem harsh, but it doesn't intend for you to pay taxes twice on your income. If you are currently reporting as income the money you are contributing to your plan, you will not have to pay taxes on those contributions when the money comes out of the plan at retirement.

If you do not know the percentages of your retirement plan contributions made with pre-tax dollars and after-tax dollars, you can:

- Contact the plan administrator, personnel manager or benefits coordinator. Ask for an accounting of pre- and after-tax contributions.

- Check the annual benefits statement. This document breaks down pre- and after-tax contributions.

The income taxes you will have to pay on retirement benefits are based on a number of factors: your tax bracket, the tax basis of the plan, your status as either the plan participant (employee) or the alternate payee (spouse of plan participant) and the type of plan you or your spouse have.

The tax basis of a retirement plan consists of money contributed to a plan that's already been taxed as income—that is, contributions for which you weren't permitted to take a deduction when you filed your taxes. Most employer contributions, plus interest earned on all contributions—from both employer and employee—are not included in basis because those dollars are not taxed until they are paid out. The plan administrator should be able to help you find the tax basis.

For IRAs and deferred annuities, special tax considerations apply.

IRAs. When you deposit money into a traditional IRA, you do not report that money as income—that is, you pay no taxes on it. This assumes that neither you nor your spouse is also an active participant in a qualified plan. If both of you are active participants in qualified plans, you can deduct your $3,000 IRA contribution if your income falls within specified limits.

Roth IRA. Unlike with regular IRAs, money you contribute to a Roth IRA is not tax deductible. But you receive the benefits tax-free when you collect at retirement. This makes Roth IRAs particularly valuable to retain in a divorce.

In general, you can also take tax-free withdrawals if you have held the account for five years or more and are under age 59½, become disabled, use up to $10,000 toward the purchase of your first home or are the beneficiary of the account.

You can convert your traditional IRA to a Roth IRA only if you have an adjusted gross income of less than $100,000. You will not have to pay the 10% penalty on early withdrawals.

Deferred annuities. The money put into a deferred annuity usually comes from your savings—or from income on which you have already been taxed. The tax basis of your annuity is the total purchase price less unpaid loans and any other tax-free amounts you received. You will pay taxes on the difference between the current account value and the tax basis. From the standpoint of income tax liability, the Roth IRA and deferred annuities are similar. Both will have a tax basis, because contributions were made with after-tax dollars.

2. Charges and Penalties

Participants in retirement plans often face charges and penalties when there is an early withdrawal—that is, when money is taken out prior to a certain date. Check your plan documents carefully or ask your plan administrator to see if these charges or penalties apply, and be sure you don't unknowingly incur them.

If a participant in a qualified retirement plan takes money out before she retires, the IRS may assess an early withdrawal penalty (also called an excise tax) as high as 10% of the amount withdrawn. There may be a state tax penalty in addition to the federal penalty.

If the holder of an IRA or an annuity withdraws money before reaching age 59½, she'll pay a 10% penalty to the IRS unless she meets certain exceptions.

Insurance companies and some investment companies impose surrender charges to discourage participants from withdrawing funds before the date specified in the contract. These can take the form of deferred sales charges on mutual funds, surrender charges on annuities, early withdrawal charges on CDs and brokerage or transaction costs.

Another tax wrinkle concerning IRAs: If the participant spouse transfers all or part of an IRA to the other spouse, neither will owe taxes on the transfer. If the participant spouse cashes out the IRA and transfers the money to the other spouse, however, the participant spouse will owe taxes on the money withdrawn.

E. Calculating the Financial Value of Plans

As we've said, any retirement plan has a Financial Value different from the Legal Value that a court assigns it. The Financial Value takes into account real-world factors like tax consequences and early withdrawal penalties. Doing the calculation that follows and entering it into the chart may seem complicated. But knowing the Financial Value of a plan will help you make a better-informed decision about where the assets should go in your divorce settlement.

The calculation is different depending on whether the plan is a defined benefit plan or is a defined contribution plan, TSA or IRA.

For each defined contribution plan, TSA or IRA plan, follow the steps below to complete the chart that follows this calculation.

1. In Column A, enter the total number of months you or your spouse have participated or did participate in the plan.

2. In Column B, enter the total number of months in which you or your spouse participated in the plan while married.

3. In Column C, enter the marital interest percentage by dividing the number in Column B by the number in Column A. For example, if you participated in a plan for 120 months and were married 72 months while participating in the plan, you would have a marital interest percentage of 60% [(72/120) x 100].

4. In Column D, enter the dollar amount of the account. (The amount should be on your statement.)

5. In Column E, enter the marital portion of the account by multiplying the amount in Column D by the percentage in Column C.

6. In Column F, enter the amount of any loan you and your spouse have taken against this retirement account. (The amount should be on your statement.) Do not include any separate loan.

7. In Column G, enter the Legal Value of your retirement plan by subtracting the amount in Column F, if any, from the amount in Column E.

8. In Column H, enter the tax basis of the retirement plan—the after-tax contributions, including nondeductible contributions made to an IRA.

9. In Column I, enter the the marital portion of the tax basis by multiplying the figure in Column H by the percentage in Column C.

10. In Column J, enter the financial value of this account. You do this as follows:

Marital Account Value *(Column E less Column I)*	$_____
Early Withdrawal Penalty*	– $_____
Taxes Due on Distribution *(Marital Account Value* *x your tax bracket)*	– $_____
Other Surrender Charges *or Penalties*	– $_____
Financial Value	$_____

*The early withdrawal penalty is the amount in Column D x 10%, or x 25% for employer-sponsored Simple IRAs you have participated in for two years or less. Be sure to add any state early withdrawal penalties.

For a defined benefit plan, follow the steps below to complete the chart that follows.

1. In Column A, enter the total number of months you or your spouse have participated or did participate in the plan.

2. In Column B, enter the total number of months in which you or your spouse participated in the plan while married.

3. In Column C, enter the marital interest percentage by dividing the number in Column B by the number in Column A. For example, if you participated in a plan for 120 months, and were married 72 months while participating in the plan, you would have a marital interest percentage of 60% [(72/120) x 100].

4. In Column D, enter the actuarial value of the plan. (You'll need to consult with the plan administrator or an actuary for this information.)

5. In Column E, enter the marital portion of the account by multiplying the value in Column D by the percentage in Column C.

6. In Column F, enter the amount of any loan you and your spouse have taken against this retirement account. (The amount should be on your statement.) Do not include any separate loan.

7. In Column G, enter the Legal Value of your retirement plan by subtracting the amount in Column F, if any, from the amount in Column E.

8. In Column H, enter the tax basis of the retirement plan—the after-tax contributions.

9. In Column I, enter the the marital portion of the tax basis by multiplying the figure in Column H by the percentage in Column C.

10. In Column J, enter the financial value of this account. You do this as follows:

Marital Account Value *(Column E less Column I)*	$_____
Taxes Due on Distribution *(Marital Account Value* *x your tax bracket)*	– $_____
Other Surrender Charges *or Penalties*	– $_____
Financial Value	$_____

Once you have completed the steps above for each retirement plan, add all the numbers in Columns D, E, F and J and enter these results in their respective columns on the "Total" line. Then, be sure to transfer the totals to the *Net Worth: Assets & Liabilities Worksheet* in Chapter 12.

Also transfer the legal value to the *Marital Balance Sheet* in Chapter 19, Section B. Any separate property (including a separate property loan) should be entered in the appropriate section on the *Marital Balance Sheet*.

CALCULATING THE FINANCIAL VALUE OF PLANS

Type of Plan	A Months of Plan Participation*	B Months of Marriage During Plan	C Marital Interest	D Dollar Amount of Account	E Marital Portion of Account	F Marital Loans Against Account**	G Legal Value	H Tax Basis	I Marital Portion of Tax Basis	J Financial Value***
EMPLOYER-SPONSORED RETIREMENT PLANS										
Qualified Plans—Defined Contribution Plans										
Salary Savings or 401(k) Plans										
Thrift Plans										
Profit-Sharing Plan										
Money Purchase Plan										
ESOPs										
TSAs										
Employer-Sponsored IRA										
SEP IRA										
SAR-SEP										
Simple IRA										
Qualified Plans—Defined Benefit Plans										
Business or Corporate Defined Benefit Plan										
GOVERNMENT-SPONSORED RETIREMENT PLANS										
Government Plans or Military Pensions										
PERSONAL RETIREMENT PLANS										
Deferred Annuities										
Personal IRA										
Traditional IRA										
Roth IRA										
TOTAL										

*Check state laws to determine the date retirement plan benefits become separate property. **If separate, do not include balance here, but be sure to include separate property loan balance on the marital balance sheet on page 19/2 in Chapter 19. ***If your state awards unvested benefits, you may wish to subtract the unvested portion.

Rolling Over Your Distribution From Your Ex-Spouse's IRA

Under IRA rules, any money you withdraw from an IRA prematurely (before age 59½) must be reinvested (referred to as a "rollover") within 60 days or it will be subject to an IRS early withdrawal penalty.

You can defer the income tax liability on the distribution by rolling over the distribution to another IRA within 60 days of the divorce. If you decide to roll over the distribution, keep in mind the following:

- You cannot roll over any portion of the distribution that is attributable to after-tax contributions of the plan participant. In other words, any nondeductible contributions that your ex-spouse made to his IRA can't be rolled over into your account. But if part of the distribution is attributable to after-tax contributions and part is attributable to before-tax contributions, you will be able to roll over a portion of the distribution.

- If you take possession of funds from your ex-spouse's IRA and *then* roll them over into your own IRA, 20% will be withheld for taxes.

- However, if the plan distribution goes directly to the new plan, then you avoid the 20% withholding on the distribution.

Even if you have someone else managing your account, it is still your responsibility to see that it is done so correctly. In a recent case, a taxpayer's account was being handled by a trustee. The trustee mistakenly transferred a rollover distribution to a brokerage account instead of an IRA. When the trustee discovered its mistake, the amount was transferred to a qualified plan, but the 60-day limit had expired. The IRS ruled that the distribution was not rolled over within the 60 days, and therefore the distribution was taxable even though the taxpayer was not at fault.

The lesson to be learned is that it is your responsibility to follow up on how your accounts are handled. Mistakes by trustees can and do occur. Failure to properly time your rollover can lead the IRS not to recognize it and to assess penalties.

F. Additional Financial Factors Affecting Retirement Plan Divisions

In most divorces, spouses keep "their" own retirement benefits in exchange for other assets. As a simplified example, if each spouse's share of the house is $75,000 and the nonemployee spouse's share of the other's retirement plan is $75,000, then the employee would keep the retirement plan while the other spouse would take the house.

Fairly dividing assets during a divorce, however, is not as simple as the above example. To truly exchange assets of equal value, you must take a variety of financial factors into account. Consider the following factors before you propose how to divide retirement benefits with your spouse.

1. Vesting

One retirement plan concept that is especially important at divorce is vesting. You've probably heard people say they'll be "fully vested" after a certain number of years or that they'll "be vested in another year." Vesting means that you are entitled to the retirement benefits your employer has contributed to the plan for you. Even if you quit your job or you are fired, you are entitled to those benefits.

Being *fully* vested means that you are entitled to all the benefits your employer has contributed. Being partially vested means that if you were to begin receiving the benefits from your employer's contribution to the plan, you'd be entitled to only a particular percentage. If the plan paid $1,000 a month upon retirement and you were 30% vested, you'd receive $300.

Vesting affects only the amount your *employer* contributes toward your retirement plan and its earnings. The contributions you make to your plan, and the earnings attributable to those contributions, always belong to you.

If you are not fully vested, consider consulting an attorney to determine whether your state characterizes nonvested retirement benefits as marital property. If it does not, then division of your plan in that state is not affected by vesting. If the state does characterize the benefits as marital property, however, and you divorce before you fully vest, you could face the awful prospect of paying your spouse a portion of the retirement benefits— even though you might *never* receive them yourself. If you are not fully vested and will potentially encounter this costly dilemma, be sure you know your rights and obligations before negotiating over your retirement plan as part of your divorce settlement. (See Section H, below.)

For example, in a state where nonvested benefits are considered marital property, the total value of your retirement plan is calculated and that amount is divided. If you want to keep the retirement plan, you might have to buy out your spouse's share or exchange it for another asset. If you're fired or change jobs, you might not receive your employer's contributions to your retirement plan, even though you paid your spouse for them.

To reduce these risks, carefully consider whether to divide your plan in the future or in the present (see Section G, below).

If you are fully vested (and therefore entitled to your employer's contribution and required to divide retirement benefits at divorce), double-check the details of your benefits package to be sure you know about any provisions that could be affected by divorce or death. In some cases, when a single (unmarried or divorced) employee dies before the age of 55, even though fully vested, that person's estate may not be entitled to the benefits.

2. Benefits in Payout Status

Once pension benefits vest, the employee may still have to wait before actually receiving the benefits. Usually, vested pensions do not pay out ("mature") until the worker reaches a certain age, such as 65. Some employees choose to continue to work even after the pension matures because the pension payments increase the longer the employee works past the maturity date. If you continue to work to prevent your ex from getting matured benefits, a court may order you to retire (or to pay your former spouse for his or her share from the benefits).

3. Double Payments

Be aware of the risk of double payments. You should not have to pay your spouse twice for the retirement benefits you receive as income. If your spouse is given a portion of your retirement benefits as part of the property settlement, you do not want your retirement benefits to be considered part of your income when alimony is calculated. To protect yourself against double dipping, remember the following: You can divide the plan or divide the stream of income, but do not divide both.

This double dipping of payments is one of the most common ways in which retirement benefits are lost at divorce. Don't let it happen to you. One way to protect yourself is to include a provision in your settlement exempting your retirement payments from being considered income for the purposes of alimony. Check with your attorney on how you can aviod this risk.

4.   Cost of Living Adjustments

Cost of Living Adjustments (COLAs) are provisions in retirement plans that provide for an increase in benefits based on your life expectancy and the formula by which benefits are paid out. A plan with a cost-of-living provision is usually more valuable than another plan without it. Check with the plan administrator to see if your retirement plan or your spouse's includes a cost-of-living provision.

5.   Access to Cash

In getting cash out of a retirement plan at divorce, the alternate payee (nonemployee spouse) holds the advantage. If you are the alternate payee, you can request that the QDRO provide for a payout when a marital property settlement becomes final. The plan administrator must withhold 20% of the amount distributed to you to offset some of the income taxes you will owe, even if you deposit it into an IRA or any other qualified pension plan within 60 days of receiving it. If the plan administrator directly rolls over the plan assets into your IRA (or another qualified plan), however, the 20% mandatory withholding rule does not apply.

If money is tight (as it often is during divorce), you may want to open a savings account with all or part of the money you receive from a retirement plan distribution. Although you'll have to pay taxes on this money, you will have easy access to these funds should you need them. Most important, you won't be hit with the 10% early withdrawal penalty that would apply if you put it into an IRA and then needed to withdraw money to live on.

If you are the plan participant (employee spouse), you probably won't get an early payout from your plan even though your spouse may. Your divorce does not change your status with respect to your benefit payments. It's rare that you will be able get to your benefits prior to the date on which the plan specifies you are to receive them. The exceptions are if you become disabled, if you quit your job or get fired or if the plan itself ends.

6.   Tax Consequences in Dividing Benefits

When dividing matured benefits in a divorce, the employee spouse must be aware of the tax risks. Many divorce settlements specify that the non-employee spouse gets a share of the other spouse's retirement benefits when the employee spouse retires. Usually, the pension plan administrator sends a check to the ex-spouse. But this means that only the retired employee pays income taxes on the benefits.

To reduce your tax burden, make sure the QDRO orders the pension plan administrator to send two checks—one to you and one to your ex-spouse. Each person pays income taxes on the benefits he or she receives. If your plan is not subject to a QDRO, it may be possible to reduce the retired person's tax liability by using the domestic relations order, marital settlement agreement or divorce agreement to specify how the benefits are to be paid.

G. The Division Decision: Now or in the Future

Taking into account all the financial factors that can affect your retirement benefits, you are ready to move on to the division decision itself. Generally, you can divide a retirement plan or take a payout in one of two ways:

Present Division. You divide the value of the plan now, at divorce, instead of later, at retirement.

Future (Deferred) Division. You divide the value of the plan at retirement or at that point in the employee's career when benefits would normally be paid out. Future divisions are most common with defined benefit plans, which promise payment in the future and are difficult to place a current value on.

Remember—no matter which approach you take, everything must be spelled out in the QDRO.

Survivor Benefits

A defined benefit (pension) plan must offer survivor benefits to the spouse of a participant employee who dies before retirement age and is vested. The surviving spouse is entitled to payments known as a qualified pre-retirement survivor annuity. An ex-spouse can be treated as the participant's current spouse for the purpose of receiving these survivor benefits. But such a provision must be included in the QDRO, or else the benefits will be lost.

If the participant dies prior to retirement, the pre-retirement survivor annuity begins payment to the survivor when the participant would have reached the earliest retirement age provided for in the plan.

Debts and Retirement Benefits After Divorce

After a divorce, some former spouses find it necessary to file for bankruptcy to discharge (eliminate) their debts. With a QDRO, retirement benefit payments are made directly from the plan to the non-employee ex-spouse. This eliminates the risk that the employee might be able to avoid the obligation to pay retirement benefits to the nonemployee ex-spouse by filing for bankruptcy. If, however, there is no QDRO, then the obligation to pay retirement benefits is a personal obligation, and the employee may be able to avoid it by filing for bankruptcy.

Even if a former spouse doesn't file for bankruptcy, paying obligations can be an overwhelming burden. Some former spouses fall behind on their support obligations. While money cannot be forcibly taken from most retirement plans to pay support, some courts have ruled that IRA funds are not insulated if an ex-spouse or the IRS seeks to collect back alimony or child support.

Furthermore, once divided, retirement plan assets are not insulated from the IRS if taxes are due on a joint return. That's true even if the parties agreed that one spouse was liable for payment of those taxes.

Here are some pros and cons of dividing each of the three main types of retirement plans either at the time of the divorce or later at retirement age. You'll see that the considerations can vary depending on whether you're the alternate payee (non-employee spouse) or the plan participant (employee spouse).

1. IRAs

IRAs are not subject to QDROs and can be divided any way the court orders. They can also be transferred from one spouse to another.

Distributing the proceeds from an IRA, however, triggers a 10% early withdrawal penalty for those under age 59½. The proceeds are also fully taxable to the participant spouse.

Transferring an IRA to a spouse without a divorce or separation agreement or a court order creates tax liability for the participant spouse. The only way to avoid the tax is for the court to order a direct transfer of the IRA from one plan to a new one for the receiving spouse.

I would like to divide the IRAs as follows:

_____

_____

_____

_____

2.   Defined Contribution Plans and TSAs

There are advantages in splitting this kind of plan now, and they are the same whether you are the alternate payee or the plan participant. If you divide the benefits now, you'll cut an economic tie to your spouse and won't need to worry about it later. In addition, consider that:

- deferred divisions are difficult for the court to supervise

- each spouse gains control over his/her share of funds, and

- it's obvious how much the plan is now worth—you don't need an actuary to figure out its future value.

But there are also advantages in waiting before you divide the plan. For both the plan participant and the alternate payee, waiting allows time for any unvested benefits to become vested. Additionally, if you have insufficient property or cash to buy out your spouse's share, then deferred division may be the only way to even up a property split. Also, because the plan participant won't receive money from the plan until later anyway, why divide it early? If you have unvested benefits and you divide now, you may end up paying more to your spouse than you receive from the plan.

I would like to divide the defined contribution plans or TSAs as follows:

_____

_____

_____

_____

3.   Defined Benefit Plans

The advantages of splitting this kind of plan at divorce rather than later depend on whether you are the plan participant or the alternate payee. For the alternate payee, the advantages are:

- you can get the money now

- vesting risk is eliminated

- there is no 10% early withdrawal penalty for distribution, and

- you avoid the risk that the plan will suffer large investment losses or that the company or plan will go bankrupt.

The plan participant should consider that:

- because the value is based on present earnings, your ex-spouse won't receive the benefit of your future work and pay increases, and

- if you outlive the mortality tables, you may end up receiving more income than the actuary predicted you would.

There are also advantages in waiting to divide this type of plan. Because benefits are based on the participant's future earnings, waiting allows the alternate payee to enjoy the fruits of those increased earnings. For the plan participant, the vesting risk is shared with the ex-spouse.

I would like to divide the defined benefit plans as follows:

_____

_____

_____

_____

H. Questions to Ask Your Attorney

Retirement plans raise many legal and financial questions. Below is a list of important questions for you to ask your attorney or research at your local law library.

1. Does my state treat retirement benefits upon divorce as marital property to be divided, or as income that may belong only to the earner? (Benefits treated as income could affect the amount you pay or receive in alimony or child support.)

2. Is a nonqualified deferred compensation plan considered income, or property subject to division?

3. What is the marital portion of our retirement benefits?

4. Must I (or my spouse) be fully vested to receive my (or my spouse's) employer's contribution to a retirement plan?

5. Does my state consider nonvested retirement plans to be marital property?

6. Does my state consider disability pension benefits to be income, or property subject to division?

7. How much experience do you have in writing Qualified Domestic Relations Orders? Do you use another firm to write them? (Some firms specialize in this area.)

8. Does my spouse's pension plan direct the distribution of assets upon my death in the event I die before receiving all of the benefits?

To get details on retirement plans held by your spouse, speak with his or her employer and, if it's a large company, the head of the human resources department. That person may refer you to the plan administrator or the trustee/custodian of the plan. The plan administrator keeps the books and records on the retirement plan, and the trustee/custodian is authorized to administer the plan assets. Begin by writing a letter to your spouse's employer. A sample is below.

Sample Letter to Spouse's Employer

Re: Marriage of _____

  County Case No. _____

  Employee's Name: _____

  Employee's Social Security #:

  _____

  Employee's Date of Birth: _____

To Whom It May Concern:

This letter is to serve as notice that I am pursuing an interest in any retirement or other deferred compensation plans available through your organization or its successors for the benefit of employees belonging to _____ (name of your spouse).

At your earliest possible convenience, I would appreciate receiving the following:

1. Summary of all Deferred Compensation Plans or stock plans that are available to employees, directors, officers or other personnel of your company for which my spouse is eligible to participate, regardless of whether s/he participated in the plan.

2. A copy of the full text of all plans for which my spouse was eligible, regardless of his/her participation therein.

3. A copy of all benefit statements for my spouse for the last five years.

4. Documentation of all stock or stock options owned by or held for the benefit of my spouse.

5. Acknowledgment that your organization has received this Notice. An acknowledgment for the Plan Administrator is below.

6. A copy of your written procedures used in determining your requirements for a Qualified Domestic Relations Order.

7. The formal names of the plan or plans.

8. The names and addresses of all plan administrators.

9. Any other documentation or information, that you believe may be of assistance in order to establish a Qualified Domestic Relations Order.

To save everyone the cost of formal discovery, I ask that you respond as soon as possible.

If you have any questions, please feel free to contact me at your convenience.

Sincerely,

_____

I consent to the release of this information.

Date: _____

Employee/Plan Participant Spouse: _____

ACKNOWLEDGMENT OF RECEIPT OF NOTICE OF ADVERSE INTEREST

I, _____, hereby acknowledge receipt of the letter dated _____, from _____ which states that s/he claims an interest in any retirement, pension or other deferred compensation plan or accounts of

_____.

Dated: _____

TITLE: _____

ORGANIZATION: _____

_____

If you don't get the answers you need, write to the plan administrator, company president or anyone else who could help you get the information you need. You might engage the services of an attorney if you're having particular problems. However you do it, persist until you get what you need. Retirement plans are too complex not to leave a "paper trail," so do not let your spouse or spouse's attorney intimidate you into thinking that the information you need does not exist. ■

CHAPTER 15

Financial Investments: How Do We Divide the Portfolio Pie?

*In divorce, when you divide the investments made by
you and your partner during marriage, it's doubtful
you'll get exactly what you want. But you should get
what you need.*

 If neither you nor your spouse has
investments, skip ahead to Chapter 16.

Objectively analyze your portfolio—that is, the
stocks, bonds, mutual funds, real estate investments,
gold, collectibles and the like that make up your
investment holdings. Then work to get the assets
that can put you in the best position to build toward
your future after divorce.

How do you know which investments will serve
you best?

Ask a dozen financial planners and you'll get
the same answer: "That depends."

Choosing the investments that will serve you
best depends on several factors—your future plans,
current age, risk tolerance, income needs and
investment experience. You should aim for investments that meet your individual needs, allow you to
sleep at night and keep your taxes to a minimum.

As you read this chapter and evaluate your
investments, keep in mind the following two
questions:

- Is the investment performing well?

- Is the investment appropriate for me?

Whether you are a novice or veteran investor,
use the formulas and tips in this chapter to select
the investments that will best support you after the

divorce. Even if you are completely unfamiliar with the investments you and your spouse share, you need not be intimidated—if you do your homework.

In some instances, you may need to consult with financial experts before making decisions at divorce, because certain investments can carry complications due to tax laws or illiquidity (not being able to sell the investment at a reasonable price). Tax advisors, stockbrokers or financial planners may be particularly useful. Whether you get help from experts or not, you can save time and money by doing the groundwork and information-gathering yourself.

A. Concepts to Consider

To get started, here are a few basic investment concepts to help you select investments when a marriage ends.

1. An Investment From Marriage May Make Little Sense When You're Single

While married, the two of you may have chosen certain investments because they met your shared goals—such as a mutual fund to help save for the down payment on a house or an annuity to increase the retirement kitty. Once you divorce, however, your goals, tax bracket and ability to withstand losses may change. Perhaps as a couple you could afford to hold on to a stock with great potential, even when its value fell. As a single person, however, such a stock may be totally unsuitable if you're looking for stable income. Similarly, a spouse in a high-income tax bracket may not want to keep an investment that generates substantial taxable interest.

2. Don't Take an Investment You Can't Live With

Does the mere mention of Wall Street give you the jitters? Can you bear to sit by and watch what happens to the bond market? Do you have the time,

energy and interest to keep up with the performance of your investments? Think about these questions carefully as you look at each asset. You should only keep an investment (like a spouse) if you can stand living with it. Don't take an asset if you don't understand its risks.

3. Use Your Divorce to Cut Your Losses

When it comes to investments, no one likes to admit to making a bad call or a poor decision—especially if your spouse warned you not to buy the loser in the first place. But you wouldn't fight to keep the awful picture Aunt Lucille gave you for a wedding present, would you? Why hold on to investments that are not doing well? Because of the emotional distress of divorce—or simple "investment inertia"—some people hang on to certain investments they ought to sell. Divorce is the perfect time to review *all* of your investments and unload those that drain your portfolio value or don't meet your long-term financial goals.

4. No Investment Is Risk Free

"Risk free" investing is one of the great illusions of the American marketplace. Regardless of what you see, hear or want to believe, every investment carries risk. (Even what were once the most trusted places for money—banks, savings and loans and insurance companies —have shown this to be true.) Ignoring risk is common among today's investors, who have been hit by a virtual avalanche of new financial products, each promising rewards that may or may not materialize. Take time to ask questions about the downside of any investment you plan to keep as part of your settlement. Keep in mind one general rule: *The greater the potential for gain, the greater the risk.*

In addition, never keep an investment that carries a greater risk than you can afford. Doing so increases the risk of loss, because you will probably sell the investment when its value drops rather than ride out its ups and downs.

Example: *In the property settlement, Cheryl received 300 shares of WOW Mutual Fund, a fund investing in small capitalization computer companies. The fund had a high return of 22% in the prior year. Her husband, Jim, convinced her that with the $14,000 worth of WOW shares, she would make more money than with the lower-return Treasury bonds he was taking as part of the settlement. Cheryl quickly learned, however, that the greater the potential for gain, the greater the risk; her $14,000 investment dropped to $8,700 the next year.*

5. Asset Options: Sell Now, Keep It Forever or Take It for a Loss

"Assume sale." Those two words sum up the best advice you can follow when deciding what to do with assets at divorce. So often, cherished investments you thought you would keep forever end up on the auction block after divorce. Ideally, you should select only those investments that financially fit your goals and needs—and you should sell together or transfer to your spouse those that do not. If you sell the investment at divorce, you share the selling costs and potential tax bite with your soon-to-be-ex-spouse. Waiting until after the divorce to unload assets means you incur all those expenses yourself.

Too often, divorcing couples overlook the simple fact that an asset they are eventually planning to sell can be sold *prior* to the divorce. They get caught up in making tradeoffs to reach a quick or supposedly fair property settlement and accept assets they don't want or intend to keep. If, however, you assume sale, you're forced to consider taxation and other costs. Then your negotiations can be based on the real cost of keeping the asset and not an illusory value. And if you do keep the asset, you know what it's truly worth.

An investment asset may provide you with a tax loss when you sell it. If it would, and if you have another asset on which you expect a gain, it may make financial sense to take the loss-producing asset in the settlement. Then you can sell the "loser" after the divorce to offset the tax gain you have from the sale of the other asset and reduce your overall tax liability. It pays therefore to know

which stocks, bonds or mutual funds carry a tax loss with them. For example, limited partnerships and rental real estate, which produce a loss because of depreciation, actually *increase* your tax liability. Be sure to consult a tax advisor before taking one of these items that show a loss.

Example: *Suppose you bought a stock for $2,000 and sold it for $1,500. Your loss is $500. If you have another stock you bought for $1,500, held for 12 months and then sold for $2,500, your gain is $1,000. If you didn't sell the first stock, you'd pay a capital gains tax of $200 on the $1,000 gain, or 20%. If you sold both assets, however, the loss partially offsets the gain and your tax liability would be 20% of $500, or $100.*

Sell Now

Elliot accepted his wife's offer of their coin collection even though he did not particularly care about the coin market and didn't really want the collection. Nevertheless, he accepted it with the illusion that by making this concession to his wife, he would speed up the settlement. Not only did the settlement proceedings drag on, but after the divorce, when he sold the collection, Elliot paid a hefty sales commission and substantial taxes on the gain—which meant Elliot received an asset of lower value than he thought he was getting. Coin collections and other collectibles did not get the benefit of a reduced capital gains rate under the Taxpayer Relief Act of 1997 and are still taxed at 28%.

---

6. Balance Security, Income and Growth

Your investments should give you more than headaches. In fact, a portfolio should balance three financial needs over your lifetime: security, income and growth.

During your divorce, analyze whether or not your investments meet these needs—and in what proportions. The degree to which you need security, income and growth will change depending on what phase of life you're in. Generally, you will want more growth than income while you are young and more income than growth when you get older.

Security. Conventional wisdom among financial advisors holds that you should have an emergency fund in place before you even consider investing. This fund should equal three to six months of your cost-of-living expenses such as mortgage, rent, utilities and food. It should be readily available in a money market fund or short-term bond fund. Disability or life insurance can also provide important sources of income or cash in the event of an emergency. Once your emergency needs are met, you can consider investments for income or growth.

Income. Income investments pay monthly, quarterly, semiannual or annual dividends or interest to supplement your salary or provide an income during retirement.

Growth. These types of investments should "make your money work for you," offering steady growth beyond what you would earn from conservative vehicles like certificates of deposit or money markets. Growth investments include individual stocks, equity mutual funds and real estate.

7. If You Don't Know the Tax Basis, the Tax Bill May Shock You

"Buy low and sell high." That cliché of the marketplace leaves out an important piece of information: When you sell high, you owe Uncle Sam taxes on the profit. Just how much you owe is determined by the amount of profit you realized on the investment. That profit can be determined once you know the tax basis of the investment.

Income vs. Growth Needs

Susan, a young executive, had just received a raise when her husband decided he wanted a divorce. Being a conservative investor, her husband had invested their money in a large number of utility stocks, which provided a steady but small flow of dividends. Because Susan's salary increase gave her a more than adequate income, she wanted cash for her share of the stocks rather than the stocks themselves. With cash in hand, she invested in several high-tech stocks that paid no dividends (and therefore did not increase her tax liability for ordinary income), but gave her what she wanted and needed: potential for appreciation or growth.

For your mutual funds and stock investments, your tax basis is the original purchase price plus the value of any dividends you reinvested in the funds or stocks, minus any commissions you paid to purchase. The tax basis for real estate is the original purchase price plus the cost of improvements you made to the property, minus any tax benefits received. Specific formulas for finding the tax basis are given throughout this chapter.

Example: *Leslie bought 100 shares of stock at $12 per share in May and another 100 shares of the same stock in December for $30 per share. Three years later, when the stock soared in value to $80 per share, Leslie decided to sell it, after holding all of the stock more than 12 months. Assuming a 20% capital gains tax rate, here's what Leslie's tax bill would look like:*

May Stocks		December Stocks	
Sell 100 shares @ $80	$ 8,000	*Sell 100 shares @ $80*	$ 8,000
Bought 100 shares @ $12	− 1,200	*Bought 100 shares @ $30*	− 3,000
Gain	$ 6,800	*Gain*	$ 5,000
(times capital gains tax rate)	x .20	*(times capital gains tax rate)*	x .20
Taxes due	$ 1,360	*Taxes due*	$ 1,000

The tax basis for the stocks purchased in May is the $12 per share price. Upon sale of these stocks, there is a greater gain, which in turn creates a bigger tax bill. For the stocks purchased in December, with the $30 per share purchase price, the gain is less, and so are the taxes. If Leslie had to sell half of the shares, she would be better off selling the December stocks rather than those she purchased in May. By doing so, she saves $360 in taxes ($1,360 – $1,000 = $360).

Suppose Leslie's spouse offers to split the 200 shares of stock. Should Leslie take the May stocks or the December stocks? Leslie would be better off taking the December stocks, on which the taxes owed are lower. The fairest settlement would be for each spouse to take 50 of the May stocks and 50 of the December stocks. Another possibility would be to sell the stocks and split the tax bill equally. In that case, the calculations would look like this:

200 shares sold @ $80/share, held more than 12 months	$16,000
Tax Basis	
100 shares @ $12 = $1,200	
100 shares @ $30 = $3,000	
	– 4,200
Total Gain	= $11,800
Capital Gains Tax Rate	x 20%
Total Taxes on Gain	= $2,360
Each Spouse's Share of Taxes Due	= $1,180
Each Spouse's Share of Proceeds from Sale of Stock	= $4,720

Keep in mind that losses and gains are netted to determine the final tax liability, and commissions paid to brokers reduce the final tax liability. This example assumes that this was the only asset Leslie and her spouse sold this year.

8.   Beware of Inflation and Inflated Claims

Nothing takes the fun out of investing faster than losing money. Yet investors often overlook the simple factor of inflation, which constantly erodes the value of their holdings. To determine the true amount of return you earn from an investment, you must consider not only taxes, but inflation as well.

Take the simple example of a $10,000 certificate of deposit paying 3% interest at a time when inflation is running 3.5% annually. At the end of a year, the CD would seem to be worth $10,300 (the $300 earned via the 3% interest payment).

Assuming a federal tax bracket of 28%, the amount due the government would equal $84, reducing the $10,300 to only $10,216. Now factor in inflation. The $10,000 loses $350 (inflation of 3.5%) a year. At the end of a year, instead of $10,300, the CD really has the purchasing power of only $9,866 ($10,216 - $350), for a stunning loss of 1.34% on the original $10,000.

Be on guard, too, for inflated or misunderstood claims. Quite commonly, investors consider only one dimension, such as the interest rate an investment pays. They often forget about the numerous other factors that affect value, such as inflation, sales charges, management fees, dividend payments and other unforeseen risks.

9.   Look to Total Return, Not Yield

The commonly misunderstood differences between yield and total return illustrate the problem of one-dimensional analysis. *Yield* represents income in the form of dividends and interest. *Total return* is the yield plus the percentage of appreciation (growth) or loss in the per share value of an investment.

Example: *Ron saw an advertisement for a mutual fund offering a yield of 9%. Later that day, his broker called to tell him about another fund with a 5% yield. Which should he buy?*

> *Ron must look beyond yield to total return. The yield represents only the dividends or interest he'll receive on his shares. The total return takes into account both the yield and the percentage increase (appreciation) or decrease (loss) in the value of the shares.*

> *Ron's broker explained that the shares in the fund yielding 9% decreased in value by 20% the previous year, meaning the total return was a minus 11% (9% - 20%). The shares in the fund yielding 5%, on the other hand, increased 8.3%, for a total return of 13.3%. Note that the higher-yield fund actually produced a lower total return.*

Tax Basis and the IRS

When spouses divorce, information concerning the tax basis of an asset must be given to the spouse who receives the asset when title (ownership) changes. Because tax consequences are so fundamental to the selection of an asset, however, you should know the tax basis before you divide your assets, not after.

B. Steps to a Settlement

Now that you have an overview of the concepts to consider when making investment choices, it is time for a plan of action for reaching decisions. Follow these steps to formulate your plan:

1. What investments do you and your spouse hold?

2. Who owns each investment?

3. What is the Legal Value or Fair Market Value of each investment?

4. What is the Financial or After-Tax/After-Sale Value of each investment?

5. Which assets should you keep?

6. How will you and your spouse divide the investments?

7. How do you feel about your decision?

To answer these questions, complete the *Investment Chart* that follows. Begin by listing your investments in the far left column, using suggestions offered in Section 1, below. As you move on through Sections 2, 3 and 4, you will find detailed instructions on how to fill in the remaining columns. Finally, when you reach Step 6 in the "Steps to a Settlement" discussion, you will return to the chart to show how you and your spouse will divide assets.

Investment Chart

Investments (Section 1)	Who Owns It H - Husband W - Wife J - Jointly (Section 2)	Legal or Equity Value (Fair Market Value–Debt) (Section 3)	Financial (After-Tax/ After-Sale) Value (Section 4)	I Keep	Spouse Keeps	Sell and Split Proceeds
Cash & Cash Equivalents						
Bank Checking Accounts 1. 2. 3. 4.						
Bank Savings Accounts 1. 2. 3. 4.						
Certificates of Deposit 1. 2. 3.						
Money Market Funds 1. 2. 3.						
Money Market Mutual Funds 1. 2. 3.						
Personal Notes Payable to You 1. 2. 3.						
Other 1. 2. 3.						

Investment Chart

Investments (Section 1)	Who Owns It H - Husband W - Wife J - Jointly (Section 2)	Legal or Equity Value (Fair Market Value–Debt) (Section 3)	Financial (After-Tax/ After-Sale) Value (Section 4)	I Keep	Spouse Keeps	Sell and Split Proceeds
Stocks and Bonds						
Common Stocks 1. 2. 3.						
Preferred Stock 1. 2.						
Mutual Funds 1. 2. 3.						
Treasury Bills 1. 2. 3.						
Government Bonds (such as Ginnie Maes) 1. 2.						
Municipal Bonds 1. ___ Mutual Funds ___ Unit Trusts ___ Individual Bonds 2. ___ Mutual Funds ___ Unit Trusts ___ Individual Bonds						
Corporate Bonds 1. 2. 3.						
EE U.S. Savings Bonds 1. 2. 3.						
Zero Coupon Bonds 1. 2. 3.						
Other 1. 2.						

Investment Chart

Investments (Section 1)	Who Owns It H - Husband W - Wife J - Jointly (Section 2)	Legal or Equity Value (Fair Market Value–Debt) (Section 3)	Financial (After-Tax/ After-Sale) Value (Section 4)	I Keep	Spouse Keeps	Sell and Split Proceeds
Real Estate						
Income or Rental Properties 1. 2.						
Real Estate Investments Trusts (REITs) 1. 2.						
Raw Land 1. 2.						
Other 1. 2.						
Insurance Investments						
Cash Value of Life Insurance Policies 1. 2. 3.						
Annuities 1. 2. 3.						
Other 1. 2.						
Limited Partnerships						
Real Estate 1. 2.						
Oil and Gas 1. 2.						
Cable Television 1. 2.						
Equipment Leasing, etc. 1. 2.						
Other 1. 2.						

Investment Chart

Investments (Section 1)	Who Owns It H - Husband W - Wife J - Jointly (Section 2)	Legal or Equity Value (Fair Market Value–Debt) (Section 3)	Financial (After-Tax/ After-Sale) Value (Section 4)	I Keep	Spouse Keeps	Sell and Split Proceeds
Collectibles						
Gold & Silver 1. 2. 3.						
Coins, Jewelry, Art & Other Valuables 1. 2. 3.						
Other 1. 2. 3.						

1. What Investments Do You and Your Spouse Hold?

Using Column 1 of the Investment Chart, list all investments owned by you, your spouse and the two of you together. If you're unsure of certain investments, check old tax returns, or call your financial planner, stockbroker, discount brokerage firm, accountant or other tax advisor. You should also check online if you or your spouse has used electronic brokerage services.

2. Who Owns Each Investment?

In Column 2, show whether the investment is owned by husband (H), wife (W) or jointly (J). Investments owned jointly—except those that are separate property—are divided at divorce. Remember: The name of the person on the investment does not necessarily determine who owns it. Most states divide marital property, even when assets are only in one spouse's name.

List the investments owned separately by you and your spouse even though they won't be divided in the settlement. As you negotiate the settlement, it is possible that your or your spouse's separate investments will be considered in terms of income needs or for alimony.

If you need more information on what constitutes separate and marital property, see Chapter 12, Section A.

3. What Is the Legal (Equity) Value of Each Investment?

With investments, the Equity or Legal Value basically equals the Fair Market Value or face value—that is, the amount the investment is worth, less any debts. (For cash or cash-like assets—such as CDs or money market accounts—the Legal Value is the same as the account balance.) The Legal Value is generally the dollar amount attorneys use when discussing investments in trying to settle your divorce. In Sections B4 and B5, below, you will take a closer look at the Financial Value of your investments.

To find the Legal or Equity Value of your investments, you often need to do no more than place a phone call.

You may, however, run into problems determining which date to use in valuing the account. As mentioned in Chapter 5, many states value portfolio assets, like houses, as close to the *date of divorce or settlement* as possible, not the *date of separation*. Be sure to ask your attorney when assets are valued in your state.

Even if your state legally values assets at the date of separation, you and your spouse can agree to another date—and you should. Stocks, bonds, mutual funds and other liquid assets, particularly, should be valued as close as possible to the date you take control of them. Otherwise, if you value assets as of the date of separation, but then don't transfer them until months or years later, you may incur losses because of market forces.

Ultimately, to get through your divorce, you will probably need to find the account balance at different times. But you can begin by filling in the amounts for the Legal Value of investments in Column 3 of the *Investment Chart*. Use the following information to help you calculate or locate the Legal Value for each investment. Some of this information may be listed on your *Net Worth Statement* from Chapter 12.

Cash and cash equivalents. For your bank checking and savings accounts, certificates of deposit and money market funds, call the bank or look at your statement. For money market mutual funds, call the fund manager or administrator. The value of personal notes will probably be found among your personal papers. Find out whether the account is pledged as security for any debt. Be sure to investigate your spouse's business, if any, and any personal loans.

Stocks and bonds. For most stocks and bonds, you can check with your broker, your discount brokerage firm or an online service. If you call a brokerage firm, ask for the trading department to check the current price of stocks or mutual funds. You can also look at the business section of the newspaper. For stocks, look in the stock market tables for the price in the column labeled "Close." That's the price the stock was selling at when the market closed the day before. Multiply this number by the number of shares you own to get a ballpark value. Get an estimate of bonds by calling a broker or discount brokerage firm. Banks can give you the value of savings bonds. For mutual funds, look in the business section of the newspaper in the column labeled "NAV," the Net Asset Value.

Real estate. For income or rental property, you can use the services of an appraiser. (See Chapter 13, Section C2.) For the value of real estate investment trusts (REITs), ask a broker or brokerage firm or check the published values in a newspaper. To find the value of raw land, check the purchase price and ask a few real estate agents to find out whether land values have gone up or down in your area. It's also helpful to know if there is a balance due on the mortgage or if the property is free and clear of debt.

⚠ Two identical pieces of property can have different values if the rents charged in one building are not the same as the rents charged in the other. Rent control laws can also affect (bring down) the value of property. A spouse trying to artificially lower the value of rental property may rent units at below-market rates on a month-to-month basis, and then raise rates (and the property's value) after the divorce. If you suspect this is happening, check previous tax returns to see what rents were charged and ask Realtors how much rent is charged for comparable units in the area.

Insurance. Call or write the insurance company or broker and ask for the policy's current value and surrender value. If you're not the owner of the policy, the insurance company may refuse to give you the information. Call your spouse, or have your attorney call your spouse's attorney to get what you need.

Limited partnerships. Investments in businesses that operate as limited partnerships are more difficult to value than, say, investments in stocks or bonds. That's because, unlike stocks, there is no conventional trading market for interests in limited partnerships.

Certain "secondary markets," however, do buy and resell limited partnership interests. But these markets may assign widely divergent values to your limited partnership interests. Ask a stockbroker or financial planner for the names of several secondary market firms. In your survey, ask for the price at which the partnership shares could be sold and if additional costs would be incurred.

There will probably be a difference between what secondary markets say the partnership interest is worth and the amount you will actually realize from its sale. And there will be an even larger difference between your original purchase price and what you could sell it for now. Generally, these markets buy partnership shares at a deeply discounted price from the amount you originally paid or might receive if held until maturity. Use the amount the firms give you to fill in *The Investment Chart*.

Limited partnerships can be complicated investments, especially when you're attempting to value and divide your interests. For additional discussion, see subsection 4(e), below.

⚠️ Do not consider the value of a limited partnership as being equal to what you paid for it. Most limited partnerships, very popular investments in the 1980s, are worth significantly less now. (In fact, some are worthless.) If you take that asset at an inflated value, you'll be getting less in your settlement than you are entitled to.

Collectibles. Gold and silver values are listed, per ounce, in the daily newspaper. Coins, jewelry, art and collectibles must be appraised. Be sure to find the wholesale or resale price, not the retail price.

4. What Is the Financial (After-Tax/ After-Sale) Value of Each Investment?

Remember: You will need to know the tax basis of your investments to calculate gains, losses and your potential tax liability when you sell. In addition, the IRS requires that when you transfer property at divorce, you must provide tax basis information to the party who will keep the asset. If you are in the

dark about investments, you may need to press matters with your spouse to get the information to figure the tax basis. You cannot make informed decisions about which investments to accept or sell in the settlement unless you know your potential tax liabilities *before* any property transfer takes place.

Knowing the tax basis will help you find the Financial Value (or After-Sale/After-Tax Value) of your investments. For most investments, you will probably enlist the services of a professional tax advisor, but the following formulas and tips should help you get a ballpark estimate of your taxes and other costs.

After calculating the Financial Value of each investment, enter that value in Column 4 of the *Investment Chart*. But first, talk to a broker, financial planner or other investment professional to find out if your investments carry any other additional or hidden costs. If they do, subtract those amounts from the Financial Value before entering the values in Column 4. Be on the lookout for:

- *Account charges.* An amount charged for having an account with a broker, brokerage house or firm.

- *Redemption fees.* What you pay to redeem or sell the investment.

- *Trading fees.* A commission for buying or selling stocks or bonds.

- *Early withdrawal penalties.* Penalties incurred for early withdrawals on CDs, life insurance annuities and other investments.

a. Cash and Cash Equivalents

Because the tax basis on cash and cash equivalent is essentially what you will liquidate them for, there are no taxes due when you cash them in. To the extent that you earn interest on checking accounts, savings accounts, money market accounts or certificates of deposit, you must report that interest as income and pay taxes on the interest the year you earned it. To estimate the interest you will earn this year, call your banker. Then simply use the Legal Value ascertained in Section B3, above, as the Financial Value, and write that amount in Column 4 of the *Investment Chart*.

b. Stocks, Bonds and Mutual Funds

Calculating taxes and other costs associated with stocks and bonds will require you to do some tedious paperwork. Old statements will have to be gathered to reconstruct trading activity that has occurred in the past (perhaps, even, over several years). Only you can decide whether it's worth it to do that work yourself or hire someone else for the job. No matter who does it, you will need this information to complete your tax return when you sell stocks or bonds. There are good software packages and websites that can help you make this calculation. Several investment calculators may be found at www.financenter.com. Some broker-age or financial planning services companies may be able to determine this figure for you using their own specialized software programs.

i. Bonds

See an accountant or tax advisor to analyze the tax aspects of bonds. The Internal Revenue Code has numerous complicated rules depending on when the bonds were purchased and the type of bonds you own. For instance, some bonds, such as municipal bonds, are tax exempt. This means their interest is free from taxes. But if you bought them at a dis-count, when you redeem them or they mature, you will have to pay capital gains tax on the difference between the purchase price and maturity value.

Also keep in mind these general rules:

- EE U.S. Savings Bonds. You can pay taxes on the interest generated on EE bonds each year, as with most investments, or when you redeem the bonds. You can defer paying taxes on the interest if you roll the bonds forward into HH bonds.

- HH Bonds. These are government bonds, on which pay you interest semiannually.

- Zero Coupon (Corporate or Municipal) Bonds. On corporate bonds, you must pay taxes on interest earned each year even though you don't receive that interest until the bond matures.

Once you talk to an accountant or other tax advisor about your bonds, enter in Column 4 their Financial Value. This value can be determined using the formula for stocks and mutual funds, below. But keep in mind that the value of bonds fluctuates with interest rates. If interest rates in the U.S. have risen since you purchased your bond, the value will be slightly less than when you bought it. If interest rates have declined, the opposite will be true: Your bond, if you go to sell it, will be worth more than when you bought it. Check your monthly statement from your brokerage account or ask your broker for the amount for which you could liquidate your bond or bonds.

ii. Stocks and Mutual Funds

Use the following formula and instructions to find the Financial Value for your stocks and mutual funds. To complete the calculations, you will need to know the following:

$ _____ *Purchase Price*

Check your confirmation statement or call your broker. Be sure to include the initial investment plus any subsequent purchases you made.

$ _____ *Dividends Reinvested*

These should be shown on your monthly statement from the brokerage firm or mutual fund company. You can also look on tax Form 1099, sent annually to you from the company, showing dividends or interest earned each tax year.

$ _____ *Commissions and Transaction Fees*

These are fees paid when you purchase stocks and mutual funds unless the mutual fund is a "no load" fund, meaning it has no commission. The amount is on your confirmation statement; if it's not, call your broker or discount brokerage firm. For "load" mutual funds, the commissions, which are automatically charged, are reflected in the Purchase Price. Ask your broker if the fund has a redemption charge or surrender charge, a fee you pay when the fund is sold.

$ _____ *Equity Value*

Enter from Column 3 of the Investment Chart.

_____ % *Tax Rate*

You will need to know your income tax bracket and how long you have held the investment to know what to put here. For everyone except those in the 15% tax bracket, if you held the stock or mutual fund for more than 12 months, enter 20% as your tax rate. If you held it less than 12 months, check with your tax preparer for your precise tax bracket.

To find the Financial (After-Sale/After-Tax) Value of stocks and mutual funds, use the following formula:

1. Find the Tax Basis by adding the Purchase Price, Reinvested Dividends and Commissions and Transaction Fees (paid at purchase).

2. Find the Adjusted Sales Price by subtracting Commissions and Transaction Fees (to be paid when you sell) from the Fair Market Value.

3. Find the Gain (or Loss) by subtracting the Tax Basis from the Adjusted Sales Price.

4. Find the Taxes Due (or Tax Refund) by multiplying the Gain (or Loss) by the capital gains rate based on your tax bracket.

5. Find the Financial Value by subtracting the Taxes Due (or adding the Tax Refund) from (or to) the Adjusted Sales Price.

Example: *Let's assume you bought 100 shares of XYZ at $10/share and it has grown to $22/share.*

1. Find the Tax Basis by adding the Purchase Price, Reinvested Dividends and Commissions and Transaction Fees (paid at purchase).

Purchase Price	$1,000
Dividends Reinvested	+ 60
Commissions & Transaction Fees	+ 65
Tax Basis	= $1,125

2. Find the Adjusted Sales Price by subtracting Commissions and Transaction Fees (to be paid when you sell) from the Equity Value.

Equity Value	$2,200
Commissions & Transaction Fees	− 68
Adjusted Sales Price	= $2,132

3. Find the Gain (or Loss) by subtracting the Tax Basis from the Adjusted Sales Price.

Adjusted Sales Price	$2,152
Tax Basis	− 1,125
Gain (or Loss)	= $1,027

(If you incur a loss on this asset, you can net it against a gain on another asset and thereby reduce your capital gains tax liability.)

4. Find the Taxes Due by multiplying the Gain by the capital gains rate based on your tax bracket.

Gain		$1,027
Capital Gains Tax Rate	x	20%
Taxes Due	=	$ 205

5. Find the Financial Value by subtracting the Taxes Due from the Adjusted Sales Price.

Adjusted Sales Price	$2,152
Taxes Due	− 205
Financial Value	= $1,947

To apply this formula to your situation, fill in the blanks below. Copy this page to use as a worksheet or to calculate the value of additional investments.

1. Find the Tax Basis by adding the Purchase Price, Reinvested Dividends and Commissions and Transaction Fees (paid at purchase).

Purchase Price		$ _____
Dividends Reinvested	+	$ _____
Commissions & Transaction Fees	+	$ _____
Tax Basis	=	$ _____

2. Find the Adjusted Sales Price by subtracting Commissions and Transaction Fees (to be paid when you sell) from the Equity Value.

Equity Value	$ _____
Commissions &	
Transaction Fees	− $ _____
Adjusted Sales Price	= $ _____

3. Find the Gain (or Loss) by subtracting the Tax Basis from the Adjusted Sales Price.

Adjusted Sales Price	$ _____
Tax Basis	− $ _____
Gain (or Loss)	= $ _____

4. Find the Taxes Due by multiplying the Gain by the capital gains rate based on your tax bracket.

Gain	$ _____
Capital Gains Tax Rate	x $ _____
Taxes Due	= $ _____

5. Find the Financial Value by subtracting the Taxes Due from the Adjusted Sales Price.

Adjusted Sales Price	$ _____
Taxes Due	− $ _____
Financial Value	= $ _____

Keep in mind that the above formula calculates only federal income taxes. In most states, you will have to pay state taxes as well.

iii. Dividing Stocks, Bonds and Mutual Funds: Consider the Tax Basis

As noted at the beginning of this section, the IRS requires that you give information about the tax basis of an asset to the person receiving it at the time of transfer. It's very important for you to understand the tax basis of an asset. If you don't, you could decide to keep investments that give you a higher tax burden than those your spouse will carry. At the least, you ought to share the tax burden equally.

Once you know the tax basis, you can calculate the taxes due if you were to sell the assets. Knowing the tax liability enables you to make an equal comparison between investment assets and other assets. This knowledge will also influence your tax strategy after the divorce, as you consider whether to sell or keep the investments.

The IRS allows three different methods to calculate the taxes. In these examples, a gain is assumed. If you have experienced a loss on your investments, the investment may be of value if you have a gain elsewhere—but only if you sell the asset immediately.

First In-First Out. If you've purchased shares of stock over several years at different prices, this method lets you sell the first batch you bought. For example, Mindy and Ryan bought 300 shares of stock at $13 per share in 1994 and another 300 shares of the same stock at $20 per share in 1996. The stock is now worth $25 per share. They decide to sell 300 shares before they divorce. But which 300?

Using the "First In-First Out" option, they would sell the 300 shares bought in 1994. They would have to pay taxes on the gain of $12 per share ($25 Fair Market Value - $13 Purchase Price = $12 Gain). Had they sold the 1996 shares, they'd owe taxes on a gain of only $5 per share ($25 Fair Market Value - $20 Purchase Price = $5 Gain). But by selling the shares that gave them a larger profit, they can split the taxes owed.

As an alternative to selling shares before the divorce, Mindy and Ryan consider splitting the 600 shares in half. It's fair on the surface. If one spouse keeps the 1994 shares, and the other keeps the 1996 shares, however, the division becomes unfair because the tax liabilities differ. They could even things up again if they divide other property to cover the tax difference.

Specific Identification. This time, assume that Mindy and Ryan bought their 600 shares at various times paying prices ranging from $13 to $20 per share. If they decide to sell 300 shares before their divorce and use the Specific Identification option, they would pinpoint precisely which 300 shares to sell—perhaps 100 bought at $13, another 100 bought at $18 and the final 100 purchased at $20 per share.

If they split the shares as part of their divorce settlement, they should consider the tax liability for the shares bought at each price. If Mindy wants 300 of the "$20 stocks"—leaving Ryan with all of the stocks purchased at $13 and $18 per share—Ryan will pay more in taxes than Mindy will pay.

Average Basis. Mindy and Ryan's third option is the Average Basis. As the name implies, this option lets them take an across-the-board average tax basis on all the shares of stock, no matter when purchased and at what price per share. They would simply take the total amount paid (and dividends reinvested) and divide it by the total number of shares owned.

Because of the difficult calculations and the fact that supporting documentation regarding reinvestments and commissions is often missing, many divorcing couples use the Average Basis to divide stocks and mutual funds. Before settling on it, however, compare it to the First In-First Out and Specific Identification options. Incorporate the calculations from this section on Tax Basis options with Financial Values when you read Sections B5 and B6, below.

Document Dividends and Reinvestments

When Evelyn divorced in 1994, she got $5,000 worth of shares in a mutual fund as part of her settlement. A savvy investor, she sold the shares in the last week of September 1997 for $10,000. Initially, it appeared Evelyn would pay taxes on the $5,000 gain: $10,000 (sales price) - $5,000 (original price) = $5,000 (gain).

But Evelyn had kept records showing every time she reinvested the dividends she received back into the fund. In adding up each reinvestment, she found that she had reinvested total dividends of $1,600 into the fund. This finding lowered her tax liability. Remember: Her tax basis is the original purchase price plus reinvested dividends. Her original $5,000 investment, plus the dividend reinvestments of $1,600, totaled $6,600. The amound of gain she had to pay taxes on,, therefore, was only $3,400, not $5,000.

---

c. Real Estate

In valuing real estate investments, you can consider many of the factors raised in Chapter 13, assuming you own a family home. If you haven't read that material, refer to it for basic formulas and an explanation of real estate terms.

Unlike the family home, however, investment properties can be hard to value. The value of the property is affected by the local economy, rental vacancy rates, rent control or stabilization laws, property management and other market forces. Nevertheless, you can estimate the Financial (After-Sale/After-Tax) Value of your real estate investments by using these guidelines.

$ _____   *REITs (Real estate investment trusts)*

A real estate investment trust company invests in a variety of holdings, which can range from apartments and hotels to office buildings and shopping centers. Because most REITs are publicly traded, their value is easily identified. Refer to the stock tables in the newspaper, or ask your broker for current values. To find the Financial Value, subtract any commissions or fees from the Fair Market Value.

$ _____ *Raw land*

Real estate agents and appraisers normally base the value of (undeveloped) land on current comparables, that is, the amount at which comparable parcels of land are currently selling. Other factors to consider in determining the real financial value of raw land are:

- how land will be affected by a city's General Plan

- the kind of building permits that have been issued in the area, and

- how land surrounding your land will be used.

Real estate agents can help you answer these questions. Also, talk with the county building permit office and the city office regarding permits and future land use. Then, make your best "guesstimate" for the value, and use that number as the Financial Value.

$ _____ *Income or rental properties*

For most income-producing property, use the formula in Chapter 13, Section C6 to determine the Financial Value. With rental property, you must also consider total depreciation taken: the amount you've deducted in taxes to account for the declining value of the property.

If you own real property, such as a residential rental, know that there is an exception to the lower capital gains rates that went into effect under the Taxpayer Relief Act of 1997. Not all the net capital gain that you have on this kind of property will qualify for the lower rate of 20% (or 10% for those in the 15% bracket). Instead, to the extent that you have taken depreciation on the property, your gain will be taxed at a maximum rate of 25%.

Example: *Jim and Carol own a rental property, which they bought in 1993 for $100,000. Over the years, they have taken $15,000 in depreciation deductions, so the property's adjusted tax basis is now $85,000. They sell the property in 1998 for $150,000, realizing a $65,000 long-term capital gain ($150,000 – $85,000 = $65,000). Assuming Jim and Carol are in the 39.6% tax bracket, $15,000 of their gain (the amount of the depreciation they have taken) will be taxed at 25%. The rest of their gain ($50,000) will be taxed at the lower rate of 20%.*

To find the Financial Value of rental real estate, you will need to know the following:

$ _____ *Fair Market Value*

Single-family homes are somewhat easier to value than commercial, industrial or multifamily dwellings. For single-family residential real estate, you can ask several real estate agents or appraisers for current comparable values. With other types of rental units, however, you will need to consult an appraiser or a broker who specializes in evaluating the type of property you have. See Chapter 13, Section C2, for information on finding an appraiser.

Real Estate Values

Property Address or Description	Fair Market Value	Current Debt on Property	Total Capital Improvements	Total Depreciation Taken
Rental house, 323 Third Street, Rye, NY	$ 100,000	$ 60,000	$ 20,000	$ 40,000
Duplex, Sun Court, Surf City, CA	$ 280,000	$ 100,000	$ 0	$ 32,000
	$	$	$	$
	$	$	$	$
	$	$	$	$

An appraiser will use one—or a combination—of these three recognized calculations:

Cost Approach. The Fair Market Value equals the amount it would cost to replace a building, plus the land's value. This approach usually applies to single-family dwellings.

Market Data Approach. Also used with single-family dwellings, this approach compares properties that all provide similar cash flows to determine the Fair Market Value.

Income Approach. The Fair Market Value is based on the cash flow a building currently generates plus an estimate of the amount it will generate in the future. Commercial, industrial or multifamily dwellings are often appraised with this approach.

Ask the appraiser which approach is being used to value your property—and why. Just as a retirement plan can be worth different amounts if appraisers use different assumptions, so too can real estate values vary if different approaches are used. Avoid disputes by making sure you and your spouse or your appraisers are basing the Fair Market Value on the same types of calculations.

When you know the Fair Market Value of your properties, use the chart below to keep track of those values. Write the address or the description by which you and your spouse will refer to the property in the first column, and the Fair Market Value in the second column. The remaining columns will be addressed as you continue reading this section.

$ _____ *Debt on Property*

The debt connected to real estate equals what you owe to any lenders (mortgages) plus any liabilities (liens) on the house. All liabilities must be paid before any cash disbursements can be made from the sale of real estate. The mortgage due is sometimes called the "payoff balance."

To find the current debt on the house, talk to your lender and check the property's title for any liens you're unaware of. (See Chapter 13, Section C3.) List the debt in Column 3 of the *Real Estate Values* chart.

$ _____ *Total Capital Improvements or Depreciation*

To find total capital improvements made or depreciation taken on rental properties, check your records or previous tax returns, or talk to your accountant or tax advisor. List the totals in the fourth column of the *Real Estate Values* chart.

_____ % *Your Tax Bracket*

By now, you have probably established your tax bracket, either by checking income tax schedules or talking with your accountant. You will need this information in the upcoming formula.

$ _____ *Cost of Sale*

In calculating how much money it takes to actually sell your rental property, you can do a quick ballpark estimate, or you can follow these steps to find as precise a figure as possible. To find this number, you'll have to include not only the costs of sale, but also the amount it will take to fix up the property and prepare it for a sale.

To get a ballpark amount for the sales cost, multiply the Fair Market Value by .07. Seven percent is an accepted estimate of what it costs to sell a house. Obviously, some sales will yield higher or lower costs of sale, but 7% will do.

To obtain a more accurate cost-of-sale figure, you need to total the following amounts:

$ _____ *Agent's Commission*

The amount a real estate agent charges you for selling property. Generally, it averages 6% of the final selling price. This fee can sometimes be negotiated down.

$ _____ *Closing Costs*

Included in these costs are escrow fees, recording costs, appraisal fees and miscellaneous expenses which can add up to thousands of dollars. A lender or real estate agent can help you figure the exact amount.

$ _____ *Attorney's Fees*

In a few states, you will need to hire an attorney to help you "close" the sale of real property. If you used an attorney when you bought the property, base your figure on that amount, taking into account the fact that most lawyers raise their fees over time. Otherwise, ask a real estate agent for an estimate.

$ _____ *Fix-up Costs*

Estimate here the amount of money you will have to spend to prepare the property for sale.

Now add all of these figures which apply to your property and fill in the Cost of Sale.

To find the Financial or After-Tax/After-Sale Value of rental Real Estate, use this formula:

1. Find the Equity by subtracting the Debt from the Fair Market Value.

2. Find the Tax Basis by adding Total Capital Improvements to the Purchase Price and then subtracting Total Depreciation taken.

3. Find the Adjusted Sales Price by subtracting the Cost of Sale from the Fair Market Value.

4. Find the Gain (or Loss) on the potential sale of the property by subtracting the Tax Basis from the Adjusted Sales Price. If you experienced a Loss, you may have no tax liability and be able to offset other Gains with your Loss to reduce your Taxes Due.

5. Determine the portion of gain related to depreciation taken. That portion will be taxed at 25%, while the remainder of the gain will be taxed at either 20% (if you are in a tax bracket above 15%) or 10% (if you are in the 15% tax bracket).

6. Find the Financial or After-Tax/After-Sale Value by subtracting Cost of Sale from the Equity and then subtracting the Taxes Due.

Example:

1. Find the Equity by subtracting the Debt from the Fair Market Value.

Fair Market Value	$100,000
Debt	– 60,000
Equity	= $ 40,000

2. Find the Tax Basis by adding Total Capital Improvements to the Purchase Price and then subtracting Total Depreciation taken.

Purchase Price		$ 50,000
Total Improvements	+	5,000
	=	55,000
Total Depreciation	–	12,500
Tax Basis	=	$ 42,500

3. Find the Adjusted Sales Price by subtracting the Cost of Sale from the Fair Market Value.

Fair Market Value		$100,000
Cost of Sale	–	7,000
Adjusted Sales Price	=	$ 93,000

4. Find the Gain (or Loss) on the potential sale of the property by subtracting the Tax Basis from the Adjusted Sales Price.

Adjusted Sales Price	=	$ 93,000
Tax Basis	–	42,500
Gain (or Loss)	=	$ 50,500

5. Find the Taxes Due by multiplying the depreciation portion of the Gain by 25% and the remaining Gain by 20% (assuming you are in the 28%+ tax bracket). Total these numbers for the Taxes Due.

Gain From Depreciation		$12,500
	x	25%
		$ 3,125
Remaining Gain		$49,500
	–	12,500
		$37,000
	x	20%
		$7,400
Taxes Due		$3,125
	+	7,400
		$10,525

6. Find the Financial or After-Tax/After-Sale Value by subtracting Cost of Sale from the Equity and then subtracting the Taxes Due.

Equity		$ 40,000
Cost of Sale	–	7,000
Taxes Due	–	13,860
Financial or After-Tax/After-Sale Value	=	$ 19,140

To apply this formula to your situation, fill in the blanks below:

1. Find the Equity by subtracting the Debt from the Fair Market Value.

Fair Market Value		$ _____
Debt	–	$ _____
Equity	=	$ _____

2. Find the Tax Basis by adding Total Capital Improvements to the Purchase Price and then subtracting Total Depreciation taken.

Purchase Price		$ _____
Total Improvements	+	$ _____
	=	$ _____
Total Depreciation	–	$ _____
Tax Basis	=	$ _____

3. Find the Adjusted Sales Price by subtracting the Cost of Sale from the Fair Market Value.

Fair Market Value		$ _____
Cost of Sale	–	$ _____
Adjusted Sales Price	=	$ _____

4. Find the Gain (or Loss) on the potential sale of the property by subtracting the Tax Basis from the Adjusted Sales Price.

Adjusted Sales Price		$ _____
Tax Basis	–	$ _____
Gain (or Loss)	=	$ _____

5. Find the Taxes Due by multiplying the depreciation portion of the Gain by 25% and the remaining Gain by 20% (assuming you are in the 28%+ tax bracket). Total these numbers for the Taxes Due.

Gain From Depreciation		$ _____
	x	25%
		$ _____
Remaining Gain		$ _____
	–	$ _____
		$ _____
	x	20%
		$ _____
Taxes Due		$ _____
	+	$ _____
		$ _____

6. Find the Financial or After-Tax/After-Sale Value by subtracting Cost of Sale from the Equity and then subtracting the Taxes Due.

Equity		$ _____
Cost of Sale	–	$ _____
Taxes Due (or Tax Refund)	–	$ _____
After-Tax/After-Sale Value	=	$ _____

Who Pays the Rent

If you or your spouse moves from the family home, you can make temporary arrangements for paying the mortgage and other bills. But what if you own rental property and the renters move? Who will pay the mortgage? Or suppose you and your spouse decide to sell the property. Who will pay for repairs? Who will be reimbursed for capital improvements to the property? You and your spouse must settle these questions. If you pay these costs alone, keep good records of every expense so that you will have a chance to get reimbursed as part of the final settlement.

d. Insurance

Buying more insurance than you need and paying too much in insurance premiums are common mistakes. At divorce, you have the opportunity to take a good look at your policies and correct these mistakes if necessary.

Whole life or universal life insurance not only provides income in the event of someone's death, but also has some investment benefits, although these benefits may be minimal compared with other investments. As you pay your premiums, a cash reserve builds up. This reserve increases over and above the premiums you pay because you earn interest on your premiums. The reserve also grows because the expenses, such as commissions paid to brokers, decrease over time. Be aware, though, that the cash value decreases if you borrow money against the policy.

Term policies, on the other hand, provide death benefits only. They have no cash buildup and therefore have no growth potential.

Choose to keep only those policies you truly need for insurance. Never surrender an essential policy or let it lapse without having replacement insurance, but do get rid of any unnecessary policies. Life insurance companies select policy-holders with care. If you have to apply for insurance in the future, you may be denied coverage because of a yet-unknown health problem. Keep in mind, however, if you surrender policies with cash value—that is, you turn them in and collect the cash—you will have to pay taxes on the interest earned. You figure the interest by subtracting the total premiums paid and the surrender charges from the cash value. The difference is the interest, and that amount is what you'd have to report to the IRS as income.

i. Annuities

Annuities are investments offered by insurance companies that are meant to provide income at retirement. Annuities are discussed in Chapter 14.

ii. Cash Value Policies

Any policy with a cash value is often called, logically enough, a "cash value policy." If you decide that your policy is not the most cost-effective for you, you can use the cash value to purchase another insurance policy that is more suitable. The benefit of buying another policy rather than taking the cash out of your current policy is that you can defer the taxes you would owe on the accrued interest. (Internal Revenue Code § 1035.) The only draw-back is that you will have to pay a commission when you purchase the new policy, and these costs will initially decrease the cash value of the new policy.

To quickly estimate the Financial Value of your insurance (a detailed analysis is not necessary), you need to obtain the following:

$ _____ *Cash Value*

Take a look at the most current policy statement and see if it shows the cash value. If it doesn't, ask your insurance agent.

$ _____ *Surrender Charges*

Again, this information should be on the current policy, or check with your agent.

$ _____ *Premiums Paid*

Check the most current policy statement or ask your agent.

Following the example in the *Value of Insurance Policy* chart, below, use the formula shown to find the Financial or After-Tax/After-Sale Value on cash value insurance policies.

e. Limited Partnerships

You may have difficulty finding an accurate value for your interests in a limited partnership. It's often hard to tell how much was invested and how much has been received in tax benefits (write-offs). We do not provide detailed information on figuring the Financial Value of limited partnerships. Instead, we urge you to consult your accountant to get an understanding of the value of these assets and to ask your broker for information on companies that

Value of Insurance Policy

	Example	*Your Policy*
Cash Value	$10,000	
Surrender Charge	– 500	
Cash Surrender Value	$9,500	
Cash Surrender Value	$9,500	
Premiums Paid	– 6,000	
Gain (or Loss)	$3,500	
Gain (or Loss)	$3,500	
Tax Bracket	x .28	
Taxes Due	$980	
Cash Surrender Value	$9,500	
Taxes Due	– 980	
Financial or After-Tax/After-Sale Value	$8,520	

specialize in secondary market sales of limited partnership units.

Also, call the general partner (and any other limited partners) to find out everything you can about the partnership, especially its economic health. Be alert to these problems with limited partnerships:

- You may not be able to divide your interest. General partners may not be willing to divide the investment in the limited partnership between you and your spouse. If you can't divide your interest, and neither of you wants to give up your interest to the other in exchange for other property, be sure you and your ex-spouse have a carefully written agreement about how taxes, bookkeeping and distribution checks will be handled after the divorce.

- A limited partnership can generate taxable income that you never receive, called phantom income. Ask the general partner whether phantom income is expected and how much of this income will be taxable.

- Some limited partnerships make requests for additional investments (called capital calls) from the limited partners. Before keeping a limited

partnership, check the original investment document, contact your accountant or ask the general partner if you may be liable for additional investments.

- All limited partnerships are risky investments, because the general partner has almost complete control over the assets of the partnership. A general partner's decision to sell an asset or allow a foreclosure can create a tax liability for you. You might call your broker or the general partner to determine when the sale of assets in the partnership is anticipated and what the tax consequences would be.

- Bookkeeping can be difficult. When the partnership sends out its IRS reporting form (K-1) each tax year, it sends only one form to each investor. The partnership usually sends only one distribution check as well. If you and your spouse are unable to divide the partnership interest, then only one of you will receive the form and the check.

Unless you've been lucky, limited partnerships are more trouble to keep after divorce than they are usually worth.

f. Collectibles

Your biggest problem in determining the Financial Value of collectibles (like art, special plates or even baseball cards) will be finding a valuation on which you and your spouse can agree. You may hear any number of conflicting values depending on who is making the appraisal.

To find the Financial Value of collectibles, first list the following:

$ _____ *Purchase Price*

Check original receipts, look at old tax returns or consult with a broker.

$ _____ *Acquisition Costs*

Did you drive to a distant city to buy the piece? Stay overnight in a hotel? Pay admission to an antique fair? Any or all of these could add to the taxable cost basis of the antique, meaning you'll owe less taxes on it when sold.

$ _____ *Improvements*

Did you restore the piece or do anything to it—such as reupholstering, refinishing or refurbishing—that increased its value?

$ _____ *Selling Price or Wholesale Value*

Ask a dealer, auctioneer or consignment shop to give you an estimate of the wholesale value of your holdings. Many people mistakenly assume that some items, such as diamonds, are worth a great deal because they consider only the retail value. But jewelers buy loose diamonds at wholesale prices and will not pay you more than that price when they buy from you.

$ _____ *Commissions*

Talk with a broker, a wholesaler or anyone familiar with the market for your item. With collectibles, the commission is as high as 30% of the sale price.

_____ *% Tax Bracket*

Consult accountant or previous tax schedules.

To find the Financial or After-Sale/After-Tax Value of collectibles, use this formula:

1. Find Tax Basis by adding Commissions (paid at purchase), Acquisition Costs, Improvements and Purchase Price.

2. Find Adjusted Sale Price by subtracting Commissions (due at sale) from the Selling Price or Wholesale Value.

3. Find Gain (or Loss) by subtracting the Tax Basis from the Adjusted Sales Price.

    (If you incur a loss on this asset, you can net it against a gain on another asset and thereby reduce your capital gains tax liability.)

4. Find Taxes Due by multiplying the Gain times the capital gains tax rate of 28%.

5. Find the Financial Value by subtracting (or adding) Taxes Due (or Tax Benefit) from (or to) the Adjusted Sale Price.

Example: *Janet and Tom had purchased a painting they now wanted to sell. It had gone down in value, so they had a loss they can net against other gains.*

1. Find Tax Basis by adding Commissions (paid at purchase), Acquisition Costs, Improvements and Purchase Price.

Purchase Price		$10,000
Acquisition Costs	+	250
Improvements	+	250
Commissions	+	500
Tax Basis	=	$11,000

2. Find Adjusted Sale Price by subtracting Commissions (due at sale) from the Selling Price or Wholesale Value.

Selling Price or Wholesale Value		$ 7,000
Commissions	–	500
Adjusted Sales Price	=	$ 6,500

3. Find Gain (or Loss) by subtracting the Tax Basis from the Adjusted Sales Price.

Adjusted Sales Price		$ 6,500
Tax Basis	–	11,000
Gain (or Loss)	=	$(4,500)

4. Find Taxes Due by multiplying the Gain times the capital gains tax rate of 28%.

Gain (or Loss)		$(4,500)
Capital Gains Tax Rate	x	28%
Taxes Due (or Benefit)	=	$(1,260)

5. Find Financial Value by subtracting the Tax Benefit from the Adjusted Sale Price.

Adjusted Sales Price		$ 6,500
Taxes Due (or Benefit)	–	($1,260)
Financial Value	=	$ 7,760

If loss is not netted against gains, you can only use up to $3,000 in losses in one year. So you would carry forward the $1,500 ($4,500 loss – $3,000 = $1,500) to the next year.

To apply this formula to your situation, fill in the blanks below:

1. Find Tax Basis by adding Commissions (paid at purchase) and Purchase Price.

Purchase Price		$ _____
Commissions	+	$ _____
Tax Basis	=	$ _____

2. Find Adjusted Sale Price by subtracting Commissions (due at sale) from the Selling Price or Wholesale Value.

Selling Price or Wholesale Value		$ _____
Commissions	–	$ _____
Adjusted Sales Price	=	$ _____

3. Find Gain (or Loss) by subtracting the Tax Basis from the Adjusted Sales Price.

Adjusted Sales Price		$ _____
Tax Basis	–	$ _____
Gain (or Benefit)	=	$ _____

4. Find Taxes Due by multiplying the Gain times the capital gains rate of 28%.

Gain		$ _____
Capital Gains Tax Rate	x	28%
Taxes Due (or Benefit)	=	$ _____

5. Find Financial Value by subtracting the Taxes Due or Benefit from the Adjusted Sale Price.

Adjusted Sales Price		$ _____
Taxes Due	–	$ _____
Financial Value	=	$ _____

5. Which Assets Should You Keep?

Once you know the Financial (or After-Tax/After-Sale) Value of investments, you have a starting point for negotiating with your spouse. The values are useful whether you want to sell your assets to the person you're divorcing, buy them for yourself or divide them between you.

The ultimate decision to keep an investment depends on many factors including your age, risk tolerance, income needs and investment experience. Asking yourself the following simple questions will help you make sound decisions about your investments.

1. Has this investment performed well?

If Yes, go to Question 2.

If No, consider these options:

___ Sell the asset before the divorce so you and your soon-to-be-ex-spouse share costs of sale, taxes and other expenses.

___ Take the asset for yourself, but only if it provides you with the benefit of a tax loss. That is, it can offset a gain you may have on another asset. You should consult a tax expert to determine your need to take any losses.

___ Offer to sell the asset to your spouse in the divorce settlement.

2. *Is this investment appropriate for me—is it providing the income, growth, liquidity or security I need?*

If Yes, how long do you plan to keep it?

___ Long Term—buy out your spouse's interest and keep this investment.

___ Short Term—consider selling before your divorce becomes final, sharing the proceeds, taxes and other costs with your spouse and then using the proceeds to purchase a similar investment.

If No, consider these options:

___ Sell before your divorce is final, sharing the proceeds, taxes and other costs with your spouse.

___ Buy out your spouse and sell immediately to take advantage of tax losses.

___ Let your spouse buy out your share or interest in the investment.

6. How Will You and Your Spouse Divide the Investments?

You are now ready to prepare your position for negotiating over investment assets. Look at the *Investment Chart* you completed earlier in this chapter and use it to show how investments will be handled in your divorce. For each investment listed in Column 1, put a check mark in one of the last three columns to show if you intend to keep the asset, have your spouse keep it or sell it and split the proceeds. If you have cash value life insurance or rental property, be sure to read the sections that follow before making a final decision about these assets.

a. Special Problems With Cash Value Life Insurance

The Financial Value of the policy isn't the only consideration with cash value life insurance. Be sure to consider the following before choosing to keep this asset in your divorce:

• What is the quality of the insurance company? You may be able to evaluate the quality of an insurance company by checking its ratings by one of the three main rating services, Standard and Poor's, Moody's and A.M. Best. But these ratings provide no guarantees. Before it folded in 1990, for example, Executive Life received an A+ rating from Best, considered the top rating company.

• What interest rate are you receiving on the premiums accruing as your cash value? Would alternative—yet safe—investments, such as corporate bonds, municipal bonds or federal government bonds, yield you more?

• Are there any loans outstanding on the policy? If so, the amount paid at death will be reduced by the outstanding loan. Before taking this asset at divorce, be sure the loans are paid back so the full amount is paid, or recognize that the death benefits will be reduced.

b. Special Problems With Rental Property

The Financial Value of the property isn't the only consideration with rental property. Be sure to ask yourself the following questions before choosing to keep this asset in your divorce:

• Where is the property located? Is it on a busy street? On the beach? Given its location, what is its potential for appreciation?

• What is the quality of the neighborhood? Is it improving or deteriorating?

• How will your property be affected by changes in the local economy?

- Are newer and nicer buildings directly competing for your renters?

- Are your rents above or below market?

- What does it cost to maintain and manage the property? Is your cash flow positive or negative? Can you afford the property when renters vacate and the income is down?

- What are the tax incentives or disincentives to keeping the property?

- What would it cost to improve the property?

- How much income can you expect the property to generate?

- When might you sell? Can you determine your rate of return over that time?

- What is the vacancy rate?

- What kind of loan do you have—fixed or adjustable rate? If it's adjustable and interest rates rise, can you still afford it?

    Your answers will help you to reach one of three conclusions:

1. The property has strong potential (the location is great, there's little rental competition, operating costs and vacancy rates are low) and it should appreciate faster than other investments I could make using the same amount of money.

    It would be a good asset to keep.

2. The property has some potential, but it's uncertain. Other investments using the same amount of money may outperform this one.

    We should probably sell now and split the proceeds, or my spouse can take it.

3. This property has little potential (operating costs are high, the location is bad and/or vacancy rates are high) and other investments have a higher probability of meeting my needs.

    We should probably sell now and split the proceeds, or my spouse can take it.

Now review all your investments—stocks, bonds, rental real estate, limited partnerships and others—and write your decisions on the *Investment Chart* earlier in this chapter.

■

CHAPTER 16

Evaluating Employee Benefits and Stock Options

*As companies get more creative in compensating their
employees, the stakes are raised in the divorce process.*

Today's employees receive more than what shows up
on the pay stub or tax form. Benefits such as stock
options, insurance, retirement plans and other
fringes are forms of compensation. And to the
extent they can be considered income to you or
your spouse, they can help determine how much
spousal and child support you are eligible to receive,
or must pay.

For divorce purposes, the key question is
whether to classify various types of employee
compensation as:

- *income*—a continuing source of money that can
  be applied to alimony and child support

- an *asset*—property of some sort that can be
  apportioned between the spouses in the settlement

- neither income nor an asset, or

- both. (For more on the distinction between
  income and assets, see Chapter 12.)

This chapter looks at different forms of employee compensation in light of their value to you
and your soon-to-be-ex-spouse in the divorce
process.

A. Employee Benefits

Employee benefits (also known as nonwage compensation) have mushroomed in recent years as
companies and nonprofit organizations have sought
to attract and retain employees. Start-up businesses,
especially, use nonwage compensation because they
may not yet generate the cash to pay competitive
salaries. Employee benefits include retirement plans,

both pension plans and deferred compensation plans; insurance coverage; disability and death benefits; employee assistance plans; educational assistance; and perks such as company cars, health club memberships and discounts at stores or hotels.

From the standpoint of divorce law, this area is far from settled. Courts can and do disagree about how to classify particular benefits at divorce. One court may say that use of a company car lowers an employee's living expenses, freeing up more money for spousal and child support; another may not. So it's important to talk to your attorney about the role that employee benefits may play in your own case.

Various types of retirement plans, employer-sponsored and otherwise, are explained in Chapter 14. In the following sections, we provide an overview of other common employee benefits and how they could affect your divorce settlement. The question that's usually at issue is whether a particular benefit can be considered taxable (or gross) income. If so, a court may take it into account in determining levels of child and spousal support. In other instances, a benefit may be regarded as a marital asset—something that gets allocated between spouses at the time of divorce.

1.   Health Insurance

The employee benefits that most affect day-to-day living are in the insurance area. Medical insurance, especially, is one of the most important benefits that are subject to a divorce court's powers. Health insurance can also cover prescriptions, therapy, dental and vision coverage and the like.

Many health insurance plans provide benefits through an insurance company, a community service organization (such as Blue Cross-Blue Shield) or a health maintenance organization (HMO). Other plans are paid directly by the employer (known as "self-funded" or "self-insured" plans).

An employer's contributions for health insurance are *not* considered taxable income to the employee. Nor does an employee report as taxable income amounts paid by the insurance company for covered medical expenses.

A court may order a parent to provide health coverage for children as part of a child support order (see Chapter 18). But this benefit is not considered an asset to divide.

2. Disability Plans

These plans protect employees against the risk that illness or injury will interrupt or terminate their ability to work. Typically, the employer offers coverage for disability under an accident or health plan.

Usually, the employer's contribution is excluded from the employee's gross income on the tax return. In the event of disability, however, amounts the employee receives are included as gross income.

Employer-sponsored disability insurance is not an asset for division between spouses at divorce. But a contribution paid by the employer may be factored into the court's calculation of child and spousal support.

3.   Group Term Life Insurance

This is an insurance policy carried by an employer to provide death benefits to employees and, occasionally, to retirees. Unless an employee is upper management, this insurance is generally available only while employed.

The employee generally excludes from taxable income the employer's contribution to the premium up to $50,000. In the event of death, the beneficiary is not taxed on the death benefits received.

Group term life insurance is not an asset that a court divides. However, the court may order a party to maintain all employer-provided life insurance, naming a former spouse or children as the beneficiary (see Chapter 10).

4.   Accidental Death or Dismemberment Insurance

Again, employer contributions to premium payments and insurance proceeds received by the employee are excluded from the employee's income.

If the employee pays the premium, the amount paid may be a factor the court considers in a child support order; however, the policy itself is not an asset to divide.

5. Medical Savings Accounts

A medical savings account involves a tax-exempt trust or custodial account established to pay medical expenses in conjunction with a health plan that carries a high deductible. Recently renamed "Archer MSAs," these accounts are available to employers with 50 or fewer employees to provide a tax-favored way to save and pay for medical expenses for their employees. The employer may pay the entire cost, or the employee may contribute to the account as well.

Any payments the employer makes to the plan are not included in the employee's gross income. If the employee contributes, the contribution is deductible from gross income on tax returns.

If an employee takes money out of an Archer MSA, this distribution is not considered part of the employee's gross income—as long as the employee used the money to pay for medical expenses and did not have other medical coverage. However, if the distribution is used for nonmedical expenses, then it is included in gross income. In addition, it's subject to a 15% tax penalty.

Any amount in an employee spouse's account on the date of separation or divorce is an asset assigned to the employee spouse. The employee spouse can be ordered to pay existing marital medical expenses with money on deposit. (See Chapter 10 for a discussion of retaining health care coverage through a spouse's employer.)

6. Dependent Care Assistance Programs

Such a program provides child care or related services for employees who need this help in order to work. Frequently, employers offer child care benefits as a choice under a cafeteria plan (see below). The program may offer direct payments to the employee, or it may involve an employer-sponsored child care center.

The employee's gross income does not include amounts contributed by the employer. This benefit is not subject to division as an asset. But the court may consider the program's value as compensation and may order an employee to provide this benefit as part of a child support order.

7. Cafeteria Plans

Cafeteria plans offer participants a choice of certain benefits—such as medical insurance, group term life, disability insurance and child care—or cash. Employees may also be given the option under a cafeteria plan to use, sell or buy additional vacation days.

Typically, in a cafeteria plan the employee elects before the beginning of the year to have his or her salary reduced. The amount of the reduction is then applied to the employee's share of the insurance premium or to cover other expenses such as child care.

The value of the benefits the employee receives is excluded from the employee's gross income. But any cash the employee receives under the plan is included in gross income.

8. Severance Plans

Severance involves payments that may be made to an employee when he or she is terminated by the employer. Whether written or informal, severance plans have two goals: to reward an employee's past service and to help the employee make ends meet during retraining or a job search. Sometimes an employer offers severance pay in exchange for the employee's promise not to sue for wrongful termination.

Severance plans, where they exist, vary from employer to employer. Some offer one week's pay for each year of service. Others have a more generous "golden parachute" policy, typically for executives. Eligibility for severance and the amount received often depend on the employee's position in the firm as well as length of service.

Severance may be paid in a lump sum, periodic payments or a combination of the two. Generally, severance payments are included in gross income.

9.   Educational Assistance Programs

These programs reimburse employees for tuition, fees and attendance at outside educational programs or institutions or provide tuition and fees for in-house seminars. Courses taken need not be related to a person's work. Such expenses paid for by an employer are not included in an employee's gross income.

10. Group Legal Services

These plans offer employees low-cost legal services such as referrals, advice and representation. They allow a group to use its collective purchasing power to negotiate lower rates from lawyers.

The employer and/or the employee pays for the cost through union dues or payroll deductions. Participation may be automatic or voluntary, and a plan may be offered independently or through a cafeteria plan.

The benefits received under group legal services plans used to be excluded from employees' income. That's no longer the case; employees must now pay taxes on any such benefits received.

11. Employee Assistance Programs

These programs cover a variety of services for employees and their families, including help for drug and alcohol abuse, stress, anxiety, depression, family problems, money and credit problems and legal problems. Usually, employers contract with a third party to provide counseling and referral services with a social worker or family counselor.

Benefits or reimbursements an employee receives under an employee assistance program may or may not be included in gross income, depending on the nature of the benefit and the employee's income level. Particular employers should be able to provide information on the tax consequences of benefits offered under the program.

B. Stock Options and Nonqualified Deferred Compensation Plans

If neither you nor your spouse has stock options, stock incentives or nonqualified deferred compensation plans (a kind of benefit usually reserved for upper management), skip ahead to the next chapter.

Stock options and other kinds of corporate incentive and compensation programs present a challenge for divorcing spouses who are trying to sort out and take control of their finances—not just because the plans themselves can be complicated, but also because there's still a lot of uncertainty over how to deal with them in the divorce process.

This section provides an overview of different kinds of plans and explains some key terms that come up in this area. If you or your spouse has such benefits, questions to keep in mind are:

- How much is the benefit worth now?
- Is the benefit something that can be divided between spouses?
- Can the benefit be transferred from one spouse to the other?
- Is the benefit considered income?
- If so, will a court take it into account in calculating alimony and/or child support?

In many cases, there are no sure answers. But you need to be aware of these issues so that you can raise them with your attorney in working out the specifics of your divorce.

If you or your spouse has stock options or other types of compensation covered in this section, you should discuss this with your divorce lawyer and also with a tax attorney or certified public accountant, since many tax considerations can be involved.

1. Types of Stock Options

Stock options are an important part of the compensation program of many corporations. The aim, in addition to compensating employees, is to encourage employees to work hard to achieve success for the firm and thus increase the value of the company's stock.

Stock options have been common perks for senior management for many years. But in recent years stock options have become part of the compensation package of many rank-and-file workers. It's estimated that about 10% of all employees now own stock options; in technology companies, the figure is about 50%.

A stock option is a right granted to an employee to purchase a certain number of shares in the company's stock at today's price sometime in the future. The stock can be sold later, when the market value may be higher.

Usually, the employee cannot exercise the right to purchase and sell stock as soon as he or she receives it. Instead, the employee must remain with the firm for a minimum period before the options vest (that is, become exercisable). When they do vest, the stock's market value presumably will have risen, thus giving the employee an automatic profit in return for having stayed with the firm through the vesting period.

As a result, employees can find themselves with potential wealth tied up in an employer's option plan. In fact, options nationally are said to represent about $1 trillion in unexercised wealth. But there is also great risk in unexercised options. That's because while the expectation is that the value of the stock will go up, sometimes it goes down quickly and significantly, as the years 2000 through 2002 have demonstrated.

Thus, while stock options are an increasingly common marital asset and often an item in contention in a divorce, they can entail substantial losses as well as gains. A divorcing spouse may have to pay additional support when his or her options go up in value, but receive no relief if they go down.

Option plans are complex, and they differ from company to company. What's more, divorce courts differ greatly on how to value options, what portion—if any—of them should be characterized as marital property and how to treat them for purposes of support.

Stock Option Documents You Need to Get

To determine what kind of stock options are involved in your case, you should obtain as much information on the options as possible. Much of this information can be obtained from the employer that granted the options. Important documents include:

- the original stock option plan statement and all amendments

- grant agreements between employer and employee (there will be one for each grant)

- employer's letter of intent to employee offering a stock option contract

- an option summary statement reflecting the status of each grant, including vesting, exercise and sales as well as changes in the number of shares resulting from stock splits (generally, the employer provides such statements annually or quarterly)

- a list of the company's monthly stock prices and dividend payments (if it's a publicly traded firm), and

- all SEC Form 10K filings, annual proxy statements or other filings with any governmental or regulatory agency during the term of employment. (These often are available at the EDGAR website at www.sec.gov; look under the EDGAR heading.)

There are varying kinds of stock options, as we discuss below. However, they have these similarities:

- Options may be exercised (the shares may be purchased) during a specified period of time and at a fixed price.

- After the vesting period, an employee will wait to exercise the option until—and *if*—the stock's market value exceeds the price at which the employee can buy it, thus guaranteeing him or her a profit.

- The employee has no risk during the vesting period because he or she has no obligation to buy the stock and has no money invested. If the value of the stock declines, the employee simply elects not to exercise the option.

Now let's look at the two broad categories of stock options: statutory and nonstatutory (also known as nonqualified stock options, or NQSOs.)

Statutory stock options are so called because they are subject to a strict set of regulations under federal statutes. For example, for the holder of the option to qualify for a favorable capital gain tax rate, either he must exercise the option within two years after the employer grants it, or after exercising the option he must hold onto the stock for at least a year.

There are two types of statutory stock options: *incentive stock options* (ISOs) and *employee stock purchase plans*. ISOs are governed by a written plan approved by the company's board of directors and stockholders. The plan lists the employees who are eligible and the number of shares available for these employees.

When an employee is granted an ISO, that's not considered income on which the employee can be taxed. Nor is it taxable income when he exercises it. (The IRS has proposed changing the income tax treatment of ISOs beginning in 2003.) After the employee sells the stock, the profit is considered a capital gain and is taxed at that rate.

Can the employee transfer the ISO to his ex-spouse upon divorce? The law says that the option itself—the right to buy the stock—can't be transferred. If it is, the option becomes a "nonqualified" option (see below). However, if the employee exercises the option first, he may transfer the ISO stock he's bought to his divorcing spouse.

Besides an ISO, the other type of qualified option is an employee stock purchase plan. Such a plan allows an employee to set aside money from her paycheck to purchase company stock, either at a discount or at market value on the date of the grant. The stock is held in trust for the employee, who receives her holdings in stock or cash when her employment ends. As with an ISO, the option to buy stock under an employee stock purchase plan cannot be transferred from one divorcing spouse to another.

Nonstatutory (or nonqualified) stock options have fewer restrictions, and the tax consequences for the employee are not as favorable. When an employee exercises her option and makes money by buying

---

Stock Option Lingo

Even to the most sophisticated investors, stock options can be confusing. Here are simple definitions of some of the key concepts:

- Stock option. A contractual right, not an obligation, to buy a certain number of shares (exercise the option) at a point in the future (the vesting date) at a specific price (the grant price).

- Grant. The issuance by an employer of the right to acquire stock at a specific time in the future at a predetermined price.

- Grant price. The price at which the shares are purchased when the option is exercised, regardless of their market price when exercised. Also know as strike price, option price or exercise price.

- Vesting. The time that must elapse before the employee fully acquires the right to exercise an option or a percentage of the option granted (for example, 25% of all total options granted over four years).

- Exercise. The exchange of an option for actual shares of the company. The employee must pay the grant price as well as the payroll taxes associated with the exercise. And when the employee sells the stock, she may be taxed on the profit made (capital gains) on the difference between the grant price and the sale price.

- Exercise date. The date after vesting when the employee purchases shares at the predetermined price under the terms of the option agreement.

- Holding period. The period of time that an employee is required to keep the stock after she purchases it and before she sells it. The holding period begins on the exercise date and ends on the day before the stock is sold.

- Expiration date. The last day the employee can exercise the option under the terms of the contract.

- Cashless exercise. This occurs when the employee simultaneously exercises his option and sells the stock she's just acquired, covering the cost of the options and the taxes due. He takes the remainder in cash instead of stock shares.

- Spread. The difference between the grant price and the market value on the exercise date.

- Gain. The difference between the grant price and the fair market value on the day the stock is sold.

stock at lower-than-market rates, that money is subject to federal income tax as well as FICA, Medicare and state and local taxes.

An NQSO can be transferred from an employee to an ex-spouse at divorce. When the ex-spouse exercises the option, she is liable for income tax, just as the employee spouse would be.

2. What Are Stock Options Worth at Divorce?

How can stock options be valued and apportioned among divorcing spouses? That question presents complex problems for family lawyers and courts, as well as for the spouses themselves.

Among the issues: Are stock options property or income, or both? Are options that vest after the couple's separation date considered marital property? If the employee spouse doesn't exercise the option until years after the divorce, does the ex-spouse deserve a portion? Is there a formula courts can use for dividing options? Should a court be able to raise levels of alimony and child support if the value of the stock increases, and reduce the support if the value falls? If an employee's option hasn't yet vested because the employee hasn't worked at the company long enough, how does that affect the value of the option?

There's not a lot of legal precedent to go on, and there are no hard and fast rules that apply to all stock option plans and in all states.

There are, however, some broad guidelines. Stock options granted to an employee spouse before the separation date generally are seen as marital property. Those granted after separation tend to be viewed as separate property of the employee spouse. In a series of California cases, the judges found that options that were granted and exercised before the separation date were community property—whereas options that were granted during marriage but not exercised until after separation entitled the ex-spouse to a partial interest, based on the amount of

time elapsed. About half the states have followed these general principles.

Courts also generally have held that recurring capital gains—including profits from exercised stock options—are income and can be used for calculating support.

What about potential income from *unexercised* options? Some courts have said that unexercised options are part of gross income and therefore can be used to help determine support payments. Courts have also said that an item can be considered both income for support purposes and property for purposes of equitable distribution. If an option is both unexercised and *unvested*, that raises more valuation questions that have no clear answer.

Courts have developed various methods for apportioning options. Sometimes, as we've seen, options can be transferred. Some courts have required the parties to hold stock options as tenants in common (for more on tenancy in common, see Chapter 12, Section C).

Still other courts have applied various methods to determine the options' present value, then ordered one spouse to give the other assets from the estate to offset the value of the options. The risk here is that later the stock's value can either fall or skyrocket, leaving each spouse feeling blessed or chagrined.

How your stock options or your spouse's options will be handled in divorce depends on many factors. There is no guarantee your situation will be treated the same as someone else's or that the court will come to the same conclusion in your case as it has in other cases or as courts have in other jurisdictions. You may need to talk at length with your lawyer about stock option issues in your case. See the sidebar "Points to Include in the Options Agreement," below, for some key points that should be covered in the settlement reached by you and your spouse.

Several websites offer information and resources on stock options. Among them are:

- www.MyStockOptions.com. This comprehensive site includes articles, a glossary, a tax guide, a tax calculator and frequently asked questions.

- www.StockOptionsCentral.com. This site provides calculators that allow you to run "what if" scenarios to determine option value and taxability.

- www.stockopter.com. While primarily a site for financial professionals, it does include a glossary and explanatory articles.

3. Nonqualified Deferred Compensation Plans

Nonqualified deferred compensation is one method by which companies have traditionally rewarded their highest-ranking executives. Far less common than stock options, these plans are generally found only in large corporations and are limited to a few executives, such as the chief executive officer, chief financial officer, president and vice presidents.

Under such a plan, the employer defers part of an executive's income now—thereby reducing the executive's current tax burden—and provides the income later, when the executive will presumably be in a lower tax bracket. Like stock options, these plans are legally complex and difficult to value and divide at divorce, or to evaluate to determine what is income available for support.

There are many kinds of nonqualified deferred compensation plans. Some look like 401(k)s, some resemble defined benefit plans (see Chapter 14) and others are merely promises by the employer to pay income to the employee in the future. A common type of plan is the SERP (Supplemental Executive Retirement Plan), or "top hat" plan, which provides additional retirement benefits to a select group of high-level managers through the use of various formulas.

Points to Include in the Options Agreement

While there are few firm rules about how to handle stock options in divorce cases, certain points ought to be covered in any agreement between you and your spouse. Here is a checklist of issues to include in your analysis:

- Identify the grants. Make sure you have all paperwork pertaining to the options as furnished by the employer, specifying the terms of the grant, the grant price, key dates and all rules that apply.

- Decide who will bear the exercise fees. An employee typically pays a fee when an option is exercised. At divorce, the fee is usually paid by whoever exercises the option, whether that's the employee or the ex-spouse.

- Agree to follow court orders and employer conditions. Both spouses should agree that the options must be exercised in a way that adheres to both the judge's ruling and the employer's terms.

- Clarify when options change or terminate. The agreement should be clear about the duration of options periods and what happens to the options if the employee leaves the company. The employer should be responsible for providing information to the parties about any changes in conditions or timetables for exercising options.

- Protect personal identification information. Do not include in any court order personal information such as address, date of birth or Social Security number. Such information should be provided to the employer and other parties by mail, certified and return receipt requested.

If you are divorcing a spouse with a non-qualified deferred compensation plan, you or your lawyer will want to request documentation from the employer. This might include the plan summary, full plan documents, employment contract and actuarial analysis.

Two factors reduce the value of these plans in divorce. Because such plans are often unfunded, there is a risk that the employee will never receive the benefits because the company goes bankrupt, reorganizes or is taken over by another company. Also, the benefit cannot be split between divorcing spouses under a QDRO. (A QDRO assures direct payment of certain benefits to the nonemployee spouse. See Chapter 14.)

C. Questions to Ask Your Attorney or Tax Specialist

1. How do our state courts treat all our employment benefits? As property? As income?

2. What do our state courts have to say about how stock options should be valued and apportioned in divorce?

■

How Will We Divide Debts?

When you divorce, you divide not only property but
debts as well. It's crucial that you and your spouse
reach an agreement about how debts will be handled.

If you are the one who is willing to assume a debt, you might ask for something in return. You may be able to make tradeoffs—perhaps getting the car or the piano in exchange for paying off credit card debts.

Before negotiating your agreement, you'll want to know what your state laws have to say about who is responsible for paying various debts in your state. (The Spousal Debt Laws chart in this chapter will help you.) You also need to be aware of the possibility that your spouse will declare bankruptcy, default or fail to live up to your agreement in some other way. Use this chapter to investigate your legal and financial position on debts and divorce.

A. General Rules on Who's Responsible for Debt

Some general rules for separated, divorced and married people having financial problems follow. Study these rules to understand which debts you or your spouse are obligated to pay and which property you or your spouse risk losing if you don't pay:

- In most states, a person is responsible for paying only the debts that he or she incurs during marriage—that is, you can't be forced to pay the bills your spouse runs up—except that both spouses are usually responsible for paying debts incurred:

- with joint accounts
- where the creditor was looking to both spouses for repayment
- for the family's necessities such as medical care, food, clothing and shelter, and
- for the children's education.

Be Aware of Medical Expenses

State statutes often expressly state that a spouse is or is not liable for the necessities of the other. Are medical expenses always considered necessities? The issue of liability for a spouse's medical debts commonly arises in court these days. And there's no clear answer. About half the courts say neither spouse is responsible for the other; the other courts say that both are responsible to each other.

- Usually, debts incurred after the separation date but before the divorce is final are the responsibility of the spouse who incurred them and must be paid by that person. There is an exception—both spouses are responsible for paying debts for the family's necessities and the children's education, regardless of who incurred them.

- A spouse is generally not responsible for paying the debts his mate incurred before marriage or after the divorce became final.

- If you or your ex-spouse agreed to pay certain joint debts as part of a divorce settlement— or a divorce decree signed by a judge requires that one spouse pay the joint debts—the agreement or decree is binding only on you and your ex. Because you were married when the joint debts were incurred, the creditor has a right to collect from both of you, and no agreement between you and your spouse can change that. If you voluntarily or involuntarily pay bills your ex-spouse was supposed to pay, your remedy is to try to get your ex to reimburse you. Complaints to the creditor will get you nowhere.

- The separately owned property of one spouse usually cannot be taken by a creditor to pay the separate debts of the other. Separate property of one spouse can be taken to pay debts you incur together, and separate property of one spouse is always available to pay that spouse's separate debts. Separate property is property owned prior to the marriage, property accumulated after divorce and property received during marriage by one spouse only, by gift or inheritance. In most non-community property states, separate property also includes wages earned by a spouse during marriage.

B. If You Live in a Community Property State

The community property states are Arizona, California, Idaho, Louisiana, Nevada, New Mexico, Texas, Washington and Wisconsin. In those states, property acquired and debts incurred during marriage—called community property and community debts—are joint. In most instances, both spouses are liable for all debts incurred by either, although there are exceptions. Here are the specific rules:

- Both spouses are generally liable for all debts incurred during marriage, unless the creditor was looking to only one spouse for repayment or the purchase in no way benefited the "community." For example, if on a credit application a spouse who bought a kayak claimed to be unmarried or stated that his spouse's income would not be used to pay the debt, his spouse would not be liable to pay for the kayak if he defaults. Similarly, if a spouse charged a trip to the Bahamas with his or her lover, the spouse who stayed at home would not be liable, as this debt does not benefit the community.

- Spouses are generally not liable for the separate debts their mate incurred before marriage or after permanent separation. However, the debtor spouse's share of all community property, including his spouse's half of the nondebtor spouse's income, can be used to pay debts he incurred before marriage.

- Community property includes all income earned during marriage, except for income earned on property owned before the marriage. This would include revenue from an income-generating piece of property or payments from a vested pension.

- Separate property is limited to property owned prior to the marriage, property accumulated after divorce (after separation, in a few states) and property received during marriage by one spouse only, by gift or inheritance.

C. Listing Your Debts

On the next page is a chart on which you can list all your debts—yours, your spouse's and your joint (marital) debts. The liabilities worksheet, which you filled out as part of your *Net Worth Statement* in Chapter 12, Section C, should contain all this data.

Instructions

Using the italicized examples as a guide, list in Column 1 all current debts you and your spouse are responsible for paying. This information can be taken from the *Assets and Liabilities Worksheet* in Chapter 12. In Column 2, write the balance owed on each debt. In Column 3, note whether the debt is your separate debt, your spouse's separate debt or a marital (joint) debt. In Column 4, write in the name of the person who will assume responsibility for paying the debt. Only in unusual circumstances will one of you be responsible for the other's separate debt. You will need to divide the marital debts, however.

You may want to make several copies of this chart in the event you negotiate back and forth about who will be responsible for paying which debts.

D. Marital Debts and Bankruptcy

For many couples, debts and divorce go together the way love and marriage once did. Unmanageable debts may serve as a catalyst for the ending of the marriage in some cases. Other couples feel the pinch as their expenses double when one spouse moves out—they maintain two households, yet their incomes stay the same.

For couples or recently divorced individuals overwhelmed by their debt burden, declaring bankruptcy may provide a way out. In most cases, bankruptcy lets you erase your debts in exchange for giving up certain property. Every state declares certain assets, such as clothing, certain equity in a home, certain equity in a car and several other items to be exempt. You get to keep exempt property when you file for bankruptcy.

Spousal Debt Chart

Debts—Example	Balance	Husband, Wife or Joint	Who Will Pay
Car Loan	$8,000	Joint	Wife
Franklin Bank Visa	$1,800	Husband	Husband
Marshall Bank Visa	$2,300	Joint	Husband
Personal Loan	$5,000	Joint	Husband
Student Loan	$10,000	Wife	Wife
USA Mastercard	$4,000	Joint	Husband

Debts	Balance	Husband, Wife or Joint	Who Will Pay

Married couples can file for bankruptcy jointly. Married persons can also file individually, and single people can file on their own. Before filing as an individual or a couple, you must understand what the different outcomes will be.

If a married couple files for bankruptcy together, they can eliminate all separate debts of the husband, all separate debts of the wife and all jointly incurred marital debts. Some debts cannot be erased (discharged) in bankruptcy. The most common ones are recent income taxes, most other taxes, student loans, child support, alimony, restitution for a crime and, in many cases, debts obtained by fraud and debts owed under a marital settlement or divorce decree.

If only one spouse files, that spouse can eliminate his or her separate debts, as well as his or her obligation to pay the marital debts. In equitable distribution states, however, the nonfiling spouse remains responsible for paying the marital debts as well as his or her own separate debts. In community property states (Arizona, California, Idaho, Louisiana, Nevada, New Mexico, Texas, Washington and Wisconsin), on the other hand, the nonfiling spouse gets the benefit of the bankruptcy discharge without filing. That is, all community debts that otherwise qualify for discharge are completely wiped out in bankruptcy. As long as the couple remains married, the nonfiling spouse will not have to pay them.

A spouse wanting to file for bankruptcy might decide to wait until after the divorce, especially if he or she agreed to pay a large share of the marital debts, perhaps in exchange for taking a greater share of the marital property. A divorced spouse must watch carefully in the event the former mate files for bankruptcy. Remember what we said at the beginning of the chapter: Dividing debts at divorce does not affect your original relationship with your creditors. Just because Mark agreed to pay back the marital debt to Sears doesn't mean that Sears cannot go after his ex-wife Sylvia for the payments.

This rule holds true in bankruptcy as well. If Mark agrees to pay the marital debts and then files for bankruptcy, the bankruptcy may wipe out Mark's obligation to pay those bills. But Sylvia, who figured she didn't have to pay them because the divorce agreement gave them to Mark, may be liable for paying, even in a community property state. (In a community property state Sylvia would only get the benefit of the discharge if she and Mark were still married.) The creditors will seek her out and, if necessary, may send the bill to a collection agency or even sue her to get paid.

In effect, a successful bankruptcy shifts the debt burden from the ex-spouse who assumed it at divorce and places it on the other ex-spouse. The Bankruptcy Code gives the nonfiling ex-spouse an opportunity to object to the discharge of the marital debts, however. Keep reading.

1. Discharging Marital Debts in Bankruptcy

Whether an obligation to pay marital debts under a divorce agreement may be discharged in bankruptcy can be tricky. Obligations owed to a spouse that were intended as support—or that are "in the nature of support"—cannot be discharged in bankruptcy. Common examples of such obligations are:

- alimony, spousal support or maintenance

- child support

- attorney's fees connected with a divorce or with modifying alimony, child support or child custody orders

- periodic payments that end upon the death or remarriage of the recipient spouse

- agreements to pay marital debts in exchange for lower alimony or child support

- debts paid to a spouse who is maintaining the primary residence of the children while there is a serious imbalance of incomes, and

- debts paid in installments over a long period of time.

Other debts assumed during divorce or separation or under a divorce agreement, divorce decree or other court order may also be nondischargeable. Debts in this category include:

- debts owed to a spouse as a result of a property division

- debts owed for costs or fees associated with a divorce, and

- an obligation to pay marital debts that clearly isn't in the "nature of support."

Whether these other types of debts remain after bankruptcy will depend on the type of bankruptcy the debtor files and whether the spouse who is owed a debt contests its discharge in the bankruptcy court.

A Carefully Worded Agreement May Protect You From an Ex-Spouse's Bankruptcy

To increase your chance that marital debts won't be discharged in the event your ex-spouse files for bankruptcy, your marital settlement agreement, order or judgment should characterize the debts as "additional child support," "alimony" or "in the nature of support." This will provide guidance to a bankruptcy judge asked to determine whether or not the ex-spouse can avoid having to pay the debts. The language of the agreement won't be binding on the judge, who can look behind the agreement to the true nature of the debts (see, for example, *In re Snipes*, 190 B.R. 450 (M.D. Fla. 1995)), but it will be evidence to the judge that you and your ex-spouse intended the debts to be nondischargeable.

2.   Types of Bankruptcies

Most people's image of bankruptcy involves a debtor going to court to get debts erased. In fact, there are two types of bankruptcies. The more familiar is liquidation bankruptcy, in which your debts are wiped out completely (referred to as Chapter 7 bankruptcy). The other type is reorganization bankruptcy, in which you partially or fully repay your debts. The reorganization bankruptcy for individuals is called Chapter 13 bankruptcy. (There are two other kinds of reorganization bankruptcy: Chapter 11 bankruptcy for businesses or for individuals with debts over $1.077 million, and Chapter 12 bankruptcy for family farmers.)

In a Chapter 7 bankruptcy, any debt arising from a separation agreement or divorce, or in connection with a marital settlement agreement, divorce decree or other court order, can be considered dischargeable. If an ex-spouse wants to challenge the discharge of the debt, she may do so in the bankruptcy court. Once the challenge is raised, the court will allow the debt to be discharged unless:

- the ex-spouse who filed bankruptcy has the ability to pay the debt from income or property that is not reasonably necessary for his support and not reasonably necessary for him to continue, preserve and operate a business, or

- discharging the debt would harm the nonfiling ex-spouse or her child more than it would benefit the filing ex-spouse.

Most courts have said that if an ex-spouse who files for bankruptcy claims he's unable to pay certain debts or would suffer greater harm if they're not erased, he must prove that in court. (See, for example, *In re Hill*, 184 B.R. 750 (N.D. Ill. 1995).) At least one court, however, has held the opposite: that it's the nonfiling ex-spouse who must convince the court otherwise. (See *In re Butler*, 186 B.R. 371 (D. Vt. 1995).)

In a Chapter 13 bankruptcy, marital debts will be discharged after the debtor completes a repayment plan. This means that all, some or none of the debts will be discharged, depending on the terms of the repayment plan approved by the bankruptcy court.

Sometimes in Chapter 7 bankruptcies, a court discharges certain debts that the debtor might have remained responsible for, if only his ex-spouse had challenged the discharge in court. On the other hand, sometimes when an ex-spouse does challenge a discharge, the court finds in favor of the debtor. How can an ex-spouse protect herself? One way is to make sure that when a spouse assumes a certain obligation upon divorce, the obligation is made subject to a security interest in that spouse's property.

Example: *Jackie and Art divorce. Jackie received a larger share of the property and gave Art a promissory note for $35,000 as an even-up payment. Jackie files for bankruptcy and asks the court to erase her obligation to make good on the note. Art fails to properly contest the discharge of the debt and therefore falls $35,000 short of getting his share of the marital property. Art could have protected himself by taking a promissory note secured by the house. This kind of note would allow him to force the sale of the house if Jackie doesn't pay. Also, this kind of note can't be erased in bankruptcy if the security interest (the note securing the house) is created at the same time the house transfers from the two spouses to the one keeping it after the marriage* (Farrey v. Sanderfoot, 500 U.S. 291 (1991).)

Bankruptcy isn't for everyone. A Chapter 7 stays on your credit record for ten years, although you can take steps to rebuild your credit and probably obtain credit in two or three years after filing. Nonetheless, bankruptcy is always a possibility for you or your spouse, unless you've already filed within the last six years. If you're overwhelmed by your debt burden, don't immediately discount bankruptcy as an option. If your spouse assumes a large share of the marital debts or owes you a large sum to even up the property division, be on the lookout for any bankruptcy filing, especially if your ex starts to complain loudly about being broke.

Make sure your divorce agreement doesn't leave you vulnerable. Promissory notes, especially unsecured notes (notes that don't give you a lien on property), are almost always wiped out in bankruptcy. You may have a little more protection with secured notes. You may be able to protect yourself by specifying in the settlement agreement that the promissory note or other payments are made in lieu of alimony. If you want to file for bankruptcy, be sure you know what's involved, and whether or not you can wipe out your debts. What's most important is that you get sound legal advice from a bankruptcy attorney or a Nolo publication.

See *How to File for Chapter 7 Bankruptcy*, by Stephen Elias, Albin Renauer, Robin Leonard & Kathleen Michon (Nolo), or *Chapter 13 Bankruptcy: Repay Your Debts*, or *Bankruptcy: Is It the Right Solution to Your Debt Problems?*, both by Robin Leonard (Nolo). The first book gives all the information necessary to decide whether to file and the forms for filing a Chapter 7 bankruptcy case. A chapter on nondischargeable debts has information on when marital debts can and cannot be wiped out. The second book contains the same information for Chapter 13 bankruptcy cases. The third will help you assess whether bankruptcy is appropriate for your situation.

E. Dividing Debts at Divorce

While it is critical that you fully understand your legal position and your options regarding your debts, do not overlook the financial realities of your situation.

In Chapter 12, you had the chance to complete *Net Worth* and *Cash Flow Statements*. If you skipped that material, you may want to go back and fill them out now. If you have already completed the *Net Worth* and *Cash Flow Statements* in Chapter 12, use this opportunity to update them. You might leave many items blank on these statements, but at least you'll get an idea of what you actually own and owe, and how much it costs you to live. This information is crucial when you divide your debts at divorce.

You have four basic options in allocating your marital debts:

- You and your spouse sell joint property to raise the cash to pay off your marital debts.

- You agree to pay the bulk of the debts; in exchange, you get a greater share of the marital property or a corresponding increase in alimony.

- Your spouse agrees to pay the bulk of the debts; in exchange, your spouse gets a greater share of the marital property or a corresponding increase in alimony.

- You and your spouse divide your property equally and divide the debts equally—that is, each of you gets half of the property and each of you agrees to pay half of the debts.

From your perspective, the first two options are much less risky than the second two possibilities. Remember the caution we have given throughout this book: *When you're conne3§ed to someone financially, you're at risk*. What happens if your spouse agrees to pay all or even half of the debts and then loses his or her job, refuses to pay or files for bankruptcy? Your credit rating will be damaged, or you will be stuck with paying debts. Then the likelihood of getting reimbursed or getting a share of the marital property originally given to your spouse will be slim or nil. So if possible, sell your joint property and pay your joint debts, or agree to pay the debts yourself.

F. Dividing Debts When There's "Nothing to Fight Over"

As your financial picture gets clearer, you may come to the unhappy conclusion that your bills and liabilities far outweigh your assets and income. Don't feel alone. Not only do most Americans live above their means, but many people going through divorce find they simply do not have enough money to make ends meet. Unlike the bitter battles for property that have stereotyped divorce cases on television, you and your partner may admit in despair that there's "nothing to fight over."

If you're in such a position, it's critical for you to take an honest look at your needs and protect your own interests. Even if you have to borrow money to get through your divorce, it could well be worth it to prevent problems later. Hiring a lawyer or financial professional now to review your situation could cost less than a huge tax bill or other debts in the future.

Extensive information on debts and creditors can be found in *Money Troubles: Legal Strategies to Cope With Your Debts*, by Robin Leonard & Deanne Loonin (Nolo).

G. Questions to Ask Your Attorney

 Debts and the fear of bankruptcy can be enough to lose sleep over during divorce. Ask your attorney the following questions so that you know the best ways to protect yourself financially.

1. Who will be legally responsible to pay which debts?

2. What can be done legally to make sure my spouse pays the debts she agrees to pay?

3. If my spouse files for bankruptcy after our divorce is final, would our property settlement protect me?

4. If my spouse makes noise about filing for bankruptcy before our divorce becomes final, should I file, too?

5. How can I stop my spouse from spending the marital assets on himself until the divorce is final?

6. If only my spouse signed the loan documents while we were married, is that still my debt?

7. If just my spouse signed the loan documents, does the creditor have a right to come after my assets once we're divorced?

H. Some Online Resources

There are many good sites, government and private, for information about debt, credit and other consumer issues. Typically, they include search mechanisms that allow you to home in on the issue most relevant for you. These sites include:

- www.ftc.gov (Federal Trade Commission)

- www.pueblo.gsa.gov (Consumer Information Center of U.S. General Services Administration)

- www.aba.com (American Bankers Association)

- www.bankrate.com

- www.cbs.marketwatch.com

■

CHAPTER

18

Alimony and Child Support: What Might I Pay or Receive?

Alimony and child support payments are often the most hotly contested issues in a divorce. These payments are often necessary when the money that used to support a single household must stretch to support two.

If neither you nor your spouse has any interest in receiving alimony, skip ahead to Section C, assuming you have children. Keep in mind that if you knowingly give up (waive) alimony, you cannot go back to court later on and try to get some. Once its waived, it's gone forever.

Unemployment checks and insurance claims can help a couple survive the loss of a job or a house or fire. But who pays the bill when the financial disaster of divorce strikes?

Somehow, household expenses must be paid. Someone must come up with the "Alimonia"—a Latin word for "food" or "support." Today the word is alimony, although it is increasingly called spousal support, maintenance or rehabilitative support. The names differ depending on which state you live in, but the impact seems to be the same everywhere: The payer feels the amount is far too much, while the recipient knows it's not enough.

Both parties may be right.

Breaking one household into two costs more than anyone thinks it will. Besides doubling the basics—mortgage or rent, utilities and phone bills—divorcing couples must admit that the choices they made as a couple may no longer be realistic. A wife who left her job to care for the children cannot retrace her steps and cover the ground she lost when she dropped out of the workforce. A husband who refused a job transfer so his wife could pursue her entrepreneurial ambitions may be stuck in a dead-end job that he can't leave without jeopardizing his pension. When you are "fired" from the job of husband or wife, no one offers you a workers' compensation check. Is it any wonder, then, that alimony often becomes a major battleground in divorce?

If you have children, the struggle to make ends meet can become even more draining. Whether you will pay or receive child support, you'll need to know what it costs. But how can parents put a price tag on their children?

That's hard to answer. It's therefore not surprising that the custodial parent (recipient) never feels he or she is receiving enough and the noncustodial parent (payer) feels hounded for support payment increases.

This chapter first takes you through the legal, financial and emotional realities of alimony and then outlines your steps to a settlement. Once you've taken care of alimony, you will follow the same steps with respect to child support.

Protect Your Parental Rights

Before making any legal moves that affect your children, make sure you are informed about your rights as a parent. Ask attorneys to get precise information about what can and will happen when custody is disputed. Make sure you know when and where all hearings or mediation sessions will take place. Better to ask too many questions than to lose your children because you misunderstood the consequences of your actions. Further, because the court will examine your custody arrangements, be prepared for any stunt your spouse may try to pull in the courtroom—such as his attorney putting the children on the stand when you both agreed not to. Don't be lulled into a false sense of security because of anything your spouse may have agreed to informally. And never move out of the family residence without a written agreement about custody.

A. Alimony—Legal, Financial and Emotional Realities

It helps to think of alimony as a separate issue, distinct from your property settlement (except if your property earns income). Especially in community property states (Arizona, California, Idaho, Louisiana, Nevada, New Mexico, Texas, Washington and Wisconsin), the need to receive or pay alimony is separate from dividing property and assets. Before reviewing the steps toward a settlement, take a few minutes to read about the legal, financial and emotional realities surrounding alimony.

1. Legal Realities

Until the 1970s, alimony was a natural extension of the financial arrangement in traditional marriages, where the husband was the breadwinner and the wife stayed home, caring for the house and children. The amount of alimony was determined by a number of factors—the needs of the spouses, their status in life, their wealth and their relative "fault" in ending the marriage. For example, if a husband was committing adultery or treating his wife with cruelty, he would pay a relatively large amount. If the wife was having an affair or treating her husband cruelly, she would receive little or no alimony.

Today, the following factors are generally considered in determining alimony:

- the recipient's needs
- the payer's ability to pay
- the age, health and standard of living of the spouses
- the length of the marriage
- each spouse's ability to earn
- the recipient's nonmonetary contributions to the marriage
- the recipient's ability to be self-supporting, and
- the tax advantages and disadvantages.

Except in marriages of long duration (usually ten years or more) or in the case of an ill or ailing spouse, alimony today usually lasts for a set period of time, with the expectation that the recipient spouse will become self-supporting.

In an effort to make alimony awards more uniform, some individual counties within states have adopted financial schedules to help judges determine the appropriate level of support. Of course, spouses can make arrangements outside of court that differ from the schedules. However, if you cannot agree on the amount, a judge will decide how much alimony will be awarded. Leaving such a decision to a judge may create a far different result from what you anticipated.

Also, in some states, especially non-community property states, the division of property can affect how much alimony is awarded. For example, if one spouse gets a house with no mortgage, plus rental properties that produce a good income, a court is not likely to award a high amount of alimony. You will have an opportunity to examine the interplay between alimony and your property division in Chapter 19.

2. Financial Realities

Generally, court-ordered alimony does not provide adequate money to live on. Often there's a big gap between the amount you will receive and what you really need, or between the amount you must pay and what you can actually afford.

To understand the financial reality of alimony, you must know what it really costs for you to live. Then you need to develop strategies for making up the difference between true living expenses and the amount you will receive or pay in alimony. As you work through Section B, below, you will look at the tax consequences of alimony as well as practical matters such as when, where and how payments should be made. Remember, alimony income is risky. It can be stopped, reduced or increased any time circumstances change.

3. Emotional Realities

Since the advent of no-fault divorce, many couples no longer vent their anger in knock-down, drag-out fights in court. That doesn't mean the anger isn't there; it just manifests itself differently. That repressed anger may lead to fights over alimony, an item directly tied to a person's survival. You may be moving along nicely in the negotiations only to find that when you get to the alimony, your spouse suddenly makes unreasonable demands or starts playing tricks. Focusing on the legal and financial questions in Section B, below, will help you guard against emotional sabotage.

B. Steps to a Settlement

As you move through your divorce, you may find that your choices about alimony are guided by the local court's financial schedules. For instance, if a schedule shows that a person in your situation should get $500 a month in alimony, your spouse will probably use that number, at least as a starting point.

While you need to be aware of any schedule used in your area, don't rely on those figures in determining the amount you will pay or receive. By answering the following questions, you can analyze the financial consequences of paying or receiving alimony.

1. How much do you need to live on?

2. What, if any, are the financial schedules for alimony in your area?

3. How much alimony do you need—or can you afford to pay?

4. Are there alternatives to paying or receiving monthly alimony?

5. What is your bottom-line decision on paying or receiving alimony?

1. How Much Do You Need to Live On?

If you've completed the *Cash Flow Statement* in Chapter 12, you have already tracked your living expenses. If not, go back now and use the statements to outline these costs. Whether you will pay or receive alimony, your goal is to get a realistic picture of your household expenses. If your spouse demands more than you feel you can afford to pay—or offers less than you feel you need to live on—you will have to document the cost of your lifestyle. Yes, that lifestyle will probably change after divorce, but for now you need to establish a baseline for expenses.

While you're documenting your own cost of living, estimate your spouse's expenses as well. You will need this information when you are negotiating. If you can't settle prior to a trial, the court will require that you each submit documentation of your income and expenses.

If You Have Children

In calculating your expenses, don't overlook the special costs generated by children, such as allowances, piano lessons, child care, braces, Little League uniforms and the like. You will need to make a list of ordinary and extra expenses. Some of those expenses may be listed on your *Cash Flow Statement* from Chapter 12. Other expenses are listed in Section D3, below.

Check the Monthly Average figures from your *Cash Flow Statement* in Chapter 12 and other documentation containing your marital costs to estimate the following:

$ _____ *My personal monthly expenses*

$ _____ *My spouse's monthly expenses*

2. What, If Any, Are the Financial Schedules for Alimony in Your Area?

As mentioned previously, a number of counties have adopted informal financial schedules to help judges—and spouses—set alimony. Be sure to ask your lawyer if your county follows such a financial schedule or guideline.

More likely, alimony is determined based on the factors listed in Section A1, above. In addition, there's a trend for courts to follow principles such as these:

• If a marriage lasted less than five years and the couple has no children, many courts will deny alimony altogether, at least on a permanent basis.

- If there are children below school age, most courts will order some alimony.

- If a marriage lasted at least eight years, most courts make an alimony award to try to assure a continuity in the standard of living for both spouses.

- In marriages that lasted at least ten years, most courts will award alimony indefinitely, or at least until the recipient dies, remarries, cohabits or no longer needs alimony.

Based on those factors, judges—and attorneys who regularly appear before those judges—estimate the amount of alimony to be paid or received. There's no universal formula or rule that applies. The amount of an alimony award, perhaps more than any other decision a judge can make, is seldom subject to challenge but often leaves ex-spouses the angriest.

To get an estimate of the amount of alimony you may have to pay or are likely to receive if the issue is presented to a judge for decision, you will need to speak to an attorney or mediator to determine local practice and custom. If you can't agree, you leave your fate to a judge whose decision may not meet your expectations.

3. How Much Alimony Do You Need— Or Can You Afford to Pay?

Figuring out how much alimony you need or can afford to pay centers on three concerns—income needs, taxes and payment practicalities.

a. Income Needs

Only a hard look at the income-alimony gap can reveal potential problems. If you come to terms with this gap, you have a better chance of closing it.

Here are a few suggestions if you, like many divorcing people, find that you run out of money before you run out of month:

- Cut expenses to reduce your debt load as much as possible.

- Do not use credit cards to finance your lifestyle.

- Take on a second job.

- Rent out part of your home to offset mortgage costs.

- Sell an asset and use the money to pay off debts.

Calculate how you would fare today if you had no option other than to pay or receive the alimony amount mandated by local custom or financial schedule. Then brainstorm about possible plans for resolving any budget problems you may face. Write your answers below.

Alimony Recipients

Monthly expenses:	$
Estimated alimony I will receive and my other net income (after taxes):	$
Difference:	$
How I will make up any shortfall:	

Alimony Payers

Monthly net income:	$
Estimated alimony I will pay and my monthly expenses:	$
Difference:	$
How I will make up any shortfall:	

Don't despair. In negotiating the overall settlement, you may get enough property or other assets to replace the loss of income caused by the divorce. You can explore this possibility in Chapter 19.

b. Taxes

To understand taxes and alimony, remember this basic rule: Alimony is tax deductible to the payer and taxable as income to the recipient, but only if the alimony is based on an agreement in writing (such as your divorce settlement papers) or is ordered by a court and very stringent rules are followed. If you do *not* want alimony to be taxed as income for the spouse receiving it, or to be a tax deduction for the spouse paying it, that preference may be spelled out in your marital settlement or separation agreement, or specified in a court order.

Factors to Consider in Making Alimony Nondeductible

A payer might not want to deduct alimony in any of the following situations:

- The payer can't use the alimony deduction—that is, if taxable income is low or if income comes from nontaxable sources, such as tax-exempt bonds, Social Security benefits, nontaxable pension benefits or nontaxable annuity payments.

- The payer expects other deductions (such as net operating loss carryovers from a business) to equal or exceed his gross income.

- The recipient is in a higher tax bracket than the payer.

- After the divorce, the recipient sold property to the payer and does not want the proceeds to be considered income.

If your taxes are particularly complicated, you will need to consult with your accountant to fully understand alimony's tax consequences. Ideally, you and your spouse (or your attorneys or accountants) should figure the tax consequences for each of you and fashion an agreement in which each person can receive the greatest number of after-tax dollars. Many attorneys and financial planners have computer programs that can make these calculations. In addition, consider the following points:

Recipients. All too often, the person receiving alimony treats it as "free" money, as in "tax free." On April 15, however, you may find yourself scrambling to pay income taxes on it. Be sure you manage your money in such a way that you put aside enough to cover this bill by making extra estimated tax payments.

You must also provide your ex-spouse with your Social Security number. If you fail to do so, the IRS can penalize you $50.

Payers. Keep careful records of the payments so you can deduct them properly. And obviously, you want to be sure the alimony award is in writing or is ordered by the court.

You can deduct alimony, even if you do not itemize your deductions. In addition, you must provide your ex-spouse's Social Security number on your tax return (and you must use Form 1040—not Form 1040A or 1040EZ). If you fail to do so, you may lose your entire alimony deduction and/or be penalized $50 for each failure to report per return.

To be deductible, alimony payments must meet the following conditions:

- There must be no obligation to pay after the death of the recipient.

- The payments must be made under a "divorce or separation instrument." These terms refer to a decree of divorce or separate maintenance, a written marital settlement or separation agreement or a court order or temporary decree.

- The payer and recipient cannot file a joint income tax return.

- The payments must be in cash for a definite amount. Cash paid to cover the rent, mortgage, taxes, tuition, health insurance or medical expenses of the recipient also qualify.

- Payments cannot be made to an ex-spouse living under the same roof after a final decree of divorce or legal separation.

- The payments cannot be disguised as child support.

The following payments qualify as alimony for tax purposes, assuming all of the preceding conditions are met:

- Premium payments on term or whole life insurance if the recipient of alimony is also the owner of the policy.

- Payments of the recipient spouse's attorney's fees.

- Payments of the recipient spouse's rent.

- One-half of the payments for mortgage (principal and interest), taxes, utilities and insurance on a residence co-owned by the payer and the recipient and held as tenants in common.

- Payments for mortgage (principal and interest), taxes and insurance on a residence owned solely by the recipient.

- Payments made after a remarriage of either spouse as long as the divorce agreement specifies that payments will continue.

- Payments made under an annulment decree, provided your state treats alimony after an annulment the same as it treats alimony after divorce.

- Some allotments for those in the military may qualify as deductions. See a military advisor for more details on this possible deduction.

The following payments are not deductible as alimony for income tax purposes, even if all of the above conditions are met:

- The fair rental value of property owned by the payer and used by the recipient.

- Payments (including mortgage, taxes and insurance premiums) to maintain property owned by the payer and used by the recipient. (These payments may qualify as a homeowner deduction for the payer, however.)

- Payments made to a recipient as the beneficiary of the payer's estate, if the payer dies. The recipient, however, must report the payments as income.

- Monthly allotments that represent an allowance for military quarters are nontaxable. In situations in which a court orders alimony paid from these allotments, the military person cannot deduct the payments. But alimony deducted from regular pay is deductible and taxable.

- If the spouses obtain a court order retroactively reclassifying equalization payments (to even up the property division) as alimony, the new "alimony" is not tax deductible.

- Payments made from a trust (alimony trust) set up to pay support, though the recipient spouse must include it as taxable income.

Alimony or Property Settlement Payments?

When your divorce settlement is being written, it is important to understand how alimony payments are structured. In some cases, the court may consider these payments as property being divided in the divorce. That matters to you because the payments may be subject to tax laws that differ from those involving a property transfer.

To qualify as alimony, the payments need not cease at remarriage, though they must terminate at death. In one case (*Prater v. Commissioner*, 95-1USTC ¶50,271 (10th Cir. 1995)), payments made by one former spouse to the other out of proceeds from an oil and gas lease were considered alimony even though there was no mention of these payments ceasing upon remarriage. The court held that even though the payments did not cease upon remarriage, the provision that they cease upon the recipient's death meant that the payments should be characterized as alimony.

In another case (*Hoover v. Commissioner* (Tax Court Memo 1995 ¶ 95,183)), the divorce decree awarded the wife the home, furnishings and "alimony as division of equity." That was because the final divorce decree did not contain a provision that all payments would cease upon death or remarriage, although the husband was to provide medical insurance until his former wife died or remarried. Because the liability for these payments did not cease upon the death of the ex-wife, payments were deemed a property settlement and not alimony, in spite of what the divorce decree called them.

Payments are regarded as part of the property settlement when:

- the sum is fixed

- the payments are not related to the payer's income

- the payments are to continue regardless of the recipient's death or remarriage

- in exchange for the payments, the recipient gave up more property than the payer or gave up some other valuable right in the property settlement, and

- the payer has put up security to insure payment.

The IRS Is Watching for "Frontloading"

Alimony is deductible by the payer in the year it's paid, as long as it hasn't been "frontloaded."

"Frontloading" does not describe a type of clothes dryer. It's a method some divorcing couples use to load up on tax-deductible alimony. Sometimes one spouse will pay a great deal of alimony the first year and then reduce it dramatically in later years. Or, a spouse will give the other some property, but call it alimony. In both cases, the IRS will want its share of money in taxes.

Example 1: Biff will be paying Kit $66,000 in total alimony. He decides to pay her $44,000 the first year and $11,000 the second and third years. Biff is clearly frontloading his payments—paying most of the alimony in the first year to get a bigger tax break. The IRS will recompute Biff's taxes at the end of the third year and slap him with a bill to recapture the tax break he got the first year.

Example 2: This time, Biff pays Kit $12,000 in cash and $30,000 for her new BMW in the first year. Even though only $12,000 was for the alimony itself, Biff deducts all $42,000 and calls all of it alimony. Biff plans to pay Kit $12,000 a year for the next two years to come up with the total $66,000. Again, Biff is clearly frontloading, and the IRS will hand him a bill at the end of the third year.

Biff could have avoided the frontloading charge by simply paying Kit $22,000 per year for each of the three years—without dramatically decreasing the amount or trying to pass off the transfer of the BMW as alimony. In general, the IRS rules against frontloading kick in if, during the first three years, the payments in one year exceed the payments in a succeeding year by more than $15,000.

Suppose, however, that Biff pays a large amount of alimony during the first year—more than $15,000—then loses his job and is able to have his payments greatly reduced. Even though he was not trying to trick the IRS, the frontload rules could nevertheless be triggered, and he could owe substantial taxes. Biff can protect himself with a tax indemnification agreement from Kit, which would make her responsible for such unintended tax consequences.

c. Payment Practicalities

If you will receive or pay alimony, you must be careful not to overlook the details involved in continuing a financial connection with your ex-spouse. Below are the questions we ask and suggestions we offer to cover payment practicalities. Whether you deal with these items as your negotiations progress or wait until the final settlement, use the spaces provided to jot down your ideas, which you can refer to later when needed. Put a check mark in front of the question once it is resolved.

_____ *How will alimony payments be made?*

_____

_____

_____

_____

If you're the recipient, you basically have four choices:

- You can wait for the proverbial "check in the mail."

- You can set up a wage deduction through your ex's employer, then have that money automatically deposited (through direct deposit plans) into your bank account.

- You can set up a voluntary account deduction through your ex's bank, then have that money automatically deposited into your bank account.

- You can have your lawyer prepare a QDRO (qualified domestic relations order) specifying that payments come directly from the payer's retirement plan.

Most recipients wait for the check, but it is becoming more common for courts to order wage assignments or garnishments, especially when the payer is also paying child support. (See Section D5, below.) Whatever you arrange, be sure the details are clearly outlined in writing.

_____ *On what day of the month will alimony payments be made?*

_____

_____

_____

_____

Payers usually find it most convenient to pay alimony shortly after receiving their salary checks or other income. If you are a recipient and payments won't arrive until after your mortgage, rent or some other large monthly bill is due, you'll need to rearrange your budget. Try to manage your cash flow so there's some money left over from the previous month. If that won't work, contact the lender and ask that your payment date be pushed ahead to correspond with your cash flow—you don't need to tell the lender you're waiting for your alimony check unless the lender pushes the question. Most lenders will make arrangements to accommodate payments.

_____ *How long will alimony payments be made?*

_____

_____

_____

_____

Records to Keep When You Pay or Receive Support

You must keep adequate records if you are paying or receiving alimony. This point cannot be over-emphasized. Frequently, after a divorce, the spouses dispute, or the IRS challenges, the amounts that were actually paid or received. Without adequate documentation, the payer may lose the alimony tax deduction and be ordered to pay back support if the other spouse makes a claim in court.

Payer

Here are suggestions of records to keep:

• list showing each payment (date, check number, place where sent)

• original checks used for payments or bank copies of your cancelled checks showing both the front and the back (keep in a safe place, such as a safe-deposit box)—be sure to note on each check (before you send it) the month for which the support is being paid, and

• a receipt signed by the recipient, if you pay in cash.

Be sure to keep these records for at least three years from the date you file the tax return deducting the payments. You might want to keep them even longer, if, for example, your ex-spouse has more than three years to sue you for any claim that you owe back support.

Recipient

Make a list that shows each payment received. Include the following information:

• date payment was received

• amount received

• check number or other document identifying the number (for example, the number of the money order)

• account number on which any check was written

• name of bank on which check is drawn or money order issued

• a photocopy of the check or money order, and

• a copy of any signed receipt you give for cash payments.

It's becoming more rare for alimony payments to be ordered indefinitely. And even in "indefinite" arrangements, alimony almost always ends if the recipient remarries or the payer retires. It usually ends if the payer dies. Sometimes, alimony lasts for a set number of years—often for the length of time it takes for the recipient to get training to reenter the workforce or, sometimes, to allow the recipient to stay home with young children.

Whatever your arrangement, pay close attention to the termination date. Suppose you are to receive alimony until September 30 of a certain year, based on the assumption that you will return to school, graduate in June of that year and use the summer to find a job. What will you do if your education and career path don't work out as planned? You can usually go back to court and ask for an extension of the alimony, *but only if you make your request before the scheduled termination date*. If you wait until after the September 30 termination date, you're probably out of luck, because the court will have "reserved jurisdiction"—kept the power to make decisions—only until September 30 of that year.

When there is no termination date, alimony is generally modifiable upward or downward depending on a former spouse's continued ability to pay and the other spouse's need.

_____ *How will you handle future economic changes, such as inflation or salary increases?*

_____

_____

_____

_____

If your alimony payment does not change, the amount it can actually buy year to year is sure to decrease. That's inflation. It's possible to take inflation into account in your alimony agreement with a COLA—Cost of Living Adjustment—clause. Some couples tie COLA increases to the rise in the Consumer Price Index (CPI); others simply choose a specific dollar amount.

Similarly, couples can avoid extended bitterness over alimony arrangements if they face the question of salary increases in advance. Will the recipient get a share of the payer's raise? Will the recipient's raise mean the alimony payment decreases? Be sure you know ahead of time how these questions will be handled.

_____ *What life or disability insurance policies will cover your ex-spouse?*

_____

_____

_____

_____

If you are dependent on someone else for your income, what will you do if that person becomes disabled or dies? If you will be the alimony recipient, you'll want to make sure you have appropriate insurance coverage on your ex-spouse. You could purchase a life insurance policy on your ex. Or your ex could buy life and disability insurance—naming you as the beneficiary—to protect your income stream. To get a tax deduction on the insurance premiums, the payer can pay the premium money to the recipient by increasing the alimony and having the recipient make the insurance payments. The alimony recipient must be the absolute owner of the policy. (Remember, however, an increase in alimony may increase the recipient's income taxes.)

_____ *What will happen if the payer tries to modify the alimony payments or stops paying altogether?*

_____

_____

_____

_____

If you are the payer and you cannot afford to pay the amount of alimony you've been ordered to pay, you must file for modification of the order with the court. At your hearing, you must show a material change in circumstances since the last court order. Your ex-spouse's cohabitation with someone of the opposite sex may qualify, especially in Alabama,

California, Connecticut, Georgia, Illinois, Louisiana, New York, Oklahoma, Pennsylvania, Tennessee and Utah, where such cohabitation raises a presumption of a decreased need for alimony.

Another common reason for changing alimony is your decreased income. Where you have voluntarily decreased your income, however—for example, you quit your job as a doctor to work in a pastry shop—the judge may instead consider your ability to earn, not your actual earnings.

If you are a recipient and your ex stops paying, you will need to go to court. Most likely, you will have to schedule a hearing in which your ex-spouse is ordered to come to court and explain why he or she isn't paying. You can also ask the court to grant you a judgment for the amount owed, or "in arrears." You can then use judgment collection methods, such as wage attachments and property liens, to try to collect the arrears.

Alimony and Bankruptcy

Alimony cannot be erased in bankruptcy. If your ex owes a substantial amount and tries to have it wiped out in bankruptcy, you will be protected so long as you follow bankruptcy laws and procedures. For more on bankruptcy and divorce, see Chapter 17, Section D.

4. Are There Alternatives to Paying or Receiving Monthly Alimony?

While financial schedules and legal guidelines help establish the amount of alimony, they don't require any certain payment arrangement. Although alimony is traditionally paid monthly, it is possible to pay it in a lump sum, periodically or combined with child support.

a. Lump Sum Alimony

A lump sum settlement of alimony upon divorce is sometimes called an alimony buyout. Before agreeing to a buyout, consider its pros and cons.

i. For the Recipient

There are four major advantages to accepting a lump sum settlement:

- You reduce the risk of depending on someone else—who could default, become disabled or die—for income. Reducing the risk of depending on someone who could default is important—alimony default rates exceed 50% in many places.

- You can use the lump sum for a down payment on a house or other purposes, such as paying bills.

- If you have no children, you can terminate any further contact with your ex-spouse.

- If the lump sum is characterized as nontaxable alimony, it is not taxable to you as the recipient.

  There are also disadvantages to a buyout:

- You lose a steady flow of income.

- Once you accept a lump sum payment, you cannot go back to court to reinstate alimony.

- You may receive less than you would have in monthly payments. You and your soon-to-be-ex-spouse may agree on a lower amount just to get rid of each other. Also, had you written a COLA (Cost of Living Adjustment) clause into your settlement, your payments would have risen over time, a consideration usually not factored into a lump sum payment.

- You run the risk of losing some or all of the lump sum payment through bad investments or other unforeseen circumstances such as a debilitating illness.

ii. For the Payer

There are three major advantages to making a lump sum settlement:

- Because writing a monthly alimony check to a former spouse can be a grating experience, which creates resentment and ill will after the divorce, a lump sum may be easier emotionally.

- If you have no children, you can end the marriage with a strong sense of finality.

- Because a buyout compresses all future payments into one present payment, the total is often discounted for taxes and is less than what would have been paid over a set number of years. For example, Mitch agrees to pay Sara $1,000 per month for the next five years, for a total of $60,000. Mitch figures inflation is around 4%, and in today's dollars, $60,000 is worth only $54,480. Mitch offers that amount less taxes in a present-day lump sum settlement.

  There are also disadvantages to a buyout:

- You have to come up with a large sum of money.

- Under standard alimony plans, payments cease if the recipient dies, remarries or, in some cases, cohabits with someone of the opposite sex. You could pay a lump sum at divorce only to watch your ex remarry in a year.

- Because a buyout cannot be renegotiated, you could end up paying more in the lump sum than might have been required. For instance, if your ex obtains a high-paying job or your income drops a great deal, you might have been able to reduce the monthly alimony payments.

- Your payment might trigger the frontloading rules, or it could look like a property settlement payment if it's paid over less than three years and the annual amount exceeds $15,000. If you are not going to pay the entire buyout in one year, the IRS could interpret the arrangement as frontloading and assess taxes at the end of the third year.

- If the lump sum settlement is less than $15,000, it would be tax deductible. Otherwise, it may trigger the frontloading rules, and a portion of it would not be tax deductible.

Transferring Assets to the Recipient in Exchange for Alimony

Certain assets, such as the house, stocks or a pension plan, could be given to your spouse in exchange for her releasing you from an obligation to pay alimony. You may want to consider this option if you do not relish the idea of making monthly alimony payments or if you are strapped for cash and the payments would make your budget tighter.

You might also consider this option if you don't want to hold assets on which you may have to ultimately pay capital gains taxes, or if you want to sever all financial ties with your soon-to-be-ex-spouse.

Exchanging property for alimony, however, means you would not get the tax deduction you get from making alimony payments. But you may nevertheless want to consider this option when negotiating the final settlement.

b. Family Support

Sometimes, alimony and child support are combined into one monthly payment called family support. Family support is child support not specified as such. Therefore, it is fully taxable to the recipient and tax deductible to the payer.

Recipients enjoy one advantage if a payer defaults. In that situation, the recipient has numerous child support collection techniques available. (See Section D5, below.) If the payer defaults on alimony payments, the only collection method in most states involves taking the payer to court. Be warned, however, that a growing number of courts are disallowing family support, not wanting to burden the child support collection bureaus with collecting what is really alimony.

Special Problems When Alimony and Child Support Are Combined Into One Payment of Family Support

If a family support payment is reduced, and the reduction is related to any of the events listed below, the amount by which the support is reduced will be treated like child support, not alimony. This can be a problem. The IRS may classify your former payments as child support, not alimony, and recompute your taxes to disallow the alimony deduction. The Internal Revenue Code does not recognize the concept of family support, classifying payments for tax purposes as either child support or alimony.

Events that can cause "family support" payments to be classified as child support include:

- a child reaching a specified age
- the death of a child
- a child leaving school
- a child leaving the household of the custodial parent, and
- a child becoming employed.

To avoid having the payments treated like child support (and losing the tax deductibility of the payments), don't base the reduction of family support on any contingency related to the child's age or needs. If you have more than one child, again, don't tie in the reduction to the date when each child reaches a certain age. Finally, don't call your support "family support" if your children are near the age of majority (usually 18 or 21).

5. What Is Your Bottom-Line Decision on Paying or Receiving Alimony?

You may have little choice about alimony payments, but you must nevertheless make decisions about them. Will you negotiate for a lump sum buyout? Will you use alimony as leverage in negotiating for other assets? Use this space to describe your bottom-line decision on alimony payments so you can easily refer to this information in Chapter 19 when you bring all your decisions to the negotiating table.

_____

_____

_____

C. Child Support—Legal, Financial and Emotional Realities

Children, unfortunately, are frequently the emotional pawns of divorce. Parents express their resentments about their mates by degrading the other parent in front of the children and by fighting over the children when dealing with custody and child support issues. Fighting scares the children and makes them feel guilty. It also wastes time, money and resources that could have been spent more positively on your children.

As difficult as it sounds, try to keep your emotions in check. This doesn't mean you should hide your feelings about your divorce from your children. It does mean that you should not take your anger out on your kids. Instead, try to include them in the process in constructive ways. By maintaining a healthy emotional attitude, you will be better equipped to deal with the legal and financial realities of child support.

1. Legal Realities

Every parent has an obligation to support his or her children, regardless of divorce. Suppose one parent has primary custody, traditionally called "physical custody," and the other has secondary custody, or "visitation rights." (See sidebar, "Legal Language Alert," below) The parent with less custody time is usually ordered to pay some child support to the custodial parent. It is assumed that the custodial parent is meeting his or her child support obligation through the custody itself. For parents with joint physical custody, the support obligation of each is often based on a number of factors, such as the ratio of each parent's income to their combined incomes, the percentage of time the child spends with each parent and who pays necessary expenses for the child.

While divorcing spouses are permitted to decide virtually all the terms of their divorce without court intervention, the court will insist on examining the child support arrangement. If the judge approves of the arrangement, the court will include it in the judgment. Some of the factors evaluated by courts in setting child support include:

- the needs of the child

- each parent's ability to earn and pay support, and

- the amount of time the child spends with each parent.

Society has become less tolerant of parents who fail to comply with child support obligations, and the federal government requires all state governments to enact laws to facilitate enforcement of child support orders. Tools for collecting child support are discussed in Section D5, below.

Legal Language Alert: Custody by Any Other Name …

Traditionally, terms such as "custodial parent" or "noncustodial parent" have been used by courts and among people in general when talking about parent-child relationships after a divorce. In light of changing family patterns, however, courts are beginning to recognize shared parenting styles and other such arrangements. Legal language is therefore changing, and terms such as "primary custody" and "secondary custody" are beginning to be used. For the time being, however, we will continue to refer to "custodial" or "noncustodial" parents until the new terms become more commonplace.

2. Financial Realities

Any legal award of child support is probably going to be less than the actual amount necessary to meet the needs of growing children. As with the gap between alimony and living expenses, you will have to devise strategies for finding the additional money not provided by child support.

Even if you receive an adequate child support award, financial reality demands that you recognize the problems caused by lack of compliance. If you are the recipient, what will you do when the check does not arrive or comes late? If you are the payer, what happens when your paycheck is suddenly garnished—or worse, you are threatened with jail for noncompliance? Don't dwell on these negative questions, but at least confront them for your children's sake.

Also keep in mind two new, but sad, trends emerging from the financial realities of divorce. Some parents have reached the painful conclusion that they cannot retain custody of their children because they do not have the resources to support them. At the same time, other parents are fighting for joint custody so they can pay less child support. To avoid these situations, you must squarely face the true costs generated by children and prepare your strongest position for negotiating your settlement and protecting the interests of your children.

The true costs of rearing children are high-lighted in Section D3, below.

3. Emotional Realities

Your children's reaction to your divorce can have a major effect on your emotional state. On all issues concerning your children—child support, custody and visitation—you and your mate may inwardly and outwardly struggle over what's best for your children.

A spouse caught up in a power struggle may try to use the children to get back at the other, causing turmoil for all. The "Disneyland Dad" (or Mom) showers the children with gifts, using financial leverage as a way of upstaging the other parent. Be aware of your own behavior, and remember that it can do more damage to the children than to anyone else. Do not let child support payments become an excuse for venting frustrations at your ex-spouse.

D. Steps to a Settlement

As you move through your divorce, you will probably find that your choices about child support are dictated by local financial guidelines. Nevertheless, by answering the following questions, you can analyze the financial consequences of paying or receiving child support:

- Who will have custody of the children?
- What are the guidelines for child support in your state?
- What does it cost to rear your children?
- How much child support do you need—or can you afford to pay?
- What is your bottom-line decision regarding custody and child support?

1. Who Will Have Custody of the Children?

Custody has two components: the legal authority to make decisions about the medical, educational, health and welfare needs of a child (legal custody), and physical control over a child (physical custody). In most states, courts now tend to award joint custody, which lets divorced parents share physical custody, legal custody or both. The most common arrangement is for legal custody to be shared, with one parent given physical custody and the other parent given visitation rights. This situation has now changed somewhat as more parents work to share time with their children.

You can work out whatever arrangement you want regarding custody. If you can't agree, you may be able to use mediation. Mediation is a nonadversarial process in which a neutral person (a mediator) meets with parents to help them resolve problems. Both parents must agree to any solution reached through mediation; the mediator cannot impose a solution on the parties. Thirty-eight states can require parents to participate in mediation before bringing a custody dispute to court. If you still can't agree (or don't use mediation) and you leave the custody decision to the court, the legal standard the court will use is "the best interests of the child." The factors courts consider in determining the best interests usually include:

- age and sex of the child

- child's preference (if the child is above a certain age, usually about 12)

- relationship of the child with the parents, siblings and any stepparent

- established living pattern for the child concerning school, home, community and the like

- mental and physical health of the child and parents (including any history of abuse), and

- lifestyle of the parents and other social factors.

2. What Are the Guidelines for Child Support in Your State?

Congress passed the Family Support Act of 1988, which required all states to adopt a statewide uniform child support formula. Parents may be able to agree on a child support amount different from that required by the state formula. However, neither the court nor the children are bound by the agreement if it is for less than the state minimum. Child support is an area in which judges have little discretion to allow support that is less than the guidelines. Remember: *All* parents are obligated to support their children, and a custodial parent cannot give up *the child's* right to receive support.

To find out how much you are likely to pay or receive, you will have to get your state's child support formula. Ask your lawyer, the local support collection division of the district attorney's office (the office obligated to enforce child support orders), a parents' support group or a court clerk.

What If Your Spouse Takes a Lower Paying Job to Reduce the Child Support Obligation?

Courts are displaying little tolerance for spouses who take lower paying jobs than those for which they are qualified. A court may "impute"—that is, assume—a higher amount of income for that spouse and base child support on that higher amount. Also, to determine support payments, a court may factor in benefits from deferred compensation, fringe benefits and certain depreciation deductions for the purpose of determining business income. California and New York courts lead the way in making it difficult for individuals to play games with income in order to hold down alimony or child support payments.

3. What Does It Cost to Rear Your Children?

The list below will alert you to items you should consider in figuring the cost of rearing children. As you review the list, calculate the average amount you spend each month. You can make this calculation by totaling the three most recent months and then dividing by three. Check the Monthly Expenses column of your *Cash Flow Statement* (see Chapter 12), look back through your checkbook or make an educated guess to find your monthly outlays.

After filling in each number, total the expenses at the end.

$ _____ *Child care*

If both parents work, child care costs must be considered. If you relied on informal babysitting arrangements with friends or relatives while married, those arrangements cannot and should not be considered permanent. If you don't know the going rate for child care in your area, investigate. You must factor the cost of competent care into your children's future. Often the court will order that child care expenses be shared by the parents to allow the custodial parent to work outside the home.

$ _____ *Education or college funds*

Even after divorce, it's possible for parents together to realize the joint goal of providing for a child's private schooling or college education. It takes planning, cooperation and agreements, but it can be done. Besides college, your children may want to receive special training for a profession or the arts. These costs can sometimes be staggering. It's necessary to recognize them now, before your settlement is negotiated.

Rising College Costs

If your children will attend college, don't forget inflation. Throughout your divorce you have to keep an eye on the future—and that includes the real-dollar costs of that future. Tallying the impact of inflation on college expenses can be an eye-opener. Suppose tuition currently averages $10,000 annually. If inflation is 4% a year and your seven-year-old enrolls as a freshman in ten years, you will need $16,010 of today's dollars to pay that $10,000 tuition.

You must also consider the fact that college tuition itself will increase. In this example, if tuition increases at 7% per year, you will need $19,672 for that freshman year (not counting any increase for inflation)—almost twice the current tuition. You will need to put your college funds in an investment vehicle that grows at a rate faster than inflation.

$ _____ *Emergency savings*

Financial planners make a standard recommendation that you have an emergency cash reserve equal to three to six months of fixed expenses. Be sure that reserve includes your children's normal expenses. You can also make your life after divorce easier if you include a cash cushion for the unexpected emergencies that only children can create.

$ _____ *Health and dental care*

Divorce affects the health care coverage of children. You and your spouse must reach an agreement as to who will carry the children on his or her health plan, who will buy coverage and how medical expenses not covered by the plan or co-payments

and deductibles will be paid. If you cannot agree, a court will make the order for you. Some states mandate that if neither parent has insurance covering the children, one parent must pay for reasonable medical insurance. Also be aware of what benefits are covered and how long they last. For more details on health care coverage for youngsters, see Section D4, below.

$ _____ *Hobbies*

Are your children involved in sports, music or ballet? Do they act in community theater? Do they want to go to summer camp? Do they expect to as they grow older? Check how much has been spent on special lessons and hobbies, or talk to parents whose children are involved in similar pursuits to get an idea of future costs. You will want your agreement to indicate who will pay for which activities and hobbies.

$ _____ *Birthdays and holidays*

Do you splurge on special occasions and birthdays? Do your children have high expectations about gifts? Depending on how many children you have, these costs can add up. You may need to readjust your budget and let your children know about the change. Under the best circumstances, you and your soon-to-be-ex-spouse might agree to a spending limit so that one partner does not use "goodies" to turn the children against the less affluent parent.

$ _____ *Total expenses for children*

4.   Health Insurance Coverage

Of all the uncertainties that result from a divorce, getting or keeping health care coverage for your children can be one of the most worrisome. To help relieve some of this worry, a federal law (P.L. 103-66, Omnibus Reconciliation Act of 1993) allows custodial parents to obtain a court order for health insurance coverage for their children through the noncustodial parent's employment insurance plan. Coverage cannot be denied by the noncustodial parent, his or her employer or the insurance company simply because the child does not live with that parent, is not claimed as a dependent or lives outside of the plan's service area.

The court order for health care for your children is called a QMCSO, a Qualified Medical Child Support Order. A QMCSO can require that:

- an employee's child is covered under an employer-provided health care plan

- the premium is deducted from the employee's paycheck

- reimbursements are made directly to the non-employee parent if that parent pays the provider

- the nonemployee parent receives information regarding the health care plan and reimbursements, and

- other health coverage is provided as specifically directed.

You will want to use a QMCSO when:

- The employee parent is or may be a recalcitrant payer.

- The employee parent's regular medical plan determines that the children are ineligible for dependent coverage if they are living with the other parent.

- The custodial parent prefers to deal directly with the plan administrator for information, forms and reimbursement.

- The employee parent selects a medical plan that is not suitable for the child. For example, if the employed parent chooses a plan with a very high deductible—not appropriate when you have children who will inevitably visit the doctor—the QMCSO gives the other parent the option of selecting a plan with a very low or no deductible.

- The employee parent wants to take advantage of favorable "family coverage" premiums.

To qualify as a QMCSO, the medical support order must:

- create the child's right to receive benefits under the group plan

- specify the employee parent's name and last known mailing address and also that of each child covered by the plan

- specify each plan and time frame to which the order applies, and

- not require the plan to provide any additional benefits not actually provided in the plan.

While the QMCSO can be valuable in making sure your children's health care is protected, it may include some of the following limitations:

- Limited coverage for a child residing outside the area served by the plan. Although the plan cannot deny coverage for this reason, it can offer only limited coverage.

- Limis on a child's ability to obtain medical coverage different from the coverage provided by the employee parent.

- Inapplicability to self-insured plans.

If you elect to use a QMCSO, the custodial parent should obtain copies of the following:

- a medical plan and summary plan description

- election forms highlighting the possible elections and open enrollment periods

- information on current beneficiary designations, and

- written material concerning plan requirements for terms of a QMCSO.

A sample QMSCO appears at the end of this chapter.

5. How Much Child Support Do You Need—Or Can You Afford to Pay?

In figuring out how much child support you need or can afford to pay, you will consider the same three items you considered with alimony—income needs, taxes and payment practicalities.

a. Income Needs

The difference between legal reality and financial reality defines your income needs for child support. By legal reality, we mean the amount set by your state's child support formula. This is the guideline amount that you are likely to pay or receive. Your lawyer or local agencies can help you determine this figure (see Section D2, above).

The financial reality is the actual cost every month of rearing your children. You came up with an estimate of this monthly total in Section D3.

For recipients. If your actual child-raising costs are higher than the amount in the legal guideline and you have no way to make up the gap, you'll have to negotiate for a higher amount. If your spouse is aware that the guidelines are lower than the amount you are asking for, you may have little leverage. Nevertheless, you can still attempt to push up the amount of support.

For payers. Recognize that the gap between what your children cost and what you have to pay has to be closed somehow. If the custodial parent has no other source of revenue, keep in mind that he or she may ask for more money from you, now and in the future. You and your spouse may be able to save yourselves time and trouble by negotiating child support from a realistic financial base right from the start. Often, divorcing couples find there is simply not enough money to meet these costs, and both spouses have to pare down their lifestyles.

b. Taxes

Child support payments have no tax consequences. They are neither deductible to the payer nor taxed as income to the recipient.

Children, however, have plenty of tax consequences. First and foremost, they are considered dependency exemptions. Parents must decide who will claim the children at tax time. Often, the noncustodial parent claims the children in exchange for paying higher support. The custodial parent must relinquish claim to the dependency exemption by signing IRS Form 8332, Release of Claim to Exemption for Child of Divorced or Separated Parents. When the parents have joint physical custody, they may each claim a child (if they have more than one) or alternate the claim year to year. No matter who claims the children as dependents, both parents must list the children's Social Security numbers on their tax returns to ensure that only one parent is claiming the children.

The following tax benefits are among those available to parents to offset the cost of raising children:

- earned income credit
- child care credit
- medical expense deductions
- head of household filing status
- dependency exemption
- child tax credit (for three or more children)
- deduction for interest on qualified education loans
- Hope and Lifetime Learning credits for tuition costs, and
- Education IRAs.

You need to be aware of these tax benefits as you make your custody and child support agreements.

Only a custodial parent is entitled to claim the child care tax credit. In general, employed custodial parents of a dependent child under the age of 13 are eligible for the credit for child care expenses incurred so that the parent can earn an income. As the custodial parent's income increases, however, the credit phases out. Keep in mind the availability of the tax credit when negotiating your agreement about who will pay child care expenses.

Any parent can claim a deduction for medical expenses actually paid, but only if those medical expenses exceed 7½% of your adjusted gross income. If your total medical expenses are high enough, you may want to allocate them to the lower wage earner so that parent can take the deduction.

Only a parent with physical custody (for more than half the time) can file as head of household. If the parents have joint legal and physical custody (and physical custody is divided 50-50), neither can file as head of household, because the dependent child resides with neither parent for more than 50% of the year.

If you have more than one minor child and share physical custody, you can specify your arrangement as 51% for one child with one parent and 51% for the other child with the other parent. Because each parent has a dependent child in the home more than 50% of the year, each parent can file as head of household.

c. Payment Practicalities

The practical matter of getting child support payments from one person to the other can create highly charged problems. Below are questions we ask and suggestions we offer to help prevent these problems. Whether you deal with these items during your negotiations or in the final settlement, use the spaces provided to jot down your ideas. You can refer to these points when needed. Put a check mark in front of the question once it is resolved.

_____   *How will child support be paid?*

_____

_____

_____

_____

You can agree to send or receive a monthly check. The court, however, may want to set up a different process.

The Family Support Act of 1988 requires that by 1994, all child support orders had to contain an automatic wage withholding provision. An automatic wage withholding order works quite simply. When the court orders you to pay child support, the court—or your child's other parent—sends a copy of the court order to your employer. The custodial parent's name and address is included with this order. At each pay period, your employer withholds a portion of your pay and sends it on to the custodial parent. Only if you and your child's other parent agree—and the court allows it—can you avoid the wage withholding and make payments directly to the custodial parent.

If you don't receive regular wages but do have a regular source of income, such as payments from a retirement fund, annuity or Social Security, the court can order the child support withheld. Instead of forwarding a copy of the order and the custodial parent's name and address to an employer, the court sends the information to the retirement plan administrator or public agency from which you receive your benefits.

The mandatory wage withholding operates differently among the states. In Texas and Vermont, for example, all current orders include automatic wage withholding, regardless of the parent's payment history. The rationale is that by not distinguishing between parents with poor payment histories and parents who have paid regularly, no parent is stigmatized.

In California, wage withholding orders are automatic as well. But parents who show a reliable history of paying child support may be exempt. And in all states, employers must withhold wages if the payer is one month delinquent in support.

A few states have set up other mechanisms to collect child support as it becomes due. For example, a judge may order a noncustodial parent to pay child support to the state's child support enforcement agency, which in turn pays the custodial parent. This program is often used where automatic wage withholding is not in effect. It may also be used for noncustodial parents without regular income (the self-employed) or when parents agree to waive the automatic wage withholding.

Some other states let judges order noncustodial parents to make payments to court clerks or court trustees who in turn pay the custodial parents. This program is mandatory in Arizona, Idaho and Kansas.

_____   *On what day of the month will payments be made?*

_____

_____

_____

_____

Most custodial parents find it convenient to pay child support shortly after being paid themselves. If you are a recipient, and payments will not arrive until after your child's monthly child care bill or health insurance premium is due, you'll need to make different arrangements. Try saving money from the previous month or contacting the creditor and negotiating a new payment schedule. Try to get your payments in sync with your cash flow. You don't need to tell the creditor you're waiting for your child support check. Creditors may be surprisingly cooperative when you contact them in advance and honestly negotiate so they are assured of getting their payments.

_____   *How long will child support payments be made?*

_____

_____

_____

_____

You must pay child support for as long as your child support court order says you must pay. If the order does not contain an ending date, in most states you must support your children until they reach age 18. A few states, however, extend the time and require you to support your children:

- until they finish high school
- until they reach 21 (for example, this is the requirement in New York)
- until they complete college, or
- if they are disabled, for as long as they are dependent.

Your child support obligation will end, however, if your child joins the military, gets married or moves out of the house to live independently, or if a court declares your child emancipated.

If you owe back support, it doesn't go away when your child turns 18 (or whatever age you are no longer liable for support). Many states give a custodial parent ten or 20 years to collect back child support—with interest.

_____   *How will you handle child support modifications?*

_____

_____

_____

_____

A court retains the power to make orders involving child support until every last dollar owed is paid. If a noncustodial parent can't afford the payments, he or she must take the offensive to change the child support order. Or, if a custodial parent can't live on the current payment, he or she needs to ask for more. As a first step, the parent wanting the change should call the other parent and try to work out an agreement. If you reach an agreement, be sure to get it in writing. You'll then need to get a judge's signature.

If you can't make satisfactory arrangements with your ex-spouse, the parent wanting the change will have to file papers with the court, schedule a hearing and then show the judge that he or she cannot afford to pay—or to live on—the ordered support. A noncustodial parent needs to understand that a court won't retroactively decrease child support, even if the noncustodial parent was too sick to get out of bed during the affected period. Once child support is owed and unpaid, it remains a debt until it is paid.

To get a judge to change a child support order, you must show a "significant change of circumstance" since the last order. What constitutes a "significant change of circumstance" depends on your situation. Generally, the condition must not have been considered when the original order was made and must affect your—or your child's or the other parent's—current standard of living.

Changes that qualify for a *noncustodial* parent include:

- your income has substantially decreased

- you have increased expenses, such as a new child

- a raise you expected—which was the basis of the last order—didn't materialize

- the custodial parent received a large inheritance, an increase in compensation or income-producing assets, or

- your child's needs have decreased—for example, she is no longer attending private school.

Changes that qualify for a *custodial* parent include:

- you have a substantial decrease in income

- you have increased expenses, such as a new child

- the noncustodial parent received a raise, large inheritance or income-producing assets, or

- your child's needs have increased—for example, he now needs ongoing counseling.

_____   *How will you handle nonpayment of child support?*

_____

_____

_____

_____

Unpaid child support (sometimes referred to as "being in arrears") accumulates when the parent doesn't pay what is owed. If the recipient is owed a great deal in arrears, he or she can go to court and ask a judge to issue a judgment for the amount due.

States' child support enforcement agencies, custodial parents, judges and district attorneys use several different methods to collect child support.

Court hearings. Failing to follow a court order is called "contempt of court." A parent owed child support can schedule a "show cause" hearing before a judge. The other parent must be served with a document ordering him or her to attend the hearing, and then must attend and explain why the support hasn't been paid. If the noncustodial parent is a no-show, the court can issue a warrant for his or her arrest, which could lead to a night or two at the county jail.

If the noncustodial parent attends the hearing, the judge can still throw him or her in jail for violating the support order. To stay out of jail, the parent must first show why the money wasn't paid and then explain why he or she didn't request a modification hearing.

Court hearings (and jail) are the second-most frequently used child support enforcement technique, after wage withholding. Throwing a parent in jail for not paying child support has proven to be somewhat effective.

Interception of income tax refunds or lottery winnings. One of the most powerful collection methods available is an interception of the payer's federal income tax refund. The custodial parent can ask the district attorney to call the Treasury Department for help. States (with income taxes) also intercept tax refunds to satisfy child support debts. In Nebraska, for example, court clerks report all child support arrears to the state for an interception of the tax refund. Also, many states with lotteries let custodial parents apply to the state for an interception of the other parent's winnings.

Property liens. In some states, a custodial parent can place a lien on the payer's real or personal property. The lien stays in effect until the payer pays up, or until the custodial parent agrees to remove the liens. The custodial parent can force the sale of the noncustodial parent's property, or can wait until the property is sold.

Posting bonds or assets to guarantee payment. Some states allow judges to require parents with child support arrears to post bonds or assets, such as stock certificates, to guarantee payment. In California, for example, if a self-employed parent misses a child support payment and the custodial parent requests a court hearing, the court *must* order the noncustodial parent to post assets (such as putting money into an escrow account) equal to one year's support or $6,000, whichever is less.

Reports to credit bureaus. If the custodial parent owes more than $1,000 in child support, that information may find its way into a credit file maintained by a credit bureau. Federal law requires child support enforcement agencies to report known child support arrears of $1,000 or more. Many child support enforcement agencies automatically send information about owed child support to credit bureaus, regardless of the amount owed.

Reporting to "most wanted" lists. States are encouraged to come up with creative ways to embarrass parents into paying the child support they owe. Most states now publish "most wanted" lists of parents who owe child support.

Refusal to renew professional licenses. Some states will not renew contractor's or professional licenses of people behind on child support. Without a license, the payer cannot legally practice his or her profession in the state.

Refusal to renew driver's license. Parents in some states are not allowed to renew a driver's license if they have not met child support obligations.

Wage and property garnishments. Child support arrears can often be collected by a wage garnishment. A wage garnishment is similar to a wage withholding—a portion of the noncustodial parent's wages is removed from the paycheck and delivered to the custodial parent. They differ, however, in one way: the amount withheld. The amount of a wage withholding is *the amount of child support ordered each month.* The amount of a wage garnishment is *a percentage of the payer's paycheck.* The amount the payer was originally ordered to pay is irrelevant.

If the wage garnishment does not cover what's owed, the custodial parent may try to get other property to cover that debt. Common property targets includes bank accounts, cars, motorcycles, boats and airplanes, houses and other real property, stock in corporations and accounts receivable. It's also possible that unemployment compensation can be withheld in some states.

District attorney assistance. In most states, a local D.A. will help—and in some states is required to help—a custodial parent who hasn't received child support.

Tapping Pension Plans to Pay Spousal and Child Support

A Qualified Domestic Relations Order (QDRO, pronounced "quadro") is a court order to the administrator of a retirement plan spelling out how the plan's benefits are to be assigned to each spouse in a divorce. (See Chapter 14, Section B for details). A QDRO can be used to collect child support and/or alimony payments from the funds in a retirement plan under certain conditions.

A QDRO is most useful when the payer is self-employed and has rights to benefits from a prior employer or when the payer changes jobs a lot. If the payer is not yet eligible for benefits, you may be able to secure payments from a defined contribution plan, such as a profit-sharing or 401(k) plan. These plans are a particularly good source for support arrears because the plan administrators normally want to make a lump sum payment, not a series of monthly payments.

If your spouse's pension plan qualifies, you can use the QDRO to collect child support and/or alimony payments. The QDRO must clearly specify how much will be paid, to whom and for how long, and the benefits must be currently available to an alternate payee (nonemployee spouse) under the terms of the plan.

If the retirement plan currently pays benefits, the QDRO operates like a garnishment of wages—that is, the money is removed from the benefits check and sent directly to the recipient. If retirement benefits are not yet being paid, the structure of the QDRO depends on the situation. If the payer is eligible to receive benefits under the plan (but has chosen to continue working), the QDRO could require that the plan make the monthly support payments. If the payer is still working, however, it is usually easier to use a wage garnishment.

Tax Problems With Using a QDRO

Child support, unlike alimony, is not taxable. Using a QDRO to collect child support from a pension plan, however, makes it taxable income to the recipient, because the tax code requires that any payments from a QDRO to a former spouse be taxed. To compensate, you can try to get the child support payments increased to allow for withholding of taxes. Otherwise, do not use this option unless no reasonable alternative exists to collect the payments.

6. What Is Your Bottom-Line Decision Regarding Custody and Child Support?

 By this point, you've worked through questions on custody and child support. Use the space below to formalize your decision by writing out what you want to accomplish regarding custody and support in the settlement negotiations.

_____

_____

_____

_____

_____

_____

_____

_____

_____

_____

E. Questions to Ask Your Attorney

1. If you live in a community property state: Will my payment of alimony before our divorce is final be deductible, or is it considered an allocation to my spouse of community income?

   If it isn't deductible, can a separation agreement or final divorce decree be written so as to make it deductible?

2. What conduct might jeopardize my right to custody of my children? Am I permitted to move away if I have custody? If I don't have custody and my ex-spouse wants to move with the children, can I fight for custody or block the move?

3. What formula is used to calculate child support in my state?

4. Does child support in my state cover all child-related expenses, including medical, clothing, allowances and child care? If not, what expenses does child support cover, and who pays for the other costs?

5. What will I do if my spouse falls behind in child support and/or alimony?

6. How does the court enforce child support and alimony orders?

7. Is it wise to arrange for "family support" payments instead of child support?

8. How will alimony or child support be affected if a parent receives government welfare benefits?

9. If my ex-spouse remarries or takes a new partner, does that affect his or her obligation to pay or receive child and/or spousal support?

Sample Qualified Medical Support Court Order

A. _____(Name of Party)_____ is ordered to maintain in full force and effect all health insurance coverage, including medical, dental, hospital and health maintenance, available at reasonable cost through employment and/or other group health insurance plan, and to pay premiums on that coverage.

_____(Name of Party)_____ is also ordered to maintain the minor child(ren) _____(Specify)_____ as alternate recipient(s), entitled to enroll in the group insurance plan, until such minor child(ren) attain majority, are emancipated, die or marry, or until further order of this Court.

B. In the event that such health insurance coverage is not available at the entry of this judgment but subsequently becomes available at no cost or reasonable cost to _____(Name of Party)_____, _____(Name of Party)__ is ordered to notify the Court and opposing party and to apply for that coverage.

C. The group health insurance plan that is the subject of this order is available through _____(Employer or Other Group)_____. Coverage is provided by _____(Name of Insurance Company)_____ and coverage is for _____(Description of the Type of Coverage Provided by the Plan)_____.

D. The employer of the plan participant (if the group health insurance is available through employment) is ordered to enroll the child(ren) as alternate recipients in the group health plan.

E. The insurance company is ordered to provide coverage to the child(ren) of the plan participant as alternate recipients even if the child(ren) were born out of wedlock, do not live with plan participant, are not claimed as dependents on the plan participant's federal income tax return or live outside of the plan's service area.

F. The insurance company is ordered to reimburse the custodial parent directly for covered medical expenses paid by the custodial parent on behalf of the alternate recipients. The insurance company shall not pay such reimbursement to the plan participant.

G. The name and last known mailing address of the party ordered to maintain health insurance (the "plan participant") are:

_____

_____

H. The name and mailing address of the alternate recipient(s) are:

_____

_____

CHAPTER 19

Negotiating and Finalizing the Best Possible Settlement

Until this stage of the divorce, you have focused on your personal, individual decisions—that is, the things you "want" in your divorce. But how will you get what you want? Through negotiation.

Negotiating the settlement is a process of offers and counteroffers between the parties to a divorce. You and your spouse may be able to compromise and reach a settlement easily, or your demands and those of your spouse may run headlong into each other. Some couples state their terms and reach a settlement in hours, while others go through years of bitter fighting.

Your settlement negotiations will probably bear an uncomfortable resemblance to the dynamics of your marriage. If your spouse has been rigid and demanding throughout your relationship, do not expect him or her to suddenly become flexible and reasonable in a settlement conference. Similarly, an uncommunicative mate will probably give you the "silent treatment" as you attempt to complete the settlement. Anticipating your spouse's most likely behavior can make it easier for you to accept and move through the negotiations.

Your decisions—and actions—become crucial in this phase, because you are playing for keeps. Once the settlement is final, it is costly, time-consuming and almost impossible to modify it. Better to make changes to the settlement before you complete it, rather than try to alter it later.

In this chapter, you will address three basic issues regarding negotiating the settlement:

- Have you done your financial homework?
- How are the offers and counteroffers made?
- How do you finalize the settlement?

A. Have You Done Your Financial Homework?

Imagine walking into a room and sitting across a table from your spouse and his attorney. The attorney smiles while going through a long list of items that your spouse is prepared to "give" you if you will simply forfeit any claim to the items that are on your spouse's much shorter list.

The attorney points out that the dollar amount on the bottom line of both lists is equal. Surely you should agree to such a fair and equitable offer.

But should you?

You can't know whether or not the offer is fair unless you've done your homework. If you've worked through the previous chapters in this book, you should be able to accept or reject your spouse's offer relatively quickly. If you haven't read the prior chapters—analyzing your assets and debts, and understanding alimony and child support—you're apt to accept an offer that is a bad financial deal for you, regardless of how "equal" the dollar amounts on the bottom line appear to be.

You must know where you stand financially before you negotiate the settlement. We cannot stress this point enough. If you have not already done so, go back and read the material relevant to your divorce from Chapters 12 (property and expenses), 13 (house), 14 (retirement plans), 15 (investments), 16 (employee benefit plans), 17 (debts) and 18 (alimony and child support). Even if your spouse has made an offer—or is preparing to counter an offer you've made—take no further steps until you have analyzed the financial consequences of any proposed settlement.

B. Tallying Your Marital Balance Sheet

In Chapter 12, you filled out the detailed *Assets and Liabilities Worksheet*. Now, as you reach the crucial point of your negotiations, that attention to detail will pay off.

You can now devise your *Marital Balance Sheet*, a key tool in arriving at a settlement. With the information you've assembled, achieving a fair division of the assets and debts—the goal of every divorce proceeding—should be infinitely easier.

Refer back to the *Assets and Liabilities Worksheet* in Chapter 12. Make note of what property is jointly owned or owned by the spouses individually. Note also the Equity or Legal Value in the last column. Then enter that information in the appropriate columns below. This will be a bit of a chore, but it's important. This is what you've been working toward.

Once you've entered that information, take a moment to study the overall picture. Think about which assets you want to keep and which ones you want to be rid of or are willing to give up. Bear in mind that what each person gets will also be an important element in deciding what, if any, amount of child support and alimony is ordered.

Begin by preliminarily dividing the property as you would ideally like to see it divided. First, consider which property each spouse would prefer to have and "deserves" to have. For example, if the Equity or Legal Value of your house is $150,000, and you and your spouse each contributed equal amounts of separate property for the down payment, you would logically have a 50-50 share of the equity, or $75,000 apiece before taxes. But if you contributed unequal amounts for the down payment, that figure may need to be adjusted. Similarly, try to determine the stake each of you has in other assets based on who acquired them and with what funds.

The assets and liabilities listed in Chapter 12 are very detailed and specific. Here you're going to be grouping them—investments, collections, real estate and so on—to get an overall sense of how they could be divided. Inequities will naturally develop. Allocate enough of the value of joint property to the spouse with the shortfall to roughly equalize the respective values. Your negotiations will determine who actually gets what. This exercise will greatly help prepare you for those negotiations.

Look at specific items of jointly owned property to identify any items that can be transferred in whole from joint names into the sole name of one party to equalize the values. Consider trading property interests of similar value—say, the wife's interest in the husband's pension for the husband's interest in the family home.

When you get to the bottom of each portion of the *Marital Balance Sheet*, check how close you've come to having equal allocations. Make note of any equalizing payment that would be required to bring the allocations into balance.

Dividing Miscellaneous Property

The bulk of your divorce may focus on splitting the miscellaneous items, such as furniture, books, electronic equipment, appliances, kitchenware, tools and the like. The easiest way to divide these items is to make a list of *everything you jointly own*—this includes wedding gifts and joint inheritances—and write your name or your spouse's name next to each item, depending on who wants what. Give the list to your spouse. Ask your spouse to note those items on which he or she disagrees with your assignment of ownership. Then sit down together and review the items in dispute. If you can't resolve your differences, here are three suggestions:

- Flip a coin. The winner gets first choice of the disputed items. Alternate selecting until the list is exhausted.

- Put the disputed items on your settlement chart and divide them as you negotiate the settlement.

- Find a mediator to help you divide what's still on the list.

This property may not be worth the time you spend fighting over it. Do not let the issue of dividing the silverware and the CD collection interfere with your negotiations over more financially significant assets such as the house or either spouse's retirement plan.

Marital Balance Sheet

Division of Jointly Owned Property

Equity or Legal Value (from Chapter 12)	Allocation to Husband	Allocation to Wife
Assets:		
Marital Home	_____	_____
Rental House	_____	_____
Real Estate	_____	_____
Investments	_____	_____
Stock Account	_____	_____
Savings	_____	_____
Checking	_____	_____
Money Fund	_____	_____
Mutual Funds	_____	_____
CDs	_____	_____
Automobile 1	_____	_____
Automobile 2	_____	_____
Furnishings	_____	_____
Art Works	_____	_____
Collections	_____	_____
	_____	_____
	_____	_____
	_____	_____
Debts:		
Credit Cards	_____	_____
Credit Line	_____	_____
Bank Loan	_____	_____
Family Loan	_____	_____
Other Debt	_____	_____
JOINT DIVISION	_____	_____
Equalizing Payment, if any	_____	_____

Husband's Property Divided

Equity or Legal Value (from Chapter 12)	Allocation to Husband	Allocation to Wife
Husband's Property	_____	_____
Equalizing Payment, if any	_____	_____

Wife's Property Divided

Equity or Legal Value (from Chapter 12)	Allocation to Husband	Allocation to Wife
Wife's Property	_____	_____
Equalizing Payment, if any	_____	_____

Summary of Property Division

Equity	To Husband	To Wife
Joint Property	_____	_____
Husband's Property	_____	_____
Wife's Property	_____	_____
Total Division	_____	_____
Overall Equalizing Payment, if any	_____	_____

When Not to Keep the House

After Janet divorced she found herself paralyzed, though not physically. Because of decisions she made during her divorce, she could not afford to move from her home.

Janet owed $60,000 to her uncle—he lent her the money so that she could buy out her husband. If Janet were to sell the house, she'd first have to pay her uncle. Then she'd have to pay taxes on any profit from the sale that exceeded $250,000. Janet wants a small condo worth less than her house. Between payments to her uncle, taxes she would owe on the profit and the lower market price of her house due to slumping real estate values in her area, she has barely enough left for a down payment on a new place.

Janet's goal is to keep her monthly house payment low. In her current home, she pays only $950 per month. After Janet repays her uncle and puts money aside for the taxes, she will have a little money left over from the sale of the house that she can use as a down payment on the condo. She'll still have to finance the deal. If she took a 30-year loan at 7.5% interest, her monthly payment would be $1,250—$300 more per month for housing than she pays now. And she simply cannot afford it on her current salary.

"It's ironic," Janet now muses. "I fought so hard to keep this house, and now I have to keep it whether I want to or not. I'm so busy at work that I hardly have time to mow the lawn, and I've had to rent out two rooms just to keep everything going. If I had it to do over again, I'd have sold the house during the divorce and started fresh."

C. How Are the Offers and Counteroffers Made?

Once you have a good grasp of your *Marital Balance Sheet*, you can begin the negotiations. In many settlements, the spouses will agree to each other's terms on several issues. To resolve the remaining issues, the couple—perhaps with the help of a mediator or their attorneys—meet or correspond until all issues are settled. Once the details are settled, they are recorded in a settlement agreement. The settlement agreement is then taken to the court for a judge's approval. Unless an agreement contains a clause leaving the children unsupported, a judge will approve the agreement as a formality.

Don't Be Discouraged

In spite of doing your financial homework and the hard work of preparing for settlement negotiations, you may still go through numerous settlement conferences in attempting to hammer out an agreement. Some cooling-off time may be needed between offers and counteroffers because of charged emotions. Take the time you need and don't give in just because you never want to see "that person" again.

Your settlement may not follow that scenario exactly. Here are several other possibilities:

Scenario 1:

You and your spouse agree to terms ➔ *file your own papers with the court* ➔ *final decree of divorce is issued* ➔ *marriage ends*

This kind of simple divorce usually takes place when couples have been married a short time and have no children or major assets to divide. If you fall into this situation, check to see if there's a good "do it yourself" divorce book written for your state. You can also use the services of an independent paralegal to help you type up your papers. Check your phone book under "attorney support" or "typing services."

Scenario 2:

You and your spouse agree to terms on some issues ➔ meet with a mediator to resolve remaining issues ➔ file papers with the court on your own or using an attorney, attorney-mediator or typing service ➔ final decree of divorce is issued ➔ marriage ends

Mediators are discussed in Chapter 7. Remember that a mediator is not an advocate—he or she is a person who helps you and your spouse arrive at a settlement you can live with. Once you settle the issues, a mediator will probably not help you file your court papers unless that person is also an attorney. You (or your spouse) can use an attorney for this, but the attorney will probably want to get more involved—find out all the issues of your case, figure out why you settled it as you did and counsel you to resolve it differently. This can mean you may have to start over. If you have a mediated settlement, you may want to file the court papers yourself.

Scenario 3:

You and your spouse—with your attorneys—agree on certain issues ➔ through your attorneys meeting or corresponding, you resolve remaining issues ➔ attorneys file papers with the court ➔ final decree of divorce is issued ➔ marriage ends

If you and your spouse cannot settle your case, you'll probably turn to the services of an attorney. The cost will rise and the issues may seem more complicated, but your interests may be better protected. Nevertheless, it is imperative that you retain absolute control over your case. Having come this far in this book, you understand the financial realities of keeping certain assets, assuming (or having your spouse assume) debts and paying or receiving alimony or child support. Be clear with your attorney as to what is an acceptable and unacceptable settlement. Give your lawyer a copy of the *Marital Balance Sheet* you completed in this chapter.

Understand What You're Getting

Judy and her husband went through an arduous negotiation process. When they couldn't agree on how to divide their property, they scheduled a trial. A few minutes before they were to go before the judge, they settled the issues in the courthouse cafeteria. Their attorneys initialed papers stipulating the terms of their agreement.

When Judy received her copy of the stipulations, she noticed that her husband's attorney had added language describing her husband's equalization payment—money owed for receiving a greater share of marital property—as a distribution of retirement benefits subject to a Qualified Domestic Relations Order (QDRO). Instead of receiving tax-free payments, Judy would be getting the payment in the form of a fully taxable distribution from the retirement plan. Judy could roll the money into an IRA to defer taxes, but she did not want a taxable asset when she and her husband had already agreed that she would receive the nontaxable equalization payment.

Fortunately, Judy reviewed the settlement agreement carefully and asked her attorney about it. Judy then demanded—and got—a correction. The equalization payment was separated from the retirement benefits, as was originally intended. Her alertness saved almost $40,000 in taxes.

Scenario 4:

You and your spouse—with your attorneys—agree on certain issues ➔ through your attorneys meeting or corresponding, you resolve some, but not all, remaining issues ➔ attorneys prepare for trial ➔ trial takes place, judge makes rulings ➔ final decree of divorce is issued ➔ marriage ends

Throughout this book, we have warned you against letting your fate be decided by a judge, and letting your marital assets be eaten up in lawyers' fees. If, however, all else fails and you must go to trial, then be prepared. Don't be afraid to ask your lawyer what will happen—and how much the lawyer's bill will be. And don't forget that you'll probably have to pay experts—actuaries, appraisers, financial planners and the like—if you're disputing asset values. If you can't agree on custody, you'll probably need to bring counselors, psychologists and others into court to testify. Be prepared for these bills.

Tips for Negotiating Your Settlement

Here are several tips to bear in mind during your negotiations:

- You may not get what you deserve, but you can get what you negotiate.

- Know the least you are willing to get, the most you are willing to give and the bottom line you are willing to agree on.

- Answer questions clearly and concisely—and without blame.

- Put yourself in your spouse's position and ask what you'd do if you were your spouse.

- Don't give in to pressure for the sake of an immediate response.

- Release tension during negotiation sessions; take deep breaths and let them out slowly.

- When difficulties or conflicts arise, use phrases that can help move things forward:
  "I appreciate what we've done so far . . ."
  "I'd like to settle this on the basis of principle, not power . . ."
  "Help me understand how you reached that conclusion . . ."
  "I'm trying to see the point you are making; would you mind clarifying it for me?"

D. How Do You Finalize the Settlement?

As mentioned earlier, once the issues are resolved and reduced to a settlement agreement, the agreement is then taken to the court for a judge's approval. Unless it leaves the children unsupported, a judge will sign the agreement.

Usually, when the agreement is taken to court, so are the papers requesting an end of the marriage. Before that, only the complaint or petition requesting that the marriage end—and an answer or response from the other spouse—have been filed. Once the couple resolves the property, debt, custody, alimony and child support issues, they also usually end their marriage. In some cases, however, you may actually be divorced before you conclude your settlement. In these cases, the divorce process is "bifurcated"—divided in two parts—so that the part ending the marriage is resolved first, and then the issues of property division, debt allocation, custody, alimony and child support are settled.

Bifurcation is usually used when one party wants to remarry and doesn't want to wait the many months or years it may take to settle the unresolved issues in the divorce. Our experience is that couples who bifurcate their divorce have little incentive to untangle their finances. Financial discussions tend to drag on, and making a clean break and planning for your own financial future may become more difficult.

If You Must Go to Trial

In some divorces, all attempts at negotiation break down and couples end up going to court. Before a trial, you will want to:

- Ask your attorney what she thinks are the pros and cons of your position and what other courts have decided in cases like yours.

- Ask which judge you will most likely get and what biases that judge tends to hold.

- Reevaluate the financial and tax implications of your options.

- Reconsider the proposals made by your spouse. Think through their merits and drawbacks.

- Think about the benefits of settling without going to court, such as saving vast legal fees, court costs and other expenses. What if you pay these expenses and lose anyway?

Do not expect a grand parade, or even a telegram announcing the end of your marriage. All you're apt to receive is a notice from the court. After all the drama of divorce, the end can be nothing more than an anticlimactic notice in the mail. You might even need to call your attorney's office or the courthouse to make sure the marriage is really over.

You can, of course, throw yourself a party to mark the occasion—or sleep in and stay under the covers, depending on how you feel about being divorced.

E. Divorce Ceremonies

Some couples craft a beautiful and touching divorce ceremony to end their marriages and begin their lives anew. An important part of any divorce ritual is to have the leader or clergy person facilitate the ex-wife and ex-husband in expressing gratitude for the best parts of their marriage. They recognize aloud what was good about the marriage and about each other. They may speak with pride and joy. Children in attendance can tell their parents how they feel about them and what their expectations are for the future. Friends can express their support and caring for both spouses.

Though it may not be for everyone, a divorce ceremony can be a powerful experience for all because it offers an opportunity to provide closure to the past and look forward to the future.

■

After the Divorce: How Do I Get From "We" to "Me"?

Congratulations … you've made it. Your divorce is over, and it's probably a tremendous relief. As far as your financial life is concerned, however, the watchword after divorce is caution—not celebration.

Just as it was important to avoid spending sprees during the divorce, it's wise to keep your expenses down once the divorce is final. You need time to adjust to your new life. The last thing you want to do is run up big bills that you can't pay.

Similarly, don't let your guard down while you wrap up the details and get ready for life as a single person—or single parent. First, you must be sure to follow through—or see that your spouse follows through—on the settlement you've worked so hard to secure. Be on the lookout, too, for people who try to pressure you into investing your money one way or another. Sit tight. You'll have plenty of time to decide what to do once you've made sure there are no loose ends from your divorce which could trip you up in the future.

A. How Do I Finish the Business of Divorce?

Forgetting to follow through on details after divorce is one of the easiest things in the world to do. It's also one of the costliest.

During the divorce, you were under tremendous stress. Now, you may be more exhausted than you realize, and that can lead you to overlook important tasks. Even if you're feeling exhilarated instead of exhausted, that state of excitement can lead to over-confidence and a lack of focus on the business at hand.

You could literally lose the property you fought to keep because of simple errors in divorce paperwork. One man lost his vacation home to his ex-wife when she sold it before the deed transferring ownership to him was recorded. Another woman had to pay off debts her ex-husband incurred because she forgot to close a joint account and he refused to pay the bills he ran up.

You've been through too much to drop the ball now. Don't put off legal and financial chores in this post-settlement phase—which is as crucial as any other part of the divorce process. Use the list below to guide you.

_____   *Title documents*

Make sure that new title documents are prepared to indicate new ownership. New deeds transferring ownership of real estate must be recorded at the county recorder's office. New registration forms changing title in a motor vehicle (car, boat and the like) must be sent to the state department of motor vehicles. Check investment accounts to see that ownership of stocks, bonds and mutual funds is properly listed.

A Rose by Any Other Name . . .

You may feel by now that you've gone through enough changes in your divorce. But there is one item which you may not mind changing: your name. Changing your name as part of the divorce process can be more efficient—and less expensive—than waiting to do it later, when you will probably have to pay court fees. Because you are changing the owner's name and address on many documents that are part of your divorce settlement, you may as well insert your new name while you're at it. You can use your birth name, use a name from a prior marriage or simply make up a new name altogether. If you're in California, you can consult *How to Change Your Name in California*, by Lisa Sedano (Nolo).

If your name changes as a result of divorce, be sure to contact the Social Security Administration by filing Form SS-5 at a local office, downloading the form from the agency's website, www.ssa.gov, or calling (800) 772-1213. It usually takes two weeks to have the change verified. A mismatch between a name on a tax return and a Social Security number could increase a tax bill and reduce the size of any refund.

_____   *Wills and other estate planning documents*

While you were married, you may have drafted a will, created a trust or taken other steps to determine who will receive your property after you die. These documents must be reviewed and changed to reflect your new status.

_____   *Insurance*

Review your health, dental and disability insurance policies. Be certain you (and your children) have adequate coverage. Also check to see if the beneficiaries of your life insurance policies are who you want them to be.

_____   *Debts*

Verify that all joint accounts are closed and that you pay all debts you agreed to cover. At the same time, contact the creditors your ex-spouse agreed to pay to make sure they are receiving payments. If they aren't, you can minimize damage to your own credit by paying the bills. You'll then have to take steps to get reimbursed from your ex-spouse. (See Section B, below.)

_____   *Deposit accounts*

Check your deposit accounts—checking, savings, money markets, certificates of deposit and treasury bills. The names on the accounts should be consistent with the decisions reached in your settlement.

Changing Joint Deposit Accounts

To change joint deposit accounts, write to the financial institution where you have your account. Here's some sample language to use:

"Please be advised that as of _____ [date], account number _____, in the names of _____, is to be closed. All assets from that account are to be transferred into a new account in the name of _____."

You and your ex-spouse must sign this form. Some banks and brokerage firms may ask for a copy of your divorce decree, but do not send it unless you're specifically requested to do so.

_____ *Children*

Make sure you understand your custody and child support agreements. If you share legal custody of your children, you should have access to their school reports, medical records and other information.

Tips for Completing the Business of Divorce

Here are a few tips for wrapping up the loose ends:

- Review settlement details. A few days after your divorce is final—after you've recovered from the euphoria or the exhaustion—meet with your lawyer or financial advisors to go over the details of your settlement. Make lists of the items that you, your attorney, your ex-spouse or others are responsible for completing. Don't leave these items to memory.

- Keep records of all payments—for alimony, child support or property exchange—you make or receive. Make copies of all checks you send or receive. Also, use a calendar or log book to show payment amounts and the date payments are made or received. You need to record these details in case you ever go to court to raise or lower support payments or to collect unpaid support.

- Make a copy of your final judgment and the settlement agreement. Put the original in a safe place, such as a safe-deposit box.

- Start a post-divorce file for essential papers. Keep your payment records and the duplicate of your final judgment and the settlement agreement in the file. If you experience problems, or need to refer to divorce papers for investment or tax purposes, everything will be located in an easy-to-find spot. On an emotional level, hunting for divorce documents can be frustrating. Avoid triggering old angers and reduce stress by keeping these documents within easy reach.

B. Can I—Or My Ex-Spouse— Change the Settlement?

Your settlement agreement contains several clauses. The main ones probably deal with property division, debt allocation, alimony, child support and custody. You may be wondering if you can change any of those provisions, or if your spouse might try the same. The two of you can *voluntarily* change the terms of your agreement. But if your ex-spouse won't cooperate, you will have to go to court. Ask your attorney for the specific rulings in your state and in your case, but below are some general guides.

Property division. It's highly unusual that a court will approve a request by one ex-spouse to change the terms of the property division after the divorce. Such a request might be approved if the ex-spouse who is asking to change the settlement agreement can show that the other ex-spouse hid assets—such as accounts receivable that should have been used to value a business. The ex-spouse will have to file a motion, schedule a court hearing and then provide convincing evidence at the hearing of the other party's wrongdoing.

Debt allocation. If your ex-spouse doesn't pay the debts he or she agreed to pay, you will no doubt need the court's assistance. You can file a motion and ask the court to order your ex to pay—and to ensure that you're paid, ask the court to have your ex turn money over to the court. To avoid damaging your own credit, however, you should go ahead and pay the bills and ask the court for an order requiring reimbursement from your ex. The court can order the reimbursement by changing any equalization payment or property distribution that hasn't yet taken place. The court might also order a wage garnishment from your ex's paycheck, or that other funds belonging to your ex be turned over to you.

Alimony. If you knowingly gave up alimony, you usually cannot go back to court and try to get some. Once it's waived, it's gone forever. If you are receiving or paying alimony, pay careful attention to the termination date. If you are the recipient and need money beyond that date, you can usually go back to court and ask for an extension of the alimony, *but you usually must make your request before the scheduled termination date.*

If you are the payer and you can't afford to pay the amount you've been ordered to pay in the settlement agreement, you must file a motion for modification with the court. See Chapter 18, Section B3.

Child support. Child support is always subject to modification by a court because the court retains power over child support until the children reach age 18 or 21 (in some states), or until whatever age your agreement specifies support must be paid. If you are the payer and can't afford the payments, or if you are the recipient and you can't live on the current payment, you must file papers with the court, schedule a hearing and show the judge that you cannot afford to pay—or to live on—the current support. See Chapter 18, Section D5.

Custody or visitation. Like child support, custody and visitation are always subject to the court's modification. The parent wanting to change custody or visitation must file papers with the court, schedule a hearing and show the judge a "significant change of circumstance" since the original order. Changing custody is usually a difficult and emotionally draining process. The court uses the standard of the "best interests of the child" and does not like to change the status quo. Unless you can show that the current custody arrangement is detrimental to your children—for example, their grades are suffering or they are depressed—you are not likely to win your court hearing.

Get It in Writing

When you want to change an existing court order affecting alimony, child support, custody or visitation, you can ask your ex-spouse to agree to the changes informally before filing papers and scheduling a court hearing. If your ex-spouse agrees on a modification, put it in writing and take it to the court for approval. The court will routinely approve it, as long as child support appears adequate. You may think that if you agree informally, getting court approval is not necessary. If relations later sour, however, not having court approval may cause great difficulty in enforcing the modified agreement.

C. What Do I Want to Do With My Life?

When your divorce is over, it's more crucial than ever to reassess where you're going financially. Rarely does anyone's post-divorce life resemble what he or she thought it would look like before the divorce. You need to adapt to changes you didn't expect.

If you have used goal-setting tools throughout your divorce, you may simply need to make minor adjustments to your basic plans. If, however, your financial position after divorce is drastically different from what you had anticipated, you may need to reevaluate your objectives, scale down your spending or take a crash course on investing wisely. Whatever your situation, don't jump into risky ventures with your share of the settlement.

1. If You Have Money to Invest

Unless you're already a successful investor, it's best to put your money in a safe parking place until you get established—personally and professionally—in your new life. It's ideal to have three to six months' worth of cost-of-living expenses in a money market fund or a certificate of deposit (CD) as an emergency fund before you do any investing.

When you feel you have your post-divorce life under control and your future plans are relatively clear, you can move some of your assets into investments where your money can work harder for you—that is, earn more return than from a money market or CD.

You may start slowly with "dollar cost averaging." With this method, you put the same amount of money into an investment on a regular basis over a long period of time. For example, you might put $200 a month into a mutual fund. Your money will buy more shares when the market is down and fewer shares when the market is high. Over time, your average cost per share will be less than your average price per share, and you'll come out ahead.

2.　If Money Is Tight

No matter how well you've planned, you may find yourself with limited resources following your divorce. Cutting costs, then, will be your major priority. Some recently divorced people find it easier to make ends meet by pooling resources. You may be able to connect with others in similar circumstances by contacting singles clubs, Parents Without Partners or groups sponsored by religious or community organizations. Setting up a baby-sitting exchange or bartering for other services with members of the group can help everyone lower expenses.

Also consider buying groceries in bulk or purchasing necessities from consumer cooperatives or warehouse distributors. To lower your housing costs, you might rent out a room or part of your home.

Avoid taking cash advances or running up the balance on credit cards if you can help it. Most credit cards carry high interest charges—and that interest is not tax deductible.

You can also try to raise cash. Below are several different suggestions.

a.　Borrow From Family or Friends

Do not feel discouraged if you have to borrow money from family or friends. Many people find they need short-term loans to get them through this transition period. In times of financial crises, some people are lucky enough to have friends or relatives who can and will help out. Be sure to give them a promissory note for the loan specifying the amount, interest rate and payment schedule.

b.　Sell a Major Asset or Many Minor Items

One of the best ways you can raise cash and keep associated costs to a minimum is to sell a major asset—or hold a garage or yard sale. Few people realize how much money may be lying around their house. Selling a hardly used car you were saving until your oldest child turns 16 or a computer system you no longer use could help you through a rough period.

c.　Cash in a Tax-Deferred Account

If you have an IRA or other tax-deferred account into which you've deposited money, consider cashing it in. You could have to pay the IRS a penalty—10% of the money you withdraw unless you qualify for the exceptions to this penalty. (See Chapter 14, Section D.) In addition, you'll owe income taxes on the money you take out. But paying these penalties to the IRS is probably better than struggling to get by.

d.　Obtain a Home Equity Loan

Many banks, savings and loans, credit unions and other lenders offer home equity loans, also called second mortgages. Lenders usually lend between 50% and 80% of the market value of a house, less what is still owed on it. Home equity loans have advantages and disadvantages. Be sure you understand all the terms before you sign up for one.

i.　Advantages

- You can obtain a closed-end loan—you borrow a fixed amount of money and repay it in equal monthly installments for a set period. Or you can obtain a line of credit—you borrow as you need the money, drawing against the amount granted when you opened the account, and repay according to your agreement.

- The interest you pay is fully deductible on your income tax return.

- Federal law requires that interest rates on adjustable rate home equity loans be capped—meaning that the rate can increase only a set amount each year as well as over the life of the loan.

ii. Disadvantages

- You are obligating yourself to make another monthly or periodic payment. If you are unable to pay, you may have to sell your house or, even worse, face the possibility of the lender foreclosing. Before you take out a home equity loan, be sure you can make the monthly payment.

- While interest is deductible and capped for adjustable rate loans, it can be high.

- You may have to pay an assortment of up-front fees for such costs as an appraisal, credit report, title insurance and points that can run to $1,000 or more. In addition, many lenders charge a yearly fee of $25 to $50.

Canceling a Home Equity Loan

If you have second thoughts after taking out a home equity loan, keep in mind that under the Federal Trade Commission's three-day cooling-off rule, you have the right to cancel a home equity loan or second mortgage until midnight of the third business day after you sign the contract. You must be given notice of your right to cancel and a cancellation form when you sign the contract.

---

e. Get Your Tax Refund Fast

Sometimes, getting a tax refund quickly will help you through a cash-flow crisis, especially if the IRS owes you a lot. Each IRS district office has a Taxpayer Advocate's Office (TAO); the offices can help callers get their refunds early. Local offices are listed in the government listing of the phone book.

3. Post-Divorce Financial Planning Tips

Financial planning strategies are often based on the idyllic picture of a couple who moves from struggling to make ends meet in their 20s to a happy retirement in their 60s. This picture hardly resembles the norm for divorced people, who must redesign their plans. Below are a few tips to help you do that.

a. Update Your Net Worth and Cash Flow Statements

Your net worth and cash flow have changed because of the property you received or exchanged during the divorce and payments you now make or receive that you didn't before. You can't realize your financial goals in the future unless you know where you're starting from. Update the *Net Worth Statement* and *Cash Flow Statement* you completed in Chapter 12.

b. Set Up a Debt Payment Plan

Pay off all debts you agreed to cover as part of your divorce settlement as quickly as possible. Create a payment schedule to match your pay periods. If you're paid on the first and 15th of the month, pay your bills then. Keep all bills in a folder. On the first of the month, take out only those bills that you will pay; write your checks, mail the bills and put the folder away until the 15th. Then do the same on the 15th. By using this system, you won't constantly think about your debts.

 For more detailed help in repaying your debts, we recommend *Money Troubles: Legal Strategies to Cope With Your Debts*, by Robin Leonard & Deanne Loonin (Nolo).

c. Make Sure You Have an Emergency Fund and an Emergency Plan

As we've recommended previously, you should have an "emergency fund" representing three to six months' worth of cost-of-living expenses. Make sure you can get to this money when you need it.

You may also want to make a contingency plan that takes into account your nonfinancial resources. Could you move in with friends or relatives—including your adult children—if you had to? Knowing you have some kind of cushion of support makes it easier to face life. Once you've been divorced, you may find yourself dwelling on the "worst cases" you can imagine. Having a contingency plan can dispel fears and let you move on.

d. Reevaluate Your Insurance

Most people fall into one of two extremes—either they have too little insurance or they have too much of the wrong kind. Now that your divorce is over, honestly revaluate your insurance coverage. Read consumer publications and check with several agents to get a good overall update on your insurance position. Consider what your new needs are with respect to health, life, disability, auto, homeowner's or renter's and personal liability coverage. If you are receiving alimony or child support, be sure to consider getting life insurance on your ex-spouse. By doing so, you and your children will not suffer financially from loss of the income stream in the event of your ex-spouse's death.

e. Keep Up With Changes in Your Tax Status

When your marital status changes, so does your tax status. Not only might you be in a different tax bracket, but tax laws themselves may change. If you're in a higher tax bracket, you need investments that provide tax-deferred or tax-free income. More likely, however, you are in a lower tax bracket and will want to take advantage of two of the best tax planning opportunities most people have: owning a house and contributing to an IRA or a 401(k) through your work.

f. Reevaluate Your Retirement Program

How much will it cost you to maintain your current lifestyle once you retire? If you and your ex-spouse divided retirement plans during divorce, be sure to do the follow-up work to secure any payments you are supposed to receive. If you have no retirement plan, go to a brokerage house and ask for a retirement projection. Do not let yourself be pushed into any investment you are not ready to make. Once you have an accurate calculation of post-retirement living costs, investigate several types of plans before choosing one that is right for you.

g. Take Care of Your Estate

Many people mistakenly assume that they do not have enough property to plan their estate. If you do not plan, however, the state will do it for you after you die. You may only need a simple will, or you might want to investigate a living trust. Consider taking these steps:

- Name a guardian for your child(ren) or be sure the guardian you did name is still appropriate. Consider parenting style, financial resources and moral and religious views.

- Talk with potential guardians before naming them in your will. They may be honored but reluctant to accept the responsibility. Designate an alternate as well in the event of death or debilitating illness of the guardian you select.

- Update your will and/or trust as needed. Changes in your life, such as another child, an increase or a loss in property, remarriage or a move to another state may necessitate changing your estate planning documents.

Nolo publishes a number of books and software programs that can help you take care of your estate. They are described in Chapter 10, Section B2.

4. Setting Goals After Divorce

Right now is the perfect time to look at your financial goals for the short and long term. Use the chart titled *Setting Goals*, below, to open up ideas about where you'd like to go in the future.

D. If You Find a New Love, Protect Your Old Assets … and Your Alimony

For some people, going through a divorce leads them to swear off the institution of marriage altogether. For others, however, a divorce represents the freedom to be with the person they truly love. If you fall into that category, be sure that you don't let Cupid blind you to the financial realities that you will face. Read the next two sections if you are considering living with or marrying someone new.

1. Cohabitation Can Be Costly

Once the divorce is over, you may be thinking about moving in with your new "significant other." Cohabitation, or living together without legally marrying, has risks and it's important that you understand them. Obviously, you will have to deal with the emotional side of your own and possibly your children's reactions to such a move. But you must recognize that you are taking legal and financial risks as well. If you and your new love acquire any assets together, be sure the title document (deed or registration) properly reflects your intentions.

Here are a couple of cautionary tales that will illustrate why it is important to be financially aware when you live with someone.

We know of a couple who cohabited for four years in Minnesota. During that time, the man used his money to purchase the home in which they lived. The title to the home was taken in "joint tenancy," which means that if one owner died before the other, the survivor automatically inherited the deceased's share of the property, even if a will or trust said something else. (See Chapter 6, Section A7.) When the couple split up, the woman sued for half the home. The man showed that he used his money to buy it. The woman claimed that he gave her a gift of half the house. The court ruled against her, stating that the house was his unless a written contract stated otherwise.

In a California case, a woman met and moved in with a new man while she was divorcing her first husband. She and her new companion bought a condominium together using joint funds. To avoid complications while negotiating her divorce property settlement, she and her companion put the title to the condominium in his name only. After her divorce was final, the woman married her companion and they moved into a larger home, renting out the condominium—for which title remained in her second husband's name alone. Twenty-seven years later, they were divorcing. The judge ruled that the condo was the property of the second husband, because title was in his name only and she could not prove any ownership interest.

In addition to getting proper titles on property, remember, too, that one companion could sue the other for a share of the assets or for alimony-like support. Given these legal and financial realities, it is in your interest to ask a lawyer's advice regarding cohabitation laws in your state before moving in with someone. We also suggest that you draft an agreement that details your understanding of your respective ownership in the property. You can incorporate this understanding into a prenuptial agreement if you later marry.

In many states, you can lose your alimony if you move in with someone new. Several states presume that someone who cohabits with a person of the opposite sex has less need for alimony. (One or two courts have applied the "spirit" of the law to cut off alimony to a woman who entered a lesbian relationship, but in virtually all other cases, alimony terminated after heterosexual cohabitation.)

If you will move in with your new partner, we recommend that you get a copy of either *Living Together: A Legal Guide for Unmarried Couples*, by Ralph Warner, Toni Ihara & Frederick Hertz (Nolo) or *A Legal Guide for Lesbian and Gay Couples*, by Hayden Curry, Denis Clifford, Robin Leonard & Frederick Hertz (Nolo). Both books cover the financial, legal, parenting, estate planning and practical concerns of couples whose living arrangements are not covered by state marital laws.

2. Prenuptial Agreements

Many couples marrying for the second time (or more) consider a prenuptial agreement before taking the plunge. These documents can be valuable planning tools if one spouse has sizable wealth and wants to preserve it for children from a prior marriage. While such agreements have a reputation of being unromantic, they can actually prevent a great deal of heartache.

Prenuptial agreements are used to protect the control, management and ownership of a family business from the prospective spouse, or to state the separate or marital nature of certain assets brought into the marriage or to be acquired in the future. Couples can also use prenuptial agreements to ensure that the laws of the state where they were married will govern in the event of a divorce, no matter where they reside in the future.

If a couple gets a divorce but does not have a prenuptial agreement, assuming they can't otherwise agree, their assets will be divided in accordance with state laws. This means that in community property states (Arizona, California, Idaho, Louisiana, Nevada, New Mexico, Texas, Washington and Wisconsin), marital property will be divided equally; in equitable distribution states (the rest), property will be split "fairly" according to the dictates of the court. If your new spouse contributed to the appreciation of assets that belonged to you alone prior to the marriage, those assets could ultimately be considered marital property subject to division at divorce.

In some cases, prenuptial agreements have been challenged by unhappy spouses and struck down in court. This can happen if the terms are too favorable to one spouse or if the agreement was signed under what the court considers unfair circumstances. If you are considering a prenuptial agreement, it is more likely to stand up if it meets these conditions:

- The terms are fair.

- It is in writing (some states require acknowledgment and attorney certification as well).

- There is a clause stating that if any provision of the agreement is invalidated, the rest of the agreement still remains in effect.

- There is a listing attached showing each spouse's assets and liabilities.

- Each spouse has had the agreement reviewed by his or her separate lawyer.

- It includes a clause stating that all agreements between the prospective spouses are included in the prenuptial agreement.

In addition to a prenuptial agreement, you can protect your separate property through more sophisticated legal tools including an irrevocable trust, revocable living trust or family limited partnership. For more information on these and other estate planning tools, see one of the many Nolo estate planning publications listed in Chapter 10, Section B2.

E. How Can I Move Beyond the Divorce?

By the time your divorce ends, you may not be sure who won or who lost. You need to give yourself time to reassess what has happened in your life. You may be so tired of the divorce process that you don't want to hear another word about money. Worse, you may feel bitter or gun-shy about moving forward. As we've said throughout this book, you must manage your money and your emotions well if you are to end the relationship with your spouse successfully.

Once you've followed up on the legal and financial details of your settlement, check your emotional state to determine what unresolved feelings you are carrying with you as you move into singlehood. If things are not what you anticipated, don't spend time and money in a continuing connection with your ex-spouse. Recognize your gains and cut your losses so you can get on with your new life.

These questions are designed to help you sort through the emotional and economic fallout of ending a marriage. Your answers can help you move on.

What changes in my financial life did I not anticipate before the final settlement?

_____

_____

_____

_____

_____

What will be different in my children's lives now that the divorce is over?

_____

_____

_____

_____

What regrets do I still have about the divorce?

_____

_____

_____

_____

_____

What financial steps do I feel good about, and what could I have done differently?

_____

_____

_____

_____

_____

How can I continue to expand the positive steps I've taken?

_____

_____

_____

_____

What can I do to avoid repeating the financial mistakes I made?

_____

_____

_____

_____

We wish you the best of luck and a speedy recovery from the process of divorce.

Setting Goals

*Instructions: Use this matrix to write your short- and long-term goals. Begin now to focus on the future—**your** future—and the memories of the past will begin to fade.*

My professional goals are:		
next six months:	next one year:	next five years:

My educational goals are:		
next six months:	next one year:	next five years:

My recreation-travel-entertainment goals are:		
next six months:	next one year:	next five years:

My plans for my children are:		
next six months:	next one year:	next five years:

My retirement goals are:		
next six months:	next one year:	next five years:

My other goals are:		
next six months:	next one year:	next five years:

Appendix: Resources Beyond the Book

This book helps you through the divorce process by giving you strategies for evaluating your assets and debts, your likelihood of paying or receiving alimony or child support and your children's custody. But you may need help beyond this book. The three best sources of legal help are a law library, lawyer or typing service.

Before discussing additional resources in detail, here's a general piece of advice: Make all decisions yourself. By reading this book, you've taken on the responsibility for getting information necessary to make informed decisions about your legal and financial affairs. If you decide to get help from others, apply this same self-empowerment principle—shop around until you find an advisor who values your competence and intelligence and recognizes your right to make your own decisions.

A. Law Libraries

Often, you can handle a legal problem yourself if you're willing to do some research in a law library. Here, briefly, are the basic steps to researching a legal question. For more detailed, but user-friendly, instructions on legal research, see *Legal Research: How to Find and Understand the Law*, by Stephen Elias & Susan Levinkind (Nolo).

1. Finding a Law Library

To do legal research, you need to find a law library that's open to the public. Public law libraries are often housed in county courthouses, public law schools and state capitals. If you can't find one, ask a public library reference librarian, court clerk or lawyer.

2. Finding a State Law That Affects Your Divorce

Laws passed by state legislatures are occasionally referred to in this book. To find a state law, or statute, you need to look in a multivolume set of books called the state code. State codes are divided into titles. Most states divide their titles by number; a few states divide them by subject, such as the civil code, family law code or finance code.

To read a law, find the state codes in your law library, locate the title you need, turn to the section number and read. If you already have a proper reference to the law—called the citation—finding the law is straightforward. If you don't have a citation, you can find the law by referring to the index in the code you're using.

After you read the law in the hardcover book, turn to the back of the book. There should be an insert pamphlet (called a pocket part) for the current or previous year. Look for the statute in the pocket part to see if it has been amended since the hardcover volume was published.

3. Going Beyond State Laws

If you want to find the answer to a legal question, rather than simply look up a law, you will need some guidance in basic legal research techniques. Good resources that may be available in your law library are:

- *Legal Research: How to Find and Understand the Law*, by Stephen Elias & Susan Levinkind (Nolo).

- *The Legal Research Manual: A Game Plan for Legal Research and Analysis*, by Christopher and Jill Wren (A-R Editions).

- *How to Find the Law*, by Morris Cohen, Robert Berring and Kent Olson (West Publishing Co.).

4. Using Background Resources

If you want to research a legal question related to family law but don't know where to begin, one of the best resources is the *Family Law Reporter*, published by the Bureau of National Affairs (BNA). This very thorough, four-volume publication covers all 50 states and the District of Columbia, and is updated weekly. It highlights and summarizes cases, new statutes and family law news. It also includes a guide to tax laws affecting family law, a summary of each state's divorce laws and a sample marital settlement agreement.

Most law libraries will have the *Family Law Reporter*. If you can't find it, however, you will need to look at materials written specifically for your state. Ask a law librarian for help.

B. Lawyers and Typing Services

A lawyer can provide you with information, guidance or legal representation. A typing service can act as a "legal secretary" if you need to have documents prepared and filed in court. Typing services *cannot* give legal advice, but they charge far less than lawyers for their services. Typing services are covered in detail in Chapter 7, Section B12.

1. Finding a Lawyer

Before explaining how to find a lawyer, let's first eliminate the types of lawyers you are not looking for:

- The expensive, flamboyant lawyer who gets his or her name in the newspaper all the time. That lawyer would probably charge you a bundle (several hundred dollars an hour) and pass your case on to a recent law school graduate who works in the office.

- The associate or partner at a giant law firm that represents big businesses. These lawyers charge $200–$400 an hour, and few know much about divorce cases or keeping costs down.

- The lawyer who won't tell you how he or she plans to handle your case and wants to make all decisions without consulting you. These lawyers are annoyed—and intimidated—by clients who know anything about the law. What they want is a passive client who doesn't ask a lot of questions and pays the bill on time each month.

What you do want is a dedicated, smart and skilled lawyer who regularly handles family law and divorce cases. The lawyer should understand that your input must be sought for every decision. This being said, here are several ways to find a lawyer:

Typing services. The best referrals will probably come from an independent paralegal listed in the Yellow Pages under "paralegals" or "typing services." Almost daily, independent paralegals refer their clients to lawyers and get feedback on the lawyers' work.

Personal referrals. This is the most common approach. If you know someone who was pleased with the services of a lawyer, call that lawyer first. If that lawyer doesn't handle divorces or can't take your case, he or she may recommend someone else. Be careful, however, when selecting a lawyer from a personal referral. A lawyer's satisfactory performance in one situation does not guarantee that the person will perform the same way in your case.

Group legal plans. Some unions, employers and consumer action organizations offer group plans to their members or employees, who can obtain comprehensive legal assistance free or for low rates. If you're a member of such a plan, check it first for a lawyer.

Prepaid legal insurance. Prepaid legal insurance plans offer some services for a low monthly fee and charge more for additional work. Participating lawyers may use the plan as a way to get clients who are attracted by the low-cost basic services, and

then sell them more expensive services. If the lawyer recommends an expensive course of action, get a second opinion before you agree.

But if a plan offers extensive free advice, your initial membership fee may be worth the consultation you receive. You can always join a plan for a specific service and then not renew.

There's no guarantee that the lawyers available through these plans are of the best caliber; sometimes they aren't. Check out the plan carefully before signing up. Ask about the plan's complaint system, whether you get to choose your lawyer and whether or not the lawyer will represent you in court.

Lawyer referral panels. Most county bar associations will give out the names of attorneys who practice in your area. But bar associations often fail to provide meaningful screening for the attorneys listed, which means those who participate may not be the most experienced or competent.

2.   What to Look for in a Lawyer

No matter what approach you take to finding a lawyer, here are three suggestions on how to make sure you have the best possible working relationship.

First, fight the urge you may have to surrender your will and be intimidated by a lawyer. You should be the one who decides what you feel comfortable doing about your legal and financial affairs. You're hiring the lawyer to perform a service for you; shop around if the price or personality isn't right.

Second, you must be as comfortable as possible with any lawyer you hire. When making an appointment, ask to talk directly to the lawyer. If you can't, this may give you a hint as to how accessible he or she is.

If you do talk directly to the lawyer, ask some specific questions. Do you get clear, concise answers? If not, try someone else. If the lawyer says little except to suggest that he or she handle the problem—with a substantial fee—watch out. You're talking with someone who doesn't know the answer and won't admit it, or someone who pulls rank on the basis of professional standing. Don't be a passive client or hire a lawyer who wants you to be one. If the lawyer admits to not knowing an answer, that isn't necessarily bad. In most cases, the lawyer must do some research.

Also, pay attention to how the lawyer responds to the fact that you have considerable information. If you read this book, you know more about divorce and money than the average person. Does the lawyer seem comfortable with that? Does the lawyer give straightforward answers to your questions—or does the lawyer want to maintain an aura of mystery about the legal system? Pay attention to your own intuition. Many lawyers are threatened when the client knows too much—or, in some cases, anything.

Once you find a lawyer you like, make an hour-long appointment to discuss your situation fully. Your goal at the initial conference is to find out what the lawyer recommends and how much it will cost. Go home and think about the lawyer's suggestions. If they don't make complete sense or if you have other reservations, call someone else.

Finally, keep in mind that the lawyer works for you. Once you hire a lawyer, you have the absolute right to switch to another—or to fire the lawyer and handle the matter yourself—at any time, for any reason.

C. Online Legal Resources

A growing number of basic legal resources are available online. Nolo's legal resources, at www.nolo.com, include a vast amount of legal information for consumers on a wide variety of legal topics and articles on legal issues.

In addition, a wide variety of secondary sources intended for both lawyers and the general public has been posted by law schools and firms. A good way to find these sources is to visit any of the following websites, each of which provides links to legal information by specific subject:

- www.findlaw.com. This legal search engine is an excellent resource for do-it-yourself legal research.
- www.yahoo.com/law/. You can find links to many legal topics.
- www.law.cornell.edu. This site is maintained by Cornell Law School's Legal Information Institute. You can find the text of some state court decisions. You can also search for material by topic.
- www.law.indiana.edu. This site is maintained by Indiana University's School of Law at Bloomington. You can search by state governments and law journals, or by topic.

D. Additional Resources

Below are names, addresses and phone numbers of organizations that may be able to offer additional assistance.

1. Attorneys, Mediators and Therapists

American Academy of Matrimonial Lawyers
150 No. Michigan Ave., Suite 2040
Chicago, IL 60601
312-263-6477 (phone)
312-263-7682 (fax)
www.aaml.org

Center for Dispute Settlement
1666 Connecticut Ave., NW, Suite 500
Washington, DC 20009
202-265-9572 (phone)
202-328-9162 (fax)

Judith Wallerstein Center for the Family
in Transition
P.O. Box 157
Corte Madera, CA 94976
415-924-5750 (phone)

American Association for Marriage and
Family Therapy
112 South Alfred St.
Alexandria, VA 22314-3061
703-838-9808 (phone)
703-838-9805 (fax)
www.aamft.org

Association for Conflict Resolution
1527 New Hampshire Ave., NW
Washington, DC 20036
202-667-9700 (phone)
202-265-1968 (fax)
www.acresolution.org

2. Child Support

National Child Support Enforcement Association
Hall of the States
444 No. Capitol St., Suite 414
Washington, DC 20001-1512
202-624-8180 (phone)
202-624-8828 (fax)
www.ncsea.org

Administration for Children and Families
U.S. Dept. of Health and Human Services
Child Support Enforcement
370 L'Enfant Promenade, SW
Washington, DC 20447
202-401-9383 (phone)
202-401-5559 (fax)
www.acf.dhhs.gov

3. Custody

Alliance for Noncustodial Parents Rights
9903 Santa Monica Blvd.
PMB 267
Beverly Hills, CA 90212
www.ancpr.org

National Congress for Fathers and Children
9454 W. Wilshire Blvd., Suite 907
Beverly Hills, CA 90212
310-247-6051 (phone)
www.ncfc.net/ncfc

4. Domestic Violence

Family Violence Prevention Fund
383 Rhode Island St., Suite 304
San Francisco, CA 94103
415-252-8900 (phone)
415-252-8991 (fax)
www.fvpf.org

5. Employment

Women Work! (National Network for Women's
Employment)
1625 K St., NW, Suite 300
Washington, DC 20006
202-467-6346 (phone)
800-235-2732 (phone)
202-467-5366 (fax)
www.womenwork.org

6. Appraisers

American Society of Appraisers
(business appraisers)
555 Herndon Parkway, Suite 125
Herndon, VA 20170
703-478-2228 (phone)
703-742-8471 (fax)
www.appraisers.org

Appraisal Institute
(real estate appraisers)
550 West Van Buren St., Suite 1000
Chicago, IL 60607
312-335-4100 (phone)
312-335-4400 (fax)
www.appraisalinstitute.com

Institute of Business Appraisers
(business appraisers)
P.O. Box 17410
Plantation, FL 33318
954-584-1144 (phone)
954-584-1184 (fax)
www.instbusapp.org

7. Tax Assistance

Internal Revenue Service (IRS)
(to obtain tax forms)
800-829-1040 (phone)
www.irs.gov

National Association of Enrolled Agents
(for a referral to an enrolled agent)
200 Orchard Ridge Dr., Suite 302
Gaithersburg, MD 20878
301-212-9608 (phone)
301-990-1611 (fax)
www.naea.org

8. Miscellaneous Financial Assistance

Financial Planning Association
(for a referral to a financial planner)
5775 Glenridge Dr., NE, Suite B 300
Atlanta, GA 30328-5364
404-845-0011 (phone)
800-322-4237 (phone)
404-854-3660 (fax)
www.fpanet.org

National Foundation for Credit Counseling
(to find a Consumer Credit Counseling office)
801 Roeder Rd., Suite 900
Silver Spring, MD 20910
800-388-2227 (phone)
www.nfcc.org

Myvesta
(for financial assistance via phone, fax, email or online)
6 Taft Court, Suite 301
Rockville, MD
800-698-3782 (phone)
www.myvesta.org

Social Security Administration
(to confirm work and benefits history)
800-772-1213
www.ssa.gov
(to get information pertaining to Social Security and women)
www.ssa.gov/women

E. Present Value Factors

This chart shows the time value of money and can help you estimate the future value of benefits, such as retirement plans. The left-hand column represents years, while the percentages across the top are rates of inflation. For example, to find the value of a $10,000-a-year payment 20 years from now with 4% inflation, follow the 20-year line to 4%. The Present Value Factor is .4564. Multiply that by $10,000, and you get $4,564, the purchasing power that $10,000 will have in two decades at that rate of inflation.

Years	1%	2%	3%	4%	5%	6%	7%
1	.9901	.9804	.9709	.9615	.9524	.9434	.9346
2	.9803	.9612	.9426	.9246	.9070	.8900	.8734
3	.9706	.9423	.9151	.8890	.8638	.8396	.8163
4	.9610	.9238	.8885	.8548	.8227	.7921	.7629
5	.9515	.9057	.8626	.8219	.7835	.7473	.7130
6	.9420	.8880	.8375	.7903	.7462	.7050	.6663
7	.9327	.8706	.8131	.7599	.7107	.6651	.6227
8	.9235	.8535	.7894	.7307	.6768	.6274	.5820
9	.9143	.8368	.7664	.7026	.6446	.5919	.5439
10	.9053	.8203	.7441	.6756	.6139	.5584	.5083
11	.8963	.8043	.7224	.6496	.5847	.5268	.4751
12	.8874	.7885	.7014	.6246	.5568	.4970	.4440
13	.8787	.7730	.6810	.6006	.5303	.4688	.4150
14	.8700	.7579	.6611	.5775	.5051	.4423	.3878
15	.8613	.7430	.6419	.5553	.4810	.4173	.3624
16	.8528	.7284	.6232	.5339	.4581	.3936	.3387
17	.8444	.7142	.6050	.5134	.4363	.3714	.3166
18	.8360	.7002	.5874	.4936	.4155	.3503	.2959
19	.8277	.6864	.5703	.4746	.3957	.3305	.2765
20	.8195	.6730	.5537	.4564	.3769	.3118	.2584
21	.8114	.6598	.5375	.4388	.3589	.2942	.2415
22	.8034	.6468	.5219	.4220	.3418	.2775	.2257
23	.7954	.6342	.5067	.4057	.3256	.2618	.2109
24	.7876	.6217	.4919	.3901	.3101	.2470	.1971
25	.7798	.6095	.4776	.3751	.2953	.2330	.1842
26	.7720	.5976	.4637	.3607	.2812	.2198	.1722
27	.7644	.5859	.4502	.3468	.2678	.2074	.1609
28	.7568	.5744	.4371	.3335	.2551	.1956	.1504
29	.7493	.5631	.4243	.3207	.2429	.1846	.1406
30	.7419	.5521	.4120	.3083	.2314	.1741	.1314
31	.7346	.5412	.4000	.2965	.2204	.1643	.1228
32	.7273	.5306	.3883	.2851	.2099	.1550	.1147
33	.7201	.5202	.3770	.2741	.1999	.1462	.1072
34	.7130	.5100	.3660	.2636	.1904	.1379	.1002
35	.7059	.5000	.3554	.2534	.1813	.1301	.0937
36	.6989	.4902	.3450	.2437	.1727	.1227	.0875
37	.6920	.4806	.3350	.2343	.1644	.1158	.0818
38	.6852	.4712	.3252	.2253	.1566	.1092	.0765
39	.6784	.4619	.3158	.2166	.1491	.1031	.0715
40	.6717	.4529	.3066	.2083	.1420	.0972	.0668
41	.6650	.4440	.2976	.2003	.1353	.0917	.0624
42	.6584	.4353	.2890	.1926	.1288	.0865	.0583
43	.6519	.4268	.2805	.1852	.1227	.0816	.0545
44	.6454	.4184	.2724	.1780	.1169	.0770	.0509
45	.6391	.4102	.2644	.1712	.1113	.0727	.0476
46	.6327	.4022	.2567	.1646	.1060	.0685	.0445
47	.6265	.3943	.2493	.1583	.1009	.0647	.0416
48	.6203	.3865	.2420	.1522	.0961	.0610	.0389
49	.6141	.3790	.2350	.1463	.0916	.0575	.0363
50	.6080	.3715	.2281	.1407	.0872	.0543	.0339

Present Value Factors

Years	8%	9%	10%	11%	12%	13%	14%
1	.9259	0.9174	0.9091	0.9009	0.8929	0.8850	0.8772
2	.8573	0.8417	0.8264	0.8116	0.7972	0.7831	0.7695
3	.7938	0.7722	0.7513	0.7312	0.7118	0.6931	0.6750
4	.7350	0.7084	0.6830	0.6587	0.6355	0.6133	0.5921
5	.6806	0.6499	0.6209	0.5935	0.5674	0.5428	0.5194
6	.6302	0.5963	0.5645	0.5346	0.5066	0.4803	0.4556
7	.5835	0.5470	0.5132	0.4817	0.4523	0.4251	0.3996
8	.5403	0.5019	0.4665	0.4339	0.4039	0.3762	0.3506
9	.5002	0.4604	0.4241	0.3909	0.3606	0.3329	0.3075
10	.4632	0.4224	0.3855	0.3522	0.3220	0.2946	0.2697
11	.4289	0.3875	0.3505	0.3173	0.2875	0.2607	0.2366
12	.3971	0.3555	0.3186	0.2858	0.2567	0.2307	0.2076
13	.3677	0.3262	0.2897	0.2575	0.2292	0.2042	0.1821
14	.3405	0.2992	0.2633	0.2320	0.2046	0.1807	0.1597
15	.3152	0.2745	0.2394	0.2090	0.1827	0.1599	0.1401
16	.2919	0.2519	0.2176	0.1883	0.1631	0.1415	0.1229
17	.2703	0.2311	0.1978	0.1696	0.1456	0.1252	0.1078
18	.2502	0.2120	0.1799	0.1528	0.1300	0.1108	0.0946
19	.2317	0.1945	0.1635	0.1377	0.1161	0.0981	0.0829
20	.2145	0.1784	0.1486	0.1240	0.1037	0.0868	0.0728
21	.1987	0.1637	0.1351	0.1117	0.0926	0.0768	0.0638
22	.1839	0.1502	0.1228	0.1007	0.0826	0.0680	0.0560
23	.1703	0.1378	0.1117	0.0907	0.0738	0.0601	0.0491
24	.1577	0.1264	0.1015	0.0817	0.0659	0.0532	0.0431
25	.1460	0.1160	0.0923	0.0736	0.0588	0.0471	0.0378
26	.1352	0.1064	0.0839	0.0663	0.0525	0.0417	0.0331
27	.1252	0.0976	0.0763	0.0597	0.0469	0.0369	0.0291
28	.1159	0.0895	0.0693	0.0538	0.0419	0.0326	0.0255
29	.1073	0.0822	0.0630	0.0485	0.0374	0.0289	0.0224
30	.0994	0.0754	0.0573	0.0437	0.0334	0.0256	0.0196
31	.0920	0.0691	0.0521	0.0394	0.0298	0.0226	0.0172
32	.0852	0.0634	0.0474	0.0355	0.0266	0.0200	0.0151
33	.0789	0.0582	0.0431	0.0319	0.0238	0.0177	0.0132
34	.0730	0.0534	0.0391	0.0288	0.0212	0.0157	0.0116
35	.0676	0.0490	0.0356	0.0259	0.0189	0.0139	0.0102
36	.0626	0.0449	0.0323	0.0234	0.0169	0.0123	0.0089
37	.0580	0.0412	0.0294	0.0210	0.0151	0.0109	0.0078
38	.0537	0.0378	0.0267	0.0190	0.0135	0.0096	0.0069
39	.0497	0.0347	0.0243	0.0171	0.0120	0.0085	0.0060
40	.0460	0.0318	0.0221	0.0154	0.0107	0.0075	0.0053
41	.0426	0.0292	0.0201	0.0139	0.0096	0.0067	0.0046
42	.0395	0.0268	0.0183	0.0125	0.0086	0.0059	0.0041
43	.0365	0.0246	0.0166	0.0112	0.0076	0.0052	0.0036
44	.0338	0.0226	0.0151	0.0101	0.0068	0.0046	0.0031
45	.0313	0.0207	0.0137	0.0091	0.0061	0.0041	0.0027
46	.0290	0.0190	0.0125	0.0082	0.0054	0.0036	0.0024
47	.0269	0.0174	0.0113	0.0074	0.0049	0.0032	0.0021
48	.0249	0.0160	0.0103	0.0067	0.0043	0.0028	0.0019
49	.0230	0.0147	0.0094	0.0060	0.0039	0.0025	0.0016
50	.0213	0.0134	0.0085	0.0054	0.0035	0.0022	0.0014

Present Value Factors

Years	15%	16%	17%	18%	19%	20%
1	0.8696	0.8621	0.8547	0.8475	0.8403	0.8333
2	0.7561	0.7432	0.7305	0.7182	0.7062	0.6944
3	0.6575	0.6407	0.6244	0.6086	0.5934	0.5787
4	0.5718	0.5523	0.5337	0.5158	0.4987	0.4823
5	0.4972	0.4761	0.4561	0.4371	0.4190	0.4019
6	0.4323	0.4104	0.3898	0.3704	0.3521	0.3349
7	0.3759	0.3538	0.3332	0.3139	0.2959	0.2791
8	0.3269	0.3050	0.2848	0.2660	0.2487	0.2326
9	0.2843	0.2630	0.2434	0.2255	0.2090	0.1938
10	0.2472	0.2267	0.2080	0.1911	0.1756	0.1615
11	0.2149	0.1954	0.1778	0.1619	0.1476	0.1346
12	0.1869	0.1685	0.1520	0.1372	0.1240	0.1122
13	0.1625	0.1452	0.1299	0.1163	0.1042	0.0935
14	0.1413	0.1252	0.1110	0.0985	0.0876	0.0779
15	0.1229	0.1079	0.0949	0.0835	0.0736	0.0649
16	0.1069	0.0930	0.0811	0.0708	0.0618	
17	0.0929	0.0802	0.0693	0.0600	0.0520	
18	0.0808	0.0691	0.0592	0.0508	0.0437	
19	0.0703	0.0596	0.0506	0.0431	0.0367	
20	0.0611	0.0514	0.0433	0.0365	0.0308	
21	0.0531	0.0443	0.0370	0.0309	0.0259	
22	0.0462	0.0382	0.0316	0.0262	0.0218	
23	0.0402	0.0329	0.0270	0.0222	0.0183	
24	0.0349	0.0284	0.0231	0.0188	0.0154	
25	0.0304	0.0245	0.0197	0.0160	0.0129	
26	0.0264	0.0211	0.0169	0.0135	0.0109	
27	0.0230	0.0182	0.0144	0.0115	0.0091	
28	0.0200	0.0157	0.0123	0.0097	0.0077	
29	0.0174	0.0135	0.0105	0.0082	0.0064	
30	0.0151	0.0116	0.0090	0.0070	0.0054	
31	0.0131	0.0100	0.0077	0.0059	0.0046	
32	0.0114	0.0087	0.0066	0.0050	0.0038	
33	0.0099	0.0075	0.0056	0.0042	0.0032	
34	0.0086	0.0064	0.0048	0.0036	0.0027	
35	0.0075	0.0055	0.0041	0.0030	0.0023	
36	0.0065	0.0048	0.0035	0.0026	0.0019	
37	0.0057	0.0041	0.0030	0.0022	0.0016	
38	0.0049	0.0036	0.0026	0.0019	0.0013	
39	0.0043	0.0031	0.0022	0.0016	0.0011	
40	0.0037	0.0026	0.0019	0.0013	0.0010	
41	0.0032	0.0023	0.0016	0.0011	0.0008	
42	0.0028	0.0020	0.0014	0.0010	0.0007	
43	0.0025	0.0017	0.0012	0.0008	0.0006	
44	0.0021	0.0015	0.0010	0.0007	0.0005	
45	0.0019	0.0013	0.0009	0.0006	0.0004	
46	0.0016	0.0011	0.0007	0.0005	0.0003	
47	0.0014	0.0009	0.0006	0.0004	0.0003	
48	0.0012	0.0008	0.0005	0.0004	0.0002	
49	0.0011	0.0007	0.0005	0.0003	0.0002	
50	0.0009	0.0006	0.0004	0.0003	0.0002	

F. Future Value Factors

This chart lets you calculate an estimate of the future value of an asset, such as a house. The figures in the first column represent the Holding Period, or number of years you would expect to retain the asset. The percentages across the top indicate the inflation rate. When you follow the two lines until they intersect, you have the Future Value Factor. For instance, if you have a $200,000 house that you expect to hold for another seven years and if you assume a 4% inflation rate, the PVF is 1.3159. Multiply that by $200,000, and you have an estimated future value of $263,180 for your house in seven years.

Years	1%	2%	3%	4%	5%	6%	7%
1	1.0100	1.0200	1.0300	1.0400	1.0500	1.0600	1.0700
2	1.0201	1.0404	1.0609	1.0816	1.1025	1.1236	1.1449
3	1.0303	1.0612	1.0927	1.1249	1.1576	1.1910	1.2250
4	1.0406	1.0824	1.1255	1.1699	1.2155	1.2625	1.3108
5	1.0510	1.1041	1.1593	1.2167	1.2763	1.3382	1.4026
6	1.0615	1.1262	1.1941	1.2653	1.3401	1.4185	1.5007
7	1.0721	1.1487	1.2299	1.3159	1.4071	1.5036	1.6058
8	1.0829	1.1717	1.2668	1.3686	1.4775	1.5938	1.7182
9	1.0937	1.1951	1.3048	1.4233	1.5513	1.6895	1.8385
10	1.1046	1.2190	1.3439	1.4802	1.6289	1.7908	1.9672
11	1.1157	1.2434	1.3842	1.5395	1.7103	1.8983	2.1049
12	1.1268	1.2682	1.4258	1.6010	1.7959	2.0122	2.2522
13	1.1381	1.2936	1.4685	1.6651	1.8856	2.1329	2.4098
14	1.1495	1.3195	1.5126	1.7317	1.9799	2.2609	2.5785
15	1.1610	1.3459	1.5580	1.8009	2.0789	2.3966	2.7590
16	1.1726	1.3728	1.6047	1.8730	2.1829	2.5404	2.9522
17	1.1843	1.4002	1.6528	1.9479	2.2920	2.6928	3.1588
18	1.1961	1.4282	1.7024	2.0258	2.4066	2.8543	3.3799
19	1.2081	1.4568	1.7535	2.1068	2.5270	3.0256	3.6165
20	1.2202	1.4859	1.8061	2.1911	2.6533	3.2071	3.8697
21	1.2324	1.5157	1.8603	2.2788	2.7860	3.3996	4.1406
22	1.2447	1.5460	1.9161	2.3699	2.9253	3.6035	4.4304
23	1.2572	1.5769	1.9736	2.4647	3.0715	3.8197	4.7405
24	1.2697	1.6084	2.0328	2.5633	3.2251	4.0489	5.0724
25	1.2824	1.6406	2.0938	2.6658	3.3864	4.2919	5.4274
26	1.2953	1.6734	2.1566	2.7725	3.5557	4.5494	5.8074
27	1.3082	1.7069	2.2213	2.8834	3.7335	4.8223	6.2139
28	1.3213	1.7410	2.2879	2.9987	3.9201	5.1117	6.6488
29	1.3345	1.7758	2.3566	3.1187	4.1161	5.4184	7.1143
30	1.3478	1.8114	2.4273	3.2434	4.3219	5.7435	7.6123
31	1.3613	1.8476	2.5001	3.3731	4.5380	6.0881	8.1451
32	1.3749	1.8845	2.5751	3.5081	4.7649	6.4534	8.7153
33	1.3887	1.9222	2.6523	3.6484	5.0032	6.8406	9.3253
34	1.4026	1.9607	2.7319	3.7943	5.2533	7.2510	9.9781
35	1.4166	1.9999	2.8139	3.9461	5.5160	7.6861	10.6766
36	1.4308	2.0399	2.8983	4.1039	5.7918	8.1473	11.4239
37	1.4451	2.0807	2.9852	4.2681	6.0814	8.6361	12.2236
38	1.4595	2.1223	3.0748	4.4388	6.3855	9.1543	13.0793
39	1.4741	2.1647	3.1670	4.6164	6.7048	9.7035	13.9948
40	1.4889	2.2080	3.2620	4.8010	7.0400	10.2857	14.9745
41	1.5038	2.2522	3.3599	4.9931	7.3920	10.9029	16.0227
42	1.5188	2.2972	3.4607	5.1928	7.7616	11.5570	17.1443
43	1.5340	2.3432	3.5645	5.4005	8.1497	12.2505	18.3444
44	1.5493	2.3901	3.6715	5.6165	8.5572	12.9855	19.6285
45	1.5648	2.4379	3.7816	5.8412	8.9850	13.7646	21.0025
46	1.5805	2.4866	3.8950	6.0748	9.4343	14.5905	22.4726
47	1.5963	2.5363	4.0119	6.3178	9.9060	15.4659	24.0457
48	1.6122	2.5871	4.1323	6.5705	10.4013	16.3939	25.7289
49	1.6283	2.6388	4.2562	6.8333	10.9213	17.3775	27.5299
50	1.6446	2.6916	4.3839	7.1067	11.4674	18.4202	29.4570

Future Value Factors

Years	8%	9%	10%	11%	12%	13%	14%
1	1.0800	1.0900	1.1000	1.1100	1.1200	1.1300	1.1400
2	1.1664	1.1881	1.2100	1.2321	1.2544	1.2769	1.2996
3	1.2597	1.2950	1.3310	1.3676	1.4049	1.4429	1.4815
4	1.3605	1.4116	1.4641	1.5181	1.5735	1.6305	1.6890
5	1.4693	1.5386	1.6105	1.6851	1.7623	1.8424	1.9254
6	1.5869	1.6771	1.7716	1.8704	1.9738	2.0820	2.1950
7	1.7138	1.8280	1.9487	2.0762	2.2107	2.3526	2.5023
8	1.8509	1.9926	2.1436	2.3045	2.4760	2.6584	2.8526
9	1.9990	2.1719	2.3579	2.5580	2.7731	3.0040	3.2519
10	2.1589	2.3674	2.5937	2.8394	3.1058	3.3946	3.7072
11	2.3316	2.5804	2.8531	3.1518	3.4785	3.8359	4.2262
12	2.5182	2.8127	3.1384	3.4985	3.8960	4.3345	4.8179
13	2.7196	3.0658	3.4523	3.8833	4.3635	4.8980	5.4924
14	2.9372	3.3417	3.7975	4.3104	4.8871	5.5348	6.2613
15	3.1722	3.6425	4.1772	4.7846	5.4736	6.2543	7.1379
16	3.4259	3.9703	4.5950	5.3109	6.1304	7.0673	8.1372
17	3.7000	4.3276	5.0545	5.8951	6.8660	7.9861	9.2765
18	3.9960	4.7171	5.5599	6.5436	7.6900	9.0243	10.5752
19	4.3157	5.1417	6.1159	7.2633	8.6128	10.1974	12.0557
20	4.6610	5.6044	6.7275	8.0623	9.6463	11.5231	13.7435
21	5.0338	6.1088	7.4002	8.9492	10.8038	13.0211	15.6676
22	5.4365	6.6586	8.1403	9.9336	12.1003	14.7138	17.8610
23	5.8715	7.2579	8.9543	11.0263	13.5523	16.6266	20.3616
24	6.3412	7.9111	9.8497	12.2392	15.1786	18.7881	23.2122
25	6.8485	8.6231	10.8347	13.5855	17.0001	21.2305	26.4619
26	7.3964	9.3992	11.9182	15.0799	19.0401	23.9905	30.1666
27	7.9881	10.2451	13.1100	16.7386	21.3249	27.1093	34.3899
28	8.6271	11.1671	14.4210	18.5799	23.8839	30.6335	39.2045
29	9.3173	12.1722	15.8631	20.6237	26.7499	34.6158	44.6931
30	10.0627	13.2677	17.4494	22.8923	29.9599	39.1159	50.9502
31	10.8677	14.4618	19.1943	25.4104	33.5551	44.2010	58.0832
32	11.7371	15.7633	21.1138	28.2056	37.5817	49.9471	66.2148
33	12.6760	17.1820	23.2252	31.3082	42.0915	56.4402	75.4849
34	13.6901	18.7284	25.5477	34.7521	47.1425	63.7774	86.0528
35	14.7853	20.4140	28.1024	38.5749	52.7996	72.0685	98.1002
36	15.9682	22.2512	30.9127	42.8181	59.1356	81.4374	111.8342
37	17.2456	24.2538	34.0039	47.5281	66.2318	92.0243	127.4910
38	18.6253	26.4367	37.4043	52.7562	74.1797	103.9874	145.3397
39	20.1153	28.8160	41.1448	58.5593	83.0812	117.5058	165.6873
40	21.7245	31.4094	45.2593	65.0009	93.0510	132.7816	188.8835
41	23.4625	34.2363	49.7852	72.1510	104.2171	150.0432	215.3272
42	25.3395	37.3175	54.7637	80.0876	116.7231	169.5488	245.4730
43	27.3666	40.6761	60.2401	88.8972	130.7299	191.5901	279.8392
44	29.5560	44.3370	66.2641	98.6759	146.4175	216.4968	319.0167
45	31.9204	48.3273	72.8905	109.5302	163.9876	244.6414	363.6791
46	34.4741	52.6767	80.1795	121.5786	183.6661	276.4448	414.5941
47	37.2320	57.4176	88.1975	134.9522	205.7061	312.3826	472.6373
48	40.2106	62.5852	97.0172	149.7970	230.3908	352.9923	538.8065
49	43.4274	68.2179	106.7190	166.2746	258.0377	398.8813	614.2395
50	46.9016	74.3575	117.3909	184.5648	289.0022	450.7359	700.2330

Future Value Factors

Years	15%	16%	17%	18%	19%	20%
1	1.1500	1.1600	1.1700	1.1800	1.1900	1.2000
2	1.3225	1.3456	1.3689	1.3924	1.4161	1.4400
3	1.5209	1.5609	1.6016	1.6430	1.6852	1.7280
4	1.7490	1.8106	1.8739	1.9388	2.0053	2.0736
5	2.0114	2.1003	2.1924	2.2878	2.3864	2.4883
6	2.3131	2.4364	2.5652	2.6996	2.8398	2.9860
7	2.6600	2.8262	3.0012	3.1855	3.3793	3.5832
8	3.0590	3.2784	3.5115	3.7589	4.0214	4.2998
9	3.5179	3.8030	4.1084	4.4355	4.7854	5.1598
10	4.0456	4.4114	4.8068	5.2338	5.6947	6.1917
11	4.6524	5.1173	5.6240	6.1759	6.7767	7.4301
12	5.3503	5.9360	6.5801	7.2876	8.0642	8.9161
13	6.1528	6.8858	7.6987	8.5994	9.5964	10.6993
14	7.0757	7.9875	9.0075	10.1472	11.4198	12.8392
15	8.1371	9.2655	10.5387	11.9737	13.5895	15.4070
16	9.3576	10.7480	12.3303	14.1290	16.1715	
17	10.7613	12.4677	14.4265	16.6722	19.2441	
18	12.3755	14.4625	16.8790	19.6733	22.9005	
19	14.2318	16.7765	19.7484	23.2144	27.2516	
20	16.3665	19.4608	23.1056	27.3930	32.4294	
21	18.8215	22.5745	27.0336	32.3238	38.5910	
22	21.6447	26.1864	31.6293	38.1421	45.9233	
23	24.8915	30.3762	37.0062	45.0076	54.6487	
24	28.6252	35.2364	43.2973	53.1090	65.0320	
25	32.9190	40.8742	50.6578	62.6686	77.3881	
26	37.8568	47.4141	59.2697	73.9490	92.0918	
27	43.5353	55.0004	69.3455	87.2598	109.5893	
28	50.0656	63.8004	81.1342	102.9666	130.4112	
29	57.5755	74.0085	94.9271	121.5005	155.1893	
30	66.2118	85.8499	111.0647	143.3706	184.6753	
31	76.1435	99.5859	129.9456	169.1774	219.7636	
32	87.5651	115.5196	152.0364	199.6293	261.5187	
33	100.6998	134.0027	177.8826	235.5625	311.2073	
34	115.8048	155.4432	208.1226	277.9638	370.3366	
35	133.1755	180.3141	243.5035	327.9973	440.7006	
36	153.1519	209.1643	284.8991	387.0368	524.4337	
37	176.1246	242.6306	333.3319	456.7034	624.0761	
38	202.5433	281.4515	389.9983	538.9100	742.6506	
39	232.9248	326.4838	456.2980	635.9139	883.7542	
40	267.8635	378.7212	533.8687	750.3783	1051.6675	
41	308.0431	439.3165	624.6264	885.4464	1251.4843	
42	354.2495	509.6072	730.8129	1044.8268	1489.2664	
43	407.3870	591.1443	855.0511	1232.8956	1772.2270	
44	468.4950	685.7274	1000.4098	1454.8168	2108.9501	
45	538.7693	795.4438	1170.4794	1716.6839	2509.6506	
46	619.5847	922.7148	1369.4609	2025.6870	2986.4842	
47	712.5224	1070.3492	1602.2693	2390.3106	3553.9162	
48	819.4007	1241.6051	1874.6550	2820.5665	4229.1603	
49	942.3108	1440.2619	2193.3464	3328.2685	5032.7008	
50	1083.6574	1670.7038	2566.2153	3927.3569	5988.9139	

G. List of Professional Advisors

Attorney:

Name: _____

Address _____

_____

Phone: _____

Fax: _____

Email: _____

Financial Planner:

Name: _____

Address _____

_____

Phone: _____

Fax: _____

Email: _____

Accountant or Other Tax Professional:

Name: _____

Address _____

_____

Phone: _____

Fax: _____

Email: _____

Stockbroker/Money Manager:

Name: _____

Address _____

_____

Phone: _____

Fax: _____

Email: _____

Banker:

Name: _____

Address _____

_____

Phone: _____

Fax: _____

Email: _____

Mortgage Broker:

Name: _____

Address _____

_____

Phone: _____

Fax: _____

Email: _____

Retirement Planning Advisor:

Name: _____

Address _____

_____

Phone: _____

Fax: _____

Email: _____

Title Company Agent:

Name: _____

Address _____

_____

Phone: _____

Fax: _____

Email: _____

Real Estate Broker:

Name: _____

Address _____

_____

Phone: _____

Fax: _____

Email: _____

Insurance Agent/Home:

Name: _____

Address _____

_____

Phone: _____

Fax: _____

Email: _____

Insurance Agent/Auto:

Name: _____

Address _____

_____

Phone: _____

Fax: _____

Email: _____

Insurance Agent/Life:

Name: _____

Address _____

_____

Phone: _____

Fax: _____

Email: _____

Other:

Name: _____

Address _____

_____

Phone: _____

Fax: _____

Email: _____

Other:

Name: _____

Address _____

_____

Phone: _____

Fax: _____

Email: _____

Other:

Name: _____

Address _____

_____

Phone: _____

Fax: _____

Email: _____

Other:

Name: _____

Address _____

_____

Phone: _____

Fax: _____

Email: _____

■

Index

CATALOG

...more from Nolo

	PRICE	CODE
Sexual Harassment on the Job	$24.95	HARS
Starting & Running a Successful Newsletter or Magazine	$29.99	MAG
Tax Savvy for Small Business	$34.99	SAVVY
Working for Yourself: Law & Taxes for the Self-Employed	$39.99	WAGE
Your Limited Liability Company: An Operating Manual (Book w/CD-ROM)	$49.99	LOP
Your Rights in the Workplace	$29.99	YRW

CONSUMER

	PRICE	CODE
Fed Up with the Legal System: What's Wrong & How to Fix It	$9.95	LEG
How to Win Your Personal Injury Claim	$29.99	PICL
Nolo's Encyclopedia of Everyday Law	$29.99	EVL
Nolo's Pocket Guide to California Law	$24.95	CLAW
Trouble-Free Travel...And What to Do When Things Go Wrong	$14.95	TRAV

ESTATE PLANNING & PROBATE

	PRICE	CODE
8 Ways to Avoid Probate	$19.95	PRO8
9 Ways to Avoid Estate Taxes	$29.95	ESTX
Estate Planning Basics	$21.99	ESPN
How to Probate an Estate in California	$49.99	PAE
Make Your Own Living Trust (Book w/CD-ROM)	$39.99	LITR
Nolo's Law Form Kit: Wills	$24.95	KWL
Nolo's Simple Will Book (Book w/CD-ROM)	$34.99	SWIL
Plan Your Estate	$44.99	NEST
Quick & Legal Will Book	$15.99	QUIC

FAMILY MATTERS

	PRICE	CODE
Child Custody: Building Parenting Agreements That Work	$29.95	CUST
The Complete IEP Guide	$24.99	IEP
Divorce & Money: How to Make the Best Financial Decisions During Divorce	$34.99	DIMO
Do Your Own Divorce in Oregon	$29.95	ODIV
Get a Life: You Don't Need a Million to Retire Well	$24.95	LIFE
The Guardianship Book for California	$39.99	GB
How to Adopt Your Stepchild in California (Book w/CD-ROM)	$34.95	ADOP
A Legal Guide for Lesbian and Gay Couples	$29.99	LG
Living Together: A Legal Guide (Book w/CD-ROM)	$34.99	LTK
Using Divorce Mediation: Save Your Money & Your Sanity	$29.95	UDMD

GOING TO COURT

	PRICE	CODE
Beat Your Ticket: Go To Court and Win! (National Edition)	$19.99	BEYT

	PRICE	CODE

The Criminal Law Handbook: Know Your Rights, Survive the System .... $34.99   KYR

Everybody's Guide to Small Claims Court (National Edition) .... $24.95   NSCC

Everybody's Guide to Small Claims Court in California .... $26.99   CSCC

Fight Your Ticket ... and Win! (California Edition) .... $29.99   FYT

How to Change Your Name in California .... $34.95   NAME

How to Collect When You Win a Lawsuit (California Edition) .... $29.99   JUDG

How to Mediate Your Dispute .... $18.95   MEDI

How to Seal Your Juvenile & Criminal Records (California Edition) .... $34.95   CRIM

Nolo's Deposition Handbook .... $29.99   DEP

Represent Yourself in Court: How to Prepare & Try a Winning Case .... $34.99   RYC

HOMEOWNERS, LANDLORDS & TENANTS

California Tenants' Rights .... $27.99   CTEN

Deeds for California Real Estate .... $24.99   DEED

Dog Law .... $21.95   DOG

Every Landlord's Legal Guide (National Edition, Book w/CD-ROM) .... $44.99   ELLI

Every Tenant's Legal Guide .... $26.95   EVTEN

For Sale by Owner in California .... $29.99   FSBO

How to Buy a House in California .... $34.99   BHCA

The California Landlord's Law Book: Rights & Responsibilities (Book w/CD-ROM) .... $44.99   LBRT

The California Landlord's Law Book: Evictions (Book w/CD-ROM) .... $44.99   LBEV

Leases & Rental Agreements .... $29.99   LEAR

Neighbor Law: Fences, Trees, Boundaries & Noise .... $26.99   NEI

The New York Landlord's Law Book (Book w/CD-ROM) .... $39.95   NYLL

Renters' Rights (National Edition) .... $24.99   RENT

Stop Foreclosure Now in California .... $29.95   CLOS

HUMOR

29 Reasons Not to Go to Law School $12.95   29R

Poetic Justice .... $9.95   PJ

IMMIGRATION

Fiancé & Marriage Visas .... $44.95   IMAR

How to Get a Green Card .... $29.95   GRN

Student & Tourist Visas .... $29.99   ISTU

U.S. Immigration Made Easy .... $44.99   IMEZ

	PRICE	CODE

MONEY MATTERS

101 Law Forms for Personal Use (Book w/CD-ROM)	$29.99	SPOT
Bankruptcy: Is It the Right Solution to Your Debt Problems?	$19.99	BRS
Chapter 13 Bankruptcy: Repay Your Debts	$34.99	CH13
Creating Your Own Retirement Plan	$29.99	YROP
Credit Repair (Quick & Legal Series, Book w/CD-ROM)	$24.99	CREP
How to File for Chapter 7 Bankruptcy	$34.99	HFB
IRAs, 401(k)s & Other Retirement Plans: Taking Your Money Out	$29.99	RET
Money Troubles: Legal Strategies to Cope With Your Debts	$29.99	MT
Nolo's Law Form Kit: Personal Bankruptcy	$24.99	KBNK
Stand Up to the IRS	$24.99	SIRS
Surviving an IRS Tax Audit	$24.95	SAUD
Take Control of Your Student Loan Debt	$26.95	SLOAN

PATENTS AND COPYRIGHTS

The Copyright Handbook: How to Protect and Use Written Works (Book w/CD-ROM)	$39.99	COHA
Copyright Your Software	$34.95	CYS
Domain Names	$26.95	DOM
Getting Permission: How to License and Clear Copyrighted Materials Online and Off (Book w/CD-ROM)	$34.99	RIPER
How to Make Patent Drawings Yourself	$29.99	DRAW
The Inventor's Notebook	$24.99	INOT
Nolo's Patents for Beginners	$29.99	QPAT
License Your Invention (Book w/CD-ROM)	$39.99	LICE
Patent, Copyright & Trademark	$39.99	PCTM
Patent It Yourself	$49.99	PAT
Patent Searching Made Easy	$29.95	PATSE
The Public Domain	$34.95	PUBL
Web and Software Development: A Legal Guide (Book w/ CD-ROM)	$44.95	SFT
Trademark: Legal Care for Your Business and Product Name	$39.95	TRD

RESEARCH & REFERENCE

Legal Research: How to Find & Understand the Law	$34.99	LRES

SENIORS

Choose the Right Long-Term Care: Home Care, Assisted Living & Nursing Homes	$21.99	ELD
The Conservatorship Book for California	$44.99	CNSV
Social Security, Medicare & Goverment Pensions	$29.99	SOA

ORDER 24 HOURS A DAY @ www.nolo.com
Call 800-728-3555 • Mail or fax the order form in this book

SOFTWARE

**Call or check our website at www.nolo.com
for special discounts on Software!**

LeaseWriter CD—Windows $129.95   LWD1
LLC Maker—Windows $89.95   LLP1
PatentPro Plus—Windows .... $399.99   PAPL
Personal RecordKeeper 5.0 CD—Windows $59.95   RKD5
Quicken Lawyer 2003 Business Deluxe—Windows $79.95   SBQB3
Quicken Lawyer 2003 Personal—Windows $79.95   WQP3

Special Upgrade Offer

Save 35% on the latest edition of your Nolo book

Because laws and legal procedures change often, we update our books regularly. To help keep you up-to-date, we are extending this special upgrade offer. Cut out and mail the title portion of the cover of your old Nolo book and we'll give you **35% off** the retail price of the NEW EDITION of that book when you purchase directly from Nolo. This offer is to individuals only.

Call us today at 1-800-728-3555

Prices and offer subject to change without notice.

Order Form

Name

Address

City

State, Zip

Daytime Phone

E-mail

Item Code	Quantity	Item	Unit Price	Total Price

Subtotal	
Add your local sales tax (California only)	
Shipping: RUSH $9, Basic $5 (See below)	
"I bought 3, ship it to me FREE!"(Ground shipping only)	
TOTAL	

Method of payment

☐ Check   ☐ VISA   ☐ MasterCard

☐ Discover Card   ☐ American Express

Account Number

Expiration Date

Signature

Shipping and Handling

Rush Delivery—Only $9

We'll ship any order to any street address in the U.S. by UPS 2nd Day Air* for only $9!

* Order by noon Pacific Time and get your order in 2 business days. Orders placed after noon Pacific Time will arrive in 3 business days. P.O. boxes and S.F. Bay Area use basic shipping. Alaska and Hawaii use 2nd Day Air or Priority Mail.

Basic Shipping—$5

Use for P.O. Boxes, Northern California and Ground Service.

Allow 1-2 weeks for delivery. U.S. addresses only.

For faster service, use your credit card and our toll-free numbers

**Call our customer service group
Monday thru Friday 7am to 7pm PST**

Phone	1-800-728-3555
Fax	1-800-645-0895
Mail	Nolo
950 Parker St.
Berkeley, CA 94710

Order 24 hours a day @ www.nolo.com

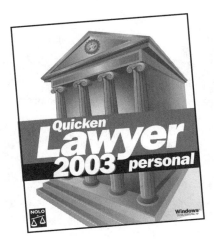

Remember:

Little publishers have big ears.
We really listen to you.

Take 2 Minutes & Give Us Your 2 cents

Your comments make a big difference in the development and revision of Nolo books and software. Please take a few minutes and register your Nolo product—and your comments—with us. Not only will your input make a difference, you'll receive special offers available only to registered owners of Nolo products on our newest books and software. Register now by:

PHONE
1-800-728-3555

FAX
1-800-645-0895

EMAIL
cs@nolo.com

or **MAIL** us
this registration card

fold here

Registration Card

NAME _____ DATE _____

ADDRESS _____

_____

CITY _____ STATE _____ ZIP _____

PHONE _____ E-MAIL _____

WHERE DID YOU HEAR ABOUT THIS PRODUCT? _____

WHERE DID YOU PURCHASE THIS PRODUCT? _____

DID YOU CONSULT A LAWYER? (PLEASE CIRCLE ONE)   YES   NO   NOT APPLICABLE

DID YOU FIND THIS BOOK HELPFUL?   (VERY)   5   4   3   2   1   (NOT AT ALL)

COMMENTS _____

_____

_____

WAS IT EASY TO USE?   (VERY EASY)   5   4   3   2   1   (VERY DIFFICULT)

We occasionally make our mailing list available to carefully selected companies whose products may be of interest to you.

❑ If you do not wish to receive mailings from these companies, please check this box.

❑ You can quote me in future Nolo promotional materials.
    Daytime phone number _____.

DIMO 6.0

Nolo in the NEWS

"Nolo helps lay people perform legal tasks without the aid—or fees—of lawyers."

—USA TODAY

Nolo books are ..."written in plain language, free of legal mumbo jumbo, and spiced with witty personal observations."

—ASSOCIATED PRESS

"...Nolo publications...guide people simply through the how, when, where and why of law."

—WASHINGTON POST

"Increasingly, people who are not lawyers are performing tasks usually regarded as legal work... And consumers, using books like Nolo's, do routine legal work themselves."

—NEW YORK TIMES

"...All of [Nolo's] books are easy-to-understand, are updated regularly, provide pull-out forms...and are often quite moving in their sense of compassion for the struggles of the lay reader."

—SAN FRANCISCO CHRONICLE

- fold here -

Place
stamp here

Nolo
950 Parker Street
Berkeley, CA 94710-9867

Attn: DIMO 6.0